Asian American X

ASIAN AMERICAN X

An Intersection of 21st Century
Asian American Voices

Edited by Arar Han and John Hsu

THE UNIVERSITY OF MICHIGAN PRESS
Ann Arbor

2007   2006   2005   2004   4   3   2   1

A CIP catalog record for this book is available from the British Library.

Library of Congress Cataloging-in-Publication Data

Asian American X : an intersection of twenty-first-century Asian
American voices / edited by Arar Han and John Hsu.
p. cm.
ISBN 0-472-09874-8 (alk. paper) — ISBN 0-472-06874-1 (pbk. : alk paper)
1. Asian Americans—Race identity.   2. Asian American's—Ethnic
identity.   3. Asian American youth—Biography.   4. Asian American
youth—Social conditions.   5. Asian Americans—Social conditions.
6. Identity (Psychology)   7. United States—Race relations.   I. Han,
Arar, 1981–   II. Hsu, John, 1980–
E184.A75A8426   2004
305.895'073—dc22   2004003463

Grateful acknowledgment is made to the following authors, publishers, and journals for permission to reprint portions of previously published materials: Wesleyan University Press for "Last Night" by Antonio Machado, *Times Alone: Selected Poems of Antonio Machado* (Middletown, CT: Wesleyan University Press, 1983); and Alvin Eng for *Rock Me, Goong Hay!,* from the punk-rap musical, "The Goong Hay Kid."

For Jamar, jte, and Rolm—who remind us that we are works in progress
And our families—so good, so beautiful, and so true

Contents

Acknowledgments

This book would have been a passing thought without the generosity of our friends and mentors: Professor Ramsay Liem, Sophia Lai, Jennie Lin, Eric Liu, and Robin Tsai refined and enriched our introduction with their sharp wisdom. Jason Schwartz deserves special mention for his helpful edits and inspirational ideas. We are also grateful to Vickie Nam and Ruben Navarrette for their advice and support from the beginning of this project; Yumi Kim for her letter-writing skills; and the numerous scholars—including Dean John Cawthorne and Professors Patrick Byrne, Eileen Chow, John Holdren, Belle Liang, Larry Ludlow, Marina McCoy, and Bill Torbert—who helped us refine our vision for this book and successfully navigate the publishing world. For their assistance with writer recruitment, their thoughtful questions, and especially their infectious enthusiasm for this project, we are indebted to many friends—Jonathan Amar, Ryan Auer, Megan Bensley, Doug Campbell, Jumi Cha, Monica Chandra, David Chen, Carol Choi, Jaime DesJardins, Jonathan Evans, Nancy Garland, Lauren Goslin, Roger Hong, Jenny Huang, Victor Huang, Megumi Itoh, Stefan Jacob, Amie Kim, Yoon Jung Lee, Stephanie Lim, Jennifer Lo, Kenneth Mah, Deborah Mascalzoni, Nitin Nohria, Xaq Pitkow, Ellen Rubinstein, Martin Sandbu, Mark Seto, Clara Shen, Grace Simmons, Tacara Soones, Irene Sun, Shauyi Tai, Cindy Uh, Stephanie Valencia, David Xiao, Mary Yang, Jia Jia Ye, and Ethan Yeh—who have made this project as much theirs as it is ours. For introducing us to the power of self-reflection through writing and guiding us toward our own style and voice, we thank our high school English teachers, especially Megan Birdsong, Robert Javier, Amy Moore, Shozo Shimazaki, and Debbie Vanni. We would also like to thank our families for their unconditional support and our siblings in particular—Susie for her administrative expertise and Jerry for his sense of humor. Finally, for taking a chance on two college kids, sharing our vision for this book, and making its publication possible, we thank Ellen McCarthy, Kelly O'Connor, and Ann Marie Schultz from the University of Michigan Press. We owe the successes in this work to all our friends and mentors; any shortcomings are wholly our own.

Introduction

Arar Han and John Y. Hsu

No one will know who we are until we know who we are!
—Malcolm X, *The Autobiography of Malcolm X*

The Origin of *Asian American X*

Before all of this—the thousands of emails, countless conversations, and the book contract that have led us here to the opening pages of *Asian American X*—we were simply old high school friends attending college in Boston, just trying to better understand ourselves. You might have called us constructively confused—groping in a cave of questions about identity and race—yet gravitating toward the light, whether through casual conversations or the books we shared.

Then, in March 2001, the *Harvard Crimson* ran Justin Fong's "The Invasian."[1]

The article was a satire accusing Asian American students at Harvard of living up to, and even reinforcing, Asian American stereotypes. According to its author, who is himself Asian American, our generation of college-aged Asian Americans represented a "segregated community of stereotypes: self-lacking males that don't have the courage to talk to anyone unless they appear just as flaccid as that image in the mirror, and a smattering of females that exist to satisfy someone's fetish."

A frenzied intercollegiate discussion immediately erupted, and we both watched in fascination. Given the provocative language of the article, most responders to "The Invasian" were furious and defensive, vigorously rebutting Fong's blanket negative portrayal of Asian American college students. More specifically, they rejected his assertion that Asian American identity is defined by sexual stereotypes and self-segregation (see Lee, *Unraveling the "Model Minority" Stereotype*). One woman opposed Fong on the grounds that such a portrayal of Asian American collective identity would fan the proliferation of hate crimes against Asian Americans.[2] Another reader suggested that Fong ought to soften his "aggressive tone," since phenomena like self-segregation could equally apply to other groups, including Caucasians.[3] Still others understood the printing of "The Invasian" as the *Crimson*'s lack of cultural sensitivity toward Asian Americans, and some fifty Harvard students staged a protest against the editorial board for printing "words which act only to undermine the efforts of other Asians who wish to defeat stereotypes constructively."[4] The *Crimson* published two apologies days later.

While we, too, found Fong's article to be excessively brash, we also identified with his emphasis on individual identity. We recognized that a grounding point of "The Invasian" was its assertion that, like all other individuals, each Asian American of our generation has the right and even the responsibility to work toward an authentic life—a life that is faithful to one's uniquely individual way of being.[5] In an attempt to reinforce this point and steer public debate away from name-calling, Arar wrote a letter to the *Crimson* that appeared four days later:

> Granted, Fong makes some egregious faux pas in his open letter, but these missteps do not justify many Asian American students' simplistic accusations that Fong has set Harvard Asian American students back ten years. Such attacks stem from a complete failure to appreciate his point that we must strive to live by the truth of our substance rather than blundering down the path of superficiality and falsehood by ignoring basic human responsibility to be true to oneself.[6]

Through the smoke of the firestorm ignited by "The Invasian," we came to recognize a central question of this challenging debate about Asian American identity: As individuals and as a collective body, who are we, and what are our definitive individual and collective features?

Understanding through Self-Evaluation

In examining ourselves, we started to explore why we identified so strongly with the individual conception of the self. What caused us to part company with many of our Asian American peers and conceptualize Fong as a liberator of sorts—taunting his fellow students out of a trap of stereotypical Asianness and daring them to step out of their racial confines to construct an original identity? Why did we believe that we had to transcend our collective identities—such as race, gender, religion, sexuality, and class—in order to realize an authentic personal identity?[7]

To answer these questions, we began to reflect on our education and upbringing. One of the very first things we realized was that neither of us had experienced much racial persecution growing up in Cupertino, California, one of the many suburban Asian American enclaves found throughout the United States today. The racial breakdown of our high school of just under two thousand students—approximately half Asian and half white, with very few Latino or black students—placed us within a critical mass of Asian students, sheltering us from the blatant racism often encountered by nonwhite students at predominantly white high schools.

As the children of white-collar professionals in Silicon Valley, we grew up with the privileges of an upper-middle-class American lifestyle. Our community placed a premium on formal education, and academic excellence was the crowning virtue; Bs were "bad," and we aimed for SAT scores above the 1500 mark, hoping to maximize our chances of getting admitted into elite colleges. Extracurricular activities included public service clubs and volunteer jobs, speech and debate camps, as well as music and sports lessons. As high school students, we were presented with many opportunities to realize our individual goals, and we were fortunate to have the support and tools with which to pursue them.

At the same time, we realized that our love of individualism was a value that was itself profoundly reinforced by our collective identities—our specific class and racial affiliations. It became clear to us that growing up in an affluent community and attending a high school in which our racial minority was a near majority not only sheltered us from economic struggle and racial strife but also required us to be individuals—to set ourselves apart from those around us. In our community, our class and race served as collective identities that kept us innocent about the experiences of the vast majority of Asian Americans, today and throughout our collective history. These particular collective identities also encouraged individualism to take root, cultivating our abilities to live as we desired and saw fit.

So we emerged from our shared reflections with not only a clearer sense of the collective identities that had advanced our individualistic tendencies but also an appreciation for how our individualism itself was deeply rooted in collective aspects of our identities. We had set out to better understand and strengthen our individual-leaning concept of identity, but ironically, our greatest insight was learning that we were who we were because of the dynamically intertwined influence of both individual *and* collective identities.

When we applied this newfound understanding to our interpretation of "The Invasian," our original question about individual and collective features of identity became firmly embedded in the context of the self: How do we—that is, Asian Americans of our generation—understand our individual and collective identities? For each of us, in what ways and situations do our individual and collective identities manifest in everyday life?

Long accustomed to borrowing answers to life's difficult questions from others, we again headed toward the library in search of answers to these new questions. Specifically, we had in mind definitive, intelligent, autoethnographic writings in the vein of Eric Liu's *The Accidental Asian,* which we had found to be especially insightful in its expression of one Asian American and his place in American society.[8] We hoped to find coherent articulations of identity for the entire terrain of college-aged Asian Americans—a set of books and essays like Liu's that we could piece together into a unified landscape. Hunting through libraries, questioning professors of Asian American studies, and scouring the Internet turned up many academic works about our generation of Asian Americans; however, we found neither an established *self*-analysis of our generation's Asian American identities nor a substantial set of autoethnographic books or essays from which we could extrapolate a broad understanding of our race and generation.

A New Generation of Asian Americans

Min Zhou and James Gatewood's "Mapping the Terrain: Asian American Diversity and the Challenges of the Twenty-First Century" gave us some demographic clues as to why we were unable to find the broad self-portrayal of Asian American college students that we sought.[9] Due in large part to the national origins quota system, Asian immigration had been restricted to a weak trickle prior to 1968, when the Hart-Cellar Act of 1965 was enacted.[10] The rising tide of Asian immigrants riding the post-Hart-

Cellar wave of migration meant that our predecessors over the last few decades were largely first-generational and thus likely to identify themselves as Asian, rather than American. As offspring of those who rode the post-Hart-Cellar wave of immigration all the way through the 1990s, our generation of collegiate Asian Americans is quantitatively larger than, and qualitatively distinct from, those of the previous three decades; sheer numbers aside, we are set apart from these mostly first-generation immigrants, for most of us are 1.5- or second-generation and thus more likely to identify ourselves as Asian *Americans*.[11] Consequently, the identity issues we face and concerns we have as ethnic Asians who have been educated and socialized in the United States are different from those of our first-generational predecessors.

Striking dissimilarities in sociopolitical environment also distinguish our generation from our counterparts over the past century. Asian Americans who lived during the first half of the twentieth century were truly second-class citizens who suffered from unconcealed racism exemplified by Yellow Peril, the immigration acts of 1924, and World War II internment camps. Their voices, unearthed by a growing tide of cultural historians, have since shaped our collective Asian American historical consciousness. Asian Americans who came of age in the 1960s and early 1970s as the children of World War II refugees, Paper Sons, and others—and were, like us, mostly 1.5- and second-generation Asian American—entered a society characterized by a spirit of revolutionary change fueled by the civil rights movement, Vietnam War draft protests, free love, and galvanizing events such as the San Francisco International Hotel struggle for affordable housing and the San Francisco State University fight for ethnic studies.[12] Their voices, influenced by their own collective experiences, alerted others to consider how racism is subtly embedded in the construction of society itself.

While we share demographic similarities with Asian Americans who came of age in the 1960s and early 1970s, our generation is growing up in a vastly different America. Our society is perhaps more racialistic than the America of the 1960s and 1970s but it is also characterized by its almost manic celebration of race and culture.[13] Like those before us, our voices will leave a distinctive legacy by creating a new chapter of history and redefining what it means to be both Asian American and American. To echo the words of Abraham Lincoln, "As our case is new, so we must think anew, and act anew."

Understanding "Asian American"

Before continuing, it is important to note that the term "Asian American" indiscriminately lumps together broadly distinct ethnicities and cultures on the basis of a vague geographical reference. Just as there is no singular Asian culture, value system, religion, or history, the internal diversity of Asian American culture is as varied as the many cultures of Asia and the stunning diversity of America. Moreover, the distinction "Asian American" often serves as a conveniently powerful mechanism to propagate stereotypes about these different people and cultures. As many of our friends have pointed out, our continued use of the category "Asian American" appears to be paradoxical—an implicit endorsement of a category we recognize as potentially harmful.

The simplest justification for our continued use of the term "Asian American" is that the category is an established part of our social vocabulary that powerfully affects everyday lives. The argument put forth by Asian American activists in the 1960s remains appropriate today: "A distinct Asian American identity [has] evolved over the years, based on the experiences of Asians in America."[14] This statement can be unpacked into three broad arguments:

- Virtually all Americans of Asian descent label themselves or are labeled by others as Asian Americans, primarily because they possess physical markers of Asian ancestries but also because of their ties to Asian culture.
- Asian Americans share a complex collective racial history riddled with targeted acts of discrimination, such as "Yellow Peril" at the turn of the twentieth century, laws restricting immigration that lasted until 1965, discriminatory educational laws, and even antimiscegenation laws.[15]
- Asian Americans are grouped together by current sociopolitical realities. In the United States, we are coclassified as a distinct people for numerous purposes, including the census, anthropological study, and admission into higher education and employment.

Our appearances, histories, and sociopolitical realities form both the reason for the legitimacy of the label "Asian American" and the basis for our collective Asian American identity. Although they represent a multitude of cultures, languages, and ethnicities, Americans of Asian descent—for reasons out of their immediate control—also belong to the group titled "Asian American" and bear its baggage.

The Urgency for Asian American Identity Discourse

After "The Invasian," we learned through self-reflection that individual identity is embedded within many collective identities. Now, we return again to the individual-collective question to reinforce the idea that we cannot fully claim to be individuals unless we know the ways in which we are not. In order to more fully exercise the freedom to be individuals, we must learn what our collective identities are and how we are tied to them; in doing so, we may also become a self-determining collective body of individuals. Most important, we must each be willing to be transformed through reflection, dialogue, and action within this collective body. As William Wei elegantly writes, it is in this "crucible of 'Asian America' that [our] individual and group identities are shaped and have integrity."[16]

Now is an appropriate time for Asian Americans in our generation to begin a dialogue on our collective identity, for we find ourselves at a point at which our body is rapidly evolving. Census 2000 results show that Asian Americans are among the fastest-growing groups in the nation, surging from 6.9 to 11.9 million—a 72 percent increase—in the past decade, growing at more than three times the rate of the entire U.S. population.[17] We are also disproportionately young and beginning to come of age in large numbers; the 1990 census revealed that over half of U.S.-born Asian Americans were under the age of fifteen.[18] Asian American out-marriage is rising as well, further complicating the composition of the future Asian America and distancing the Asian America of today from the Asian America of the past. Approximately one-third of second-generation Asian Americans and over one-half of third-generation Asian Americans marry non-Asians, and if current projections hold, one in three Asian Americans will be multiracial by the year 2070.[19] Furthermore, Asian Americans are becoming increasingly visible—and powerful—in the media, whether as influential political figures, celebrities, or mainstream sports players.[20] All of these changes point to one end, which is also our beginning: We have arrived at a moment in which the events and experiences of the past have collided with the sociopolitical reality of the present. The future of what it means to be Asian American, and even

American, lies in the successful reconciliation of past and present. Therein lies a crucial dialogue we have coined the "Asian American X."

The Making of *Asian American X*

Asian American X intends to serve as a nexus for a dialogue of our past, present, and future as a collective body of Asian Americans. The thirty-five voices we selected to begin the dialogue were chosen from among 170 proposed essays received in response to an emailed call for papers circulated to undergraduate Asian American organizations at over sixty universities between April 2001 and July 2002. These essays are the result of four rounds of cuts: The first two rounds emphasized clarity and complexity of articulation, and the latter two were conducted with an eye for diverse representation of ethnicity, socioeconomic status, gender, generation, regional affiliation, and especially experiences and themes.

The essays in *Asian American X* are primarily written by first- to third-generation Americans who are in college and hail from middle-class backgrounds. It is likely that these writers are a self-selecting sample of our generation of Asian Americans, since all are attending, have attended, or plan to attend college. Indeed, there are significant groups of Asian Americans—for instance, those who have not the resources or opportunity to continue their education after high school—whose voices are not represented here directly and thus are in danger of becoming further marginalized. In the meantime, as we collectively work to increase their opportunities, those groups of Asian Americans who do not speak directly to us will find voice through the words of our authors, many of whom take careful note of the internal diversity of Asian America and of the need for a truly inclusive dialogue on Asian American identity.

The means by which our authors articulate their identities vary as much as their topics. Some choose to speak to their readers through lists and poetry, others through song and prose. Shiuan Butler's "Reminiscings" chooses the former, creating a top-ten list of life-changing moments interspersed with poems, illuminating a range of experiences from losing her virginity ("My first time having sex killed like hell") to reuniting with her brother after fifteen years. Frederick Macapinlac's "Doppelgänger" adopts an existential style to examine the impact of race, class, and popular culture on cultural identity in high school, explaining, in Macapinlac's characteristically conversational diction, that "if you don't want to identify yourself with your culture, there is no way to change it." Other authors choose to ground their essays in one decisive moment. Sunita Puri's "1984" centers around her childhood memory of the assassination of Prime Minister Indira Gandhi, while Jeremiah Torres's "Label Us Angry" takes off from an instance of racism—"to them, we looked like lowlifes, chinks, gangsters, and punks"—and May Chang's "Being Oil" delves into the clash between her Hmong heritage and American schooling through her experience of running away from home. A few authors choose to explore the intersection of racial identity with another collective identity: Priscilla Chan comments on how "being Asian in Chinatown meant climbing over more hurdles to even get to the same starting point" in "Drawing the Boundaries"; Francine Di, who writes about breaking stereotypes as an Asian American jazz musician, wishes that "people, in any country, of any race, [would] see [her] as a singer—not an Asian, not an American—just a singer," in "The Jazzian Singer"; Uyen-Khanh Quang-Dang writes that "simply being a little bigger than all my best friends was . . . devastating to me" as she probes the connection between Asian American body-image expectations and eating disorders in "Thin Enough to Be Asian"; and Michael Kim notes that given the opportunity, he "would wish upon everyone in the world a coming-out experience" as he explores the intricacies of his gay, Christian, and Asian American identities in "Out and About: Coming of Age in a Straight White World."

These essays are not intended to be a comprehensive standard of "the" Asian American experience. Neither is this book presented as a review of all Asian American experiences, for no single book could possibly encompass the whole of Asian America. We are not interested in trying to achieve a superficial representation of Asian America; rather, *Asian American X* provides an array of well-articulated identity essays whose collective intent is to contribute to the ongoing evolution of American culture by promoting discussion about who Asian Americans of our generation are and how we ought to understand ourselves within our current American context.

We have chosen not to divide this collection into sections that would place our authors into groups like country of origin, age, gender, socioeconomic status, or generation. An organizational scheme emphasizing such categories would undermine our attempt to explore the Asian American collective identity, since they would present the temptation for readers to focus their attention solely on the slivers that appeared to be personally relevant. In addition, while reclaiming one's ethnic history can be empowering, *Asian American X* does not intend to spotlight or emphasize differences among Asian Americans, for that may serve to fragment the overall dialogue. Instead, it focuses on examining both our differences and our similarities to achieve an inclusive understanding of our Asian American identity. We also decided against creating other categories, such as sectioning the book into positive or negative takes on being Asian American, or according to stages of identity development. Groupings like the first quickly become difficult or fuzzy, and partitions like the second would place us in the presumptuous and uncomfortable position of rank-ordering the essays and endorsing the false notion that there is only one hierarchical path of self-knowing. Such groupings would also introduce a top-down conceptualization of identity that could preclude the possibility of a necessarily bottom-up dialogue.

Ultimately, we decided to order the essays to form a conversation among themselves. Each essay serves as a response to the experiences, themes, and ideas discussed in the previous pieces and also presents new topics that are considered in following essays. We have refrained from infusing our own interpretations and meanings into the essays by way of editorial comments. The most immediate reason for this is that we believe that these are excellent essays that speak strongly for themselves. Inspired by Henry Louis Gates Jr.'s careful rendering of *The Bondwoman's Narrative*, we have kept our editorial hand to a minimum, requesting only broad structural revisions from our contributors or taking the liberty of minor cosmetic editing.[21] We have labored to present the reader with a set of powerfully written, compelling, original expressions of identity in their entirety. To that end, we have been scrupulous to avoid edits that could potentially narrow the scope of these essays. Our goal is to deliver to the reader a set of excellent data in the form of identity essays that are free of academic jargon and abstract theory and are enlightening and pleasurable to read. At the same time, each story, or "research text," is narrated from a critically introspective perspective, making for a collection that could easily be studied in the classroom.[22]

All works of self-examination hint at the central issue of being that historian Stephen Schloesser calls the "inexorable dialectic" of humanity: to know oneself in a way that "builds on the past but does not become a captive of it."[23] It is this dialectic that so many writers before us have joined. It is this dialectic whose inexorability led us to recognize the need for a critical dialogue on Asian American identity, to embark on the self-reflective journey that became this book, and finally to mark this intersection of voices with *Asian American X*.

We now offer to you the result of our work to strengthen our individual and collective identities within the constantly evolving, fluid nature of American identity. It is by reexamining the roots of our identities and the foundations of our country that we may emerge as unified individuals, mutually strengthened by compassion and sincere respect toward all those around us. Particularly during these precarious times of amplified hope and fear, we hope that others will join us in expanding and developing this dialogue to create a new American identity: "something more complex than either a melting pot or a confederation of separate but equal groups."[24]

Let's begin here—the Asian American "X."

Notes

1. Justin Fong, "The Invasian," *Harvard Crimson*, March 15, 2001, available at <http://www.thecrimson.com/fmarchives/fm_03_15_2001/article6U.html>.

2. "Hate crimes . . . are fueled by discrimination and stereotypes. From where do people get hate, discrimination and stereotypes? From articles like Fong's, articles that perpetuate that cycle of hate and misunderstanding." Christine Ho, "Stereotypes Spur Hate," *Harvard Crimson*, March 19, 2001, available at <http://www.thecrimson.com/article.aspx?ref=103650>.

3. "True, Asians do tend to stick together and share similar tastes in music, clothes, etc. But, what group doesn't? Even so, who cares? Besides, when did this 'sticking to your own' concept become an exclusively Asian phenomenon?" J. Patrick Gatdula, "Style of 'The Invasian' Needlessly Offensive," *Harvard Crimson*, March 19, 2001, available at <http://www.thecrimson.com/article.aspx?ref= 103650>.

4. Elliott Balch, "Students March on *Crimson* to Protest Article," *Harvard Crimson*, March 20, 2001, available at <http://www.thecrimson.com/article.aspx?ref=103665>; Robin Tang, "Invasian Insensitive," *Harvard Crimson*, March 19, 2001, available at <http://www.thecrimson.com/article.aspx?ref=103650>.

5. K. Anthony Appiah, "Identity, Authenticity, Survival," in *Multiculturalism*, ed. Amy Gutmann (Princeton: Princeton University Press, 1994), 152.

6. Arar Han, "Fong Is Right," *Harvard Crimson*, March 19, 2001, available at <http://www.thecrimson.com/article.aspx?ref=103650>.

7. For a discussion on race, identity, and the authentic life, refer to Appiah, "Identity, Authenticity, Survival," 149–63.

8. "Autoethnography" is defined as "an autobiographical genre of writing and

research that displays multiple layers of consciousness, connecting the personal to the cultural," in Carolyn Ellis and Arthur P. Bochner, "Autoethnography, Personal Narrative, Reflexivity," in *Handbook of Qualitative Research*, ed. N. Denzin and Y. Lincoln (Thousand Oaks, Calif.: Sage, 2000), 733–68. See Eric Liu, *The Accidental Asian* (New York: Random House, 1998).

9. Min Zhou and James Gatewood, "Mapping the Terrain: Asian American Diversity and the Challenges of the Twenty-First Century," *Asian American Policy Review* 9 (2000): 5–29.

10. The Hart-Cellar Act of 1965 enabled rapid acceleration of immigration from Asia by abolishing the national origins quota system, and between 1971 and 1996, a total of 5.8 million Asians were admitted as legal immigrants (not counting refugees). More than two-thirds were family-sponsored migrations and about one-fifth was employer-sponsored skilled labor. See Zhou and Gatewood, "Mapping the Terrain," 7.

11. The term "1.5 generation" is defined as "immigrants and refugees born abroad but educated and socialized in the US"; see <http://www.imdiversity.com /article_detail.asp?Article_ID=807>.

12. For a description and history of Paper Son immigration, see <http:// angelisland.org/immigr02.html>. Liz Del Sol, "Finding Our Common Interests: Personal Reflections about the Asian American Movement," in *Asian Americans: The Movement and the Moment*, ed. S. Louie and G. Omatsu (Los Angeles: UCLA Asian American Studies Center Press, 2001), 139–45.

13. J. K. Bernhard, M. L. Lefebvre, K. M. Kilbride, G. Chud, and R. Lange, "Troubled Relationships in Early Childhood Education: Parent-Teacher Interactions in Ethnoculturally Diverse Child Care Settings," *Early Education and Development* 19, no.1 (1998): 7–28.

14. William Wei, *The Asian American Movement* (Philadelphia: Temple University Press, 1993), 47.

15. For a description, see Ronald Takaki, *Strangers from a Different Shore* (Boston: Back Bay Books, 1998), 101–2, 330–31.

16. Wei, *The Asian American Movement*, 47.

17. See <http://www.census.gov/Press-Release/www/2003/cb03–16.html>.

18. Zhou and Gatewood, "Mapping the Terrain," 12–13. The value goes to 75 percent if one looks solely at new immigrant groups and excludes Japanese Americans.

19. Gregory Rodriguez, "Mongrel America," *Atlantic Monthly*, January/February 2003, 95–97.

20. Examples of political figures include Secretary of Labor Elaine Chao, New York City councilman John Liu, two-term governor of Washington Gary Locke, and Secretary of Transportation Norman Mineta. Celebrities include Dean Cain, Tia Carrere, Jackie Chan, Ann Curry, Ang Lee, Lisa Ling, Lucy Liu, The Rock, Ming-Na Wen, Russell Wong, John Woo, and Rick Yune. Mainstream sports players include Michael Chang, Amy Chow, Michelle Kwan, Jeanette Lee, Greg Louganis, Grace Park, Tiger Woods, and Kristi Yamaguchi.

21. Hannah Crafts, *The Bondwoman's Narrative,* ed. Henry Louis Gates (New York: Warner Books, 2002).

22. L. Richardson, "Writing: A Method of Inquiry," in *Handbook of Qualitative Research,* ed. N. K. Denzin and Y. S. Lincoln (Thousand Oaks, Calif.: Sage, 1994), 516–29.

23. Stephen Schloesser, personal conversation (March 2001); Kofi Annan, "Address to the Summit of the Organization of African Unity," 9 July 2001, available at <http://www.dfa.gov.za/docs/annan.html> (12 July 2001).

24. Rodriguez, "Mongrel America," 97.

Bibliography

Annan, Kofi. "Address to the Summit of the Organization of African Unity." July 9, 2001. Available at <http://www.dfa.gov.za/docs/annan.html>. Accessed July 12, 2001.

Appiah, K. Anthony. "Identity, Authenticity, Survival." In *Multiculturalism,* ed. Amy Gutmann, 149–63. Princeton: Princeton University Press, 1994.

Balch, Elliott. "Students March on *Crimson* to Protest Article." *Harvard Crimson.* March 20, 2001. Available at <http://www.thecrimson.com/article.aspx?ref=103665>.

Bernhard, J. K., M. L. Lefebvre, K. M. Kilbride, G. Chud, and R. Lange. "Troubled Relationships in Early Childhood Education: Parent-Teacher Interactions in Ethnoculturally Diverse Child Care Settings." *Early Education and Development* 19, no.1 (1998): 7–28.

Crafts, Hannah. *The Bondwoman's Narrative.* Ed. Henry Louis Gates. New York: Warner Books, 2002.

Del Sol, Liz. "Finding Our Common Interests: Personal Reflections about the Asian American Movement." In *Asian Americans: The Movement and the Moment,* ed. S. Louie and G. Omatsu, 139–45. Los Angeles: UCLA Asian American Studies Center Press, 2001.

Ellis, Carolyn, and Arthur P. Bochner. "Autoethnography, Personal Narrative, Reflexivity." In *Handbook of Qualitative Research,* ed. N. Denzin and Y. Lincoln, 733–68. Thousand Oaks, Calif.: Sage, 2000.

Fong, Justin. "The Invasian." *Harvard Crimson.* March 15, 2001. Available at <http://www.thecrimson.com/fmarchives/fm_03_15_2001/article6U.html>.

Gatdula, J. Patrick. "Style of 'The Invasian' Needlessly Offensive." *Harvard Crimson.* March 19, 2001. Available at <http://www.thecrimson.com/article.aspx?ref=103650>.

Han, Arar. "Fong Is Right." *Harvard Crimson.* March 19, 2001. Available at <http://www.thecrimson.com/article.aspx?ref=103650>.

Ho, Christine. "Stereotypes Spur Hate." *Harvard Crimson.* March 19, 2001. Available at <http://www.thecrimson.com/article.aspx?ref=103650>.

Lee, Stacey J. *Unraveling the "Model Minority" Stereotype*. New York: Teachers College Press, 1996.

Liu, Eric. *The Accidental Asian*. New York: Random House, 1998.

Richardson, L. "Writing: A Method of Inquiry." In *Handbook of Qualitative Research*, ed. N. K. Denzin and Y. S. Lincoln, 516–29. Thousand Oaks, Calif.: Sage, 1994.

Rodriguez, Gregory. "Mongrel America." *Atlantic Monthly*, January/February 2003, 95–97.

Schloesser, Stephen. Personal conversation. March 2001.

Takaki, Ronald. *Strangers from a Different Shore*. Boston: Back Bay Books, 1998.

Tang, Robin. "Invasian Insensitive." *Harvard Crimson*. March 19, 2001. Available at <http://www.thecrimson.com/article.aspx?ref=103650>.

Wei, William. *The Asian American Movement*. Philadelphia: Temple University Press, 1993.

X, Malcolm. *The Autobiography of Malcolm X*. 2d ed. Chicago: African American Images, 1989.

Zhou, Min, and James Gatewood. "Mapping the Terrain: Asian American Diversity and the Challenges of the Twenty-First Century." *Asian American Policy Review* 9 (2000): 5–29.

1 Label Us Angry

Jeremiah Torres

It hurts to know that the most painful and shocking event of my life happened in part because of my race—something I can never change. On October 23, 1998, my friend and I experienced what would forever change our perceptions of our hometown and society in general.

We both attended elementary, middle, and high school in the quiet, prosperous, seemingly sophisticated college town of Palo Alto. In the third grade, we happily sang "It's a Small World," holding hands with the children of professors, graduate students, and professionals of the area, oblivious to our diversity in race, culture, or experience. Our small world grew larger as we progressed through the school system, each year learning more about what made us different from each other. But on that October evening, the world grew too large for us to handle.

Carlos and I were ready for a night out with the boys. It was his seventeenth birthday, and we were about to celebrate at the pool hall. I pulled out of the Safeway driveway as a speeding driver delivered a jolting honk. I followed him out, speeding to catch up with him, my immediate anger getting the better of me.

We lined up at the stoplight, and the passenger, a young white man dressed for the evening, rolled down his window; I followed. He looked irritated.

"He wasn't honking at you, you stupid fuck!"

His words slapped me across the face. I opened my stunned mouth, only to deliver an empty breath, so I gave him my middle finger until I could return some angry words. He grimaced and reached under his seat to pull out a bottle of mace, spraying it directly in my face, barely missing Carlos, who witnessed the bizarre scene in shock. It burned.

"Take that you fucking lowlifes! Stupid chinks!"

Carlos instinctively bolted out the door at those words. He started pound-
ing the white guy without a second thought, with a new anger he had never
known or felt before. Pssssht! The white guy hit Carlos point blank in the
face with the mace. He screamed; tires squealed; "fuck you's" were
exchanged.

We spent the next ten minutes half-blind, clutching our eyes in the burning pain, cursing in raging anger that made us forget for moments the intense,
throbbing fire on our faces. I crawled out of my car to follow Carlos's
screams and curses, opening my eyes to the still, spectating traffic surrounding us. I stumbled to the sidewalk, where Carlos pounded the ground and
recalled the words of the white guy. We needed water.

I stumbled further to a nearby house that had lights in the living room. I
doorbelled frantically, but nobody answered. I appealed to the traffic for
help. They just watched, forming a new route around my car to continue
about their evening. The mucous membranes in our sinuses cut loose, and we
spit every few seconds to sustain our gasping breaths. After nearly five minutes of appeals, a kind woman stopped to call the cops and give us water to
quench the burning.

The cops came within minutes with advice for dealing with the mace. We
tried to identify the car and the white guy who had sprayed us, and they sent
out the obligatory all points bulletin. They questioned us soon after, asking if
we were in a gang. I returned a blank stare with a silent "no." Apparently,
two Filipino teenagers finding trouble on a Friday evening raised suspicions
of a new Filipino gang in Palo Alto—yeah, all five of us.

I often ask myself if it would have been different had I been driving a
BMW and dressed in an ironed polo shirt and slacks, like a typical Palo Alto
kid. Maybe then the white guy would not have been afraid and called us
lowlifes and chinks. I don't think so. He wasn't afraid of us; he initiated the
curses and maced us from a safe distance. He reached out to hurt us because
he was having a bad day and we looked different.

That night was our first encounter with overt racism that stems from a
hatred of difference. We hadn't seen it through the smiles and happy songs of
elementary school or the isolated cliques of middle and high school, but now
we knew it was there. We hadn't seen it through the clean-cut, sophisticated
facade of the Palo Alto white guy, but now we knew it was there. The

"lowlife," "chink," and "gangster" labels made us different, marginalizing us from the town we called home.

Those labels made us angry, but we hesitated to project that anger. At first, we didn't tell anyone except our closest friends, afraid our parents would find out and react irrationally by locking us in our rooms to keep us away from trouble. But then we realized that the trouble had found us, and we decided to voice our anger.

We wrote an anonymous article in the school newspaper narrating the incident and the underlying racism that had come to surface. We noted that the incident wasn't purely racial, or a hate crime, but proof that racist tendencies still exist, even in open-minded suburban towns like Palo Alto. Parents, students, and teachers were shocked, maybe because they knew the truth in what we were saying. Many asked if it was Carlos and me who had been maced, but I responded, "Does it matter? What matters is that some people in this town still can't accept diversity. It's sad." We confronted the community with an issue previously reserved for hypothetical classroom discussions and brought it into the open. It was the least we could do to release our anger and expose its roots, hoping for a change in those who chose to label us.

After the article, Carlos and I took different routes. I continued with my studies, complying with my regimen of high school classes and activities as my anger subsided. I tried to lay the incident aside, having exposed it and promoted self-inspection and possible change in others through writing. Carlos remained angry. Why not? He got a face full of mace and racist labels for his seventeenth birthday. He alienated himself from the white majority and returned the mean gestures of the white guy to the yuppie congregation of Palo Alto. He became an outsider. Whenever someone would look at him funny, he would stare back, sometimes too harshly.

On the day after finals, he was making his way through the front parking lot of school when a parent looked at him funny. He stared back. The parent called him a punk. Carlos exploded. He cursed and gestured all he could at the father, and when he sped away in his Suburban, Carlos followed. Carlos couldn't keep up with the Suburban, so he took a quarter from his pocket and threw it at the back window, shattering it to pieces. Carlos ran away when the cops came to school.

Within two days, students had identified Carlos as the perpetrator, and he was suspended from school as the father called his lawyer, indicting Carlos of "assault with the intent to hurt." Weeks passed until a court hearing, and Carlos attended anger management counseling, but he was still angry—angry that he was being tried over throwing a quarter and that once again "the white guys were winning." His mother scraped up the little money she had to spare to afford him a lawyer for the trial, but there was no contesting the father's accusations. Carlos was sentenced to a night in juvenile hall and two hundred hours of community service over some angry words and throwing a quarter. He became a convicted felon.

He had learned once again that he couldn't win against the labels thrown at him, the labels that hurt him more than the mace or the night in juvy, and so he became more of an outsider. In both cases, the labels distanced us from the "normal" Palo Altans: white, clean-cut, wealthy. That division didn't always exist, however; it was created by the generalizations "normal" Palo Altans made through labels. To them, we looked like lowlifes, chinks, gangsters, and punks. In truth, we were two Filipino Americans headed toward Stanford and Berkeley, living in a town that swiftly disowned us with four reckless labels after raising us for ten years. Label us angry.

Jeremiah Torres is from Palo Alto, California, and studies symbolic systems at Stanford University.

2 1984

Sunita Puri

What I remember most vividly about the party is the colors.

I could not have been more than five years old—in fact, I was definitely five because I remember jumping off of my father's lap when he began yelling and pointing at the television, shocked beyond belief at the horrific images of mass executions of Sikhs following Prime Minister Indira Gandhi's assassination in 1984. Sikhs, a religious group marked visually by their turbans and beards, were targeted in numerous riots across Delhi because Gandhi had been assassinated by previously loyal Sikh bodyguards. I remember much of my father's anger and frustration during that year—the year that the Delhi he knew collapsed under the twin threats of India's second Partition and the advent of terrorism in Punjab, our homeland.

The colors on the television set were both conveniently foreign and eerily familiar. Above all, shockingly frightening. I had never seen the bright red that I saw spilling out of a murdered Sikh sprawled facedown in a dusty Delhi street. The dark blue of his cloth turban, now unraveled beside him, lay somewhere between the sky blue of the Smurfs that I knew and the deep blue of deep sea trenches that threatened to swallow me when I examined pictures of the ocean. The camera suddenly zoomed in on the face of one man who, exhausted, backed away from the Sikh man that he had helped to beat to death. I remember the color of his eyes: a strange, possessed yellow, immediately reminding me of the time I took too many B-vitamin tablets (the chewy, fruit-flavored Flintstones kind) and urinated a thick, deep yellow fluid. I had known only comfortable colors: the fluffy pink of my bedroom, the inviting gray of my cat, the soft black of my mother's hair.

I looked desperately for any sort of familiarity in the room. But the room, full of only my father's friends (who were necessarily male, in keeping with the unspoken Indian tradition of segregating guests by gender at large gatherings), was unfamiliar to all my senses: sight, sound, touch. I grabbed my father's arm and pulled at it, exclaiming, "Daddy! Daddy! I want apple juice!" His arm was strangely cold, and he yanked it away from me, murmuring "Choop karo!" to silence me. Usually, I would get some reaction from another uncle in the room when I acted cute, but this time not even my tinny child's voice could unglue the pairs of eyes in the room from the television. I saw the dark brown eyes of my father's friends lighten slightly as tears welled up and were promptly blinked away. A teardrop flickered in the dim yellow light as it fell from Gurdeep ji. I watched it drop to the lush brown carpet, memorizing its exact location.

I left the room quietly, stumbling over my first *salwar kameez*, a Punjabi dress with baggy trousers and a long, elaborately decorated top that extended like a nightgown to my stubby knees. My grandmother had recently brought the outfit as a present for me when she came to visit and to take care of my brother and me so that my mother could resume her medical residency. It shone a light purple, covered with multicolored sequins in elaborate Gujarati patterns throughout.

A Punjabi girl in Gujarati colors. I was many Indias, all at once. A different India (which I never understood) was a room away, on an old television set.

I made my way through my auntie's kitchen, following a familiar path to the tiny refrigerator in her garage where she kept cold Cokes and Sprites for me to enjoy. As I weaved through an assorted bunch of aunties scrambling to prepare *pulao, sabzis,* and dal for dinner, I found myself stopping just to look at their saris. Some Kashmiri, golden-blue silk shining brightly despite the dimness of the overhead lighting. Some very Rajasthani, with prominent red and green patterns reminding me of pictures of Rajput princes I had seen adorned with very authoritative colors. Some South Indian varieties, made of cotton in light, feminine colors. Lavenders, pastel greens, blues.

And some truly Punjabi. Like my mother's. The image of her hunching over a steaming pot of *pulao,* her long hair draped like a curtain over her slightly plump form, never leaves me. I remember her sari so clearly: a bright, regal purple splashed with dots of yellow, green, magenta. It gleamed in the dim light, drawing attention to the curve of her hips and the slight part of her back and stomach that was visible beneath her *choli* and the *paloo* of the sari itself. Even though I only looked at her briefly, I remember the wonder with which I gazed at the part of her stomach I could see. It was something I had never before seen. Her skin there, truly an amalgamation of our Punjabi-AfghaniCentralAsian history, was two shades lighter than the rest of her, layered in two slight folds that reminded me of the doughy *aata* she used to make chapatis. Two beads of sweat dropped from her forehead onto the part of her sari nearest to her stomach, startling me out of my gaze. As she wiped her forehead, I caught a glimpse of her *choli*, stained with sweat and fragrant with the scent of garam masala, cumin, salt, and *haldi*, combined with okra and onions.

A PunjabiAfghaniCentralAsian in a spotted sari in Indiana. Many lands at once.

After grabbing my Coke, I wandered around the house until dinnertime, when I was too afraid to eat because I did not want to disturb the beautiful appearance of the carefully prepared and garnished food. Usually, at home, my mother would prepare my dinner plate for me, forcing me to eat the quantities of dal, chapatis, and *sabzis* that she found appropriate for a growing girl. I was appalled at the luxury of choosing my own food and portion sizes. It was an unexpected freedom. I carefully dug the serving spoon into the corners of the okra, *matter paneer*, and *rajma* that were not covered with sprigs of parsley garnish.

At dinner, the men were surprisingly quiet while the women chatted excitedly about moving (one of the aunties had gotten a new job in Florida and was leaving soon), news from relatives, and marriage alliances for their older daughters. I listened eagerly, interested especially in how they switched back and forth between Punjabi and English. I never understood why. All of a sudden, Gurdeep ji screamed, "Shut up!"

The table fell silent. I had no idea what had happened, or why. The colors and fragrance of my food seemed to fade into one big black and white scentless mass. The background—the people, the food, the table, the place—vanished, leaving only Gurdeep ji and his angry eyes gazing around.

"Do you know what has happened? DO YOU?"

Gurdeep ji shouted as if nobody was there. I did not look up.

"They have taken our country. They have destroyed my home. YOUR home. Do you not know? Do you not care?" He made no mention of who "they" were. Or where his "home" was. I had always assumed it was at 467 Lakewood Avenue, number four, right down the block from us. Flecks of *sabzi* stuck to his long black beard, interspersing it with tiny red globs full of *masalas*. His lips trembled beneath his beard.

Gurdeep ji got up and left the table. I remember him slamming down his barely used fork before leaving, and looking at it long after he had left as if I might find some explanation, or some words, left on its pokey ends. His napkin crumpled in his empty seat, stained with his fingerprints made with the sauces of the vegetable dishes he had eaten with his hands. We always ate with our hands, using forks and knives only to get at a few remaining peas, some isolated onions. And even then, we used utensils reluctantly. I miss that freedom of gathering around tables with elders and eating with my hands while they coached me on proper technique to pick up and consume rice topped with spiced yogurt. Gurdeep ji was the one who taught me best, showing me how to eat with my hands without spilling on myself or my napkin. Years later, when I would run from my second-grade class at lunch because I was being teased for eating my rice and yogurt with my hands, I would want so badly to find him, to run to him for comfort and bury myself in his beard. Now, as I heard him collect his shoes and coat and close the front door, I wished that I could run to him, to tell him that nobody was going to destroy his home because if they did I would get angry at them.

We ate the rest of the meal in silence. My father spoke up at one point to inform the women of what they had missed on the news. Silence followed. I looked up and saw everything in black and white.

The next day, I went to kindergarten still in a daze, still confused about what had happened and why. What was this home that Gurdeep ji was talking about? Who was the dead man on television? Why was he killed? I had tried to ask my father about it the previous night, but to no avail. He waved off my questions, put me to bed early without making sure that I had brushed my teeth and said my prayers, and talked with my mother long into the night.

At school, we happened to be discussing current events. Somebody mentioned an occurrence in her neighborhood, and another person mentioned something that had happened at the hospital where his mother worked. All spoke brightly, about happy events. I raised my hand.

"My Uncle Gurdeep's house was destroyed, but I dunno who did it."

The teacher looked at me. "Suh-nee-duh, are you sure? What do you mean by 'destroyed'?"

"I dunno. He said it was though."

"Where is your Uncle Goor-teep from?"

I realized that I was angry at her for mispronouncing his name and my name, but I didn't know then what to do. After all, what does a brown child say to a white woman with authority?

"467 Lakewood Avenue."

"Well, I didn't hear anything about that or read it in the papers," she said. "Are you sure?"

I looked at her, angry, and said, "Yes, I'm sure."

Everyone in the class, who had nodded eagerly and listened to what the other students had said, made no reaction to anything I said. The teacher then asked, "Do you mean what happened in In-dee-yuh this past week? Is that what you are talking about?"

"Maybe." I honestly was not sure.

"Well, that's a completely different problem," she said, speaking slowly. Turning to the rest of the class, she said, "In-dee-yuh is a place where people are really wild. They kill each other all the time."

At first, her comments did not register. I was so used to nodding at and accepting whatever the teacher said. ("Never question her, Sunita," my mother would tell me. "She is giving you knowledge. She is there to help you. It doesn't matter if you like her or not. What is there to like or dislike?") Just do your work. Behave. Don't talk in class. If you mess up, it's your fault—not the teacher's. She has the right to punish you, to question you. Because of this very typically Indian attitude toward teachers and education, I had just learned to do whatever I was told, not to be critical of it.

But in the midst of my internal nodding, I noticed blond heads turning and staring at me. Even the girls I pushed on the swingset or rode the merry-go-round with looked at me as if I were a headless monster. Their blue and brown eyes gazed emptily at me—almost as they had when I was the new kid in town, when they looked like they had never seen a nonwhite kid before. (Well, actually, in this part of Indiana they probably hadn't.)

Just then, I became aware.

As my teacher walked up to the board to point out where India was on the pathetic map in the classroom, I wanted so desperately to say something, to say no, this is not a country where we kill each other, it is a country of beautiful saris, of food and culture that you could never imagine, of men with turbans who eat with their hands and enjoy it. Looking back, I am surprised that

I had the reaction that I did, and the capability to remember this incident, but the feeling of foreignness, of being an outsider, of being looked at as Someone Who Killed Others, was very real, and very frightening.

There, I was the Punjabi girl in Rajasthani colors. Many Indias at once.

Here, I was the girl from the Place Where Wild People Killed Each Other. One "In-dee-yuh."

I have been Here and There since then, separating the two as best as I could. I learned the words "stereotype," "racism," and "Orientalism" long after those two days in 1984 had passed. But I will always remember the feelings of anger, confusion, and vulnerability in that innocent, sterile classroom that were my own first definitions of these terms, my first experience of a specific type of racial ignorance that I never learned about in classrooms.

It was the kind that allowed little White Girls to say to me that I was brown because my skin was just really dirty. "Just scrub really hard!" they said. "It'll be as white as ours!"

It was the kind that forced Gurdeep ji to cut his hair, his sacred hair, and to take off his turban or lose his job.

It was the kind that made my parents frightened to eat in public because they didn't know how to use a knife and fork (no silverware in their Darya Ganj or Ludhiana) or to pronounce names of dishes that forced their tongues to move in unfamiliar ways.

I can never forget 1984. It revisits me every day, in the glances I draw from disapproving white people who think I should "just assimilate," "be normal," and remove my *bindi* and *salwar kameez*, replacing them instead with "all-American" jeans and T-shirts. (While they themselves begin to follow Madonna's example and sport *bindis* and skirts made of sari fabric—sold at your nearest Urban Outfitters or Gap. Because "looking Indian" is suddenly "in"—and profitable for the ever-exploitative fashion industry that pays Indians hardly anything to produce goods later sold at sky-rocketing prices.)

It hovers in the condescending voices of people who think Yale's cultural houses, orientation programs for minority students, and ethnic counselors should be eliminated because they "cause" segregation. (Yet these people seek our ethnic groups' endorsements when they run for student body president, promising to draw university attention to "ethnic issues," and only bother to find out the location of the cultural houses when they host parties because all of a sudden *bhangra* remixes or salsa dancing—not the groups who produce the music—matter to them.)

It is the weight on people's eyelashes when they dramatically drop their eyes, shake their heads disapprovingly, open their eyes slowly, and say, "It's *such* a pity that Indian people kill each other all the time. I always thought it was such a peaceful country!" (Yet they say nothing when white Americans kill innocent Sikhs after 9/11 and the Sikh community itself must pay for ads visually distinguishing Sikhs from Muslims. Isn't *this* supposed to be a peaceful country for all people—Sikhs and Muslims included?)

How do I pronounce this anger?

They mispronounce my pain.

Sunita Puri is from Los Angeles, California, and graduated from Yale University with a degree in social and cultural anthropology. She is currently studying South Asian history at Oxford University on a Rhodes Scholarship.

3 Death of a Butterfly

Felix Poon

The sun soothingly shined,
reflecting off the bright and blinding beach,
which consisted of an infinite abyss
of millions of white grains
and a single yellow one—
tranquil as the lapping waves
blown by the calming breeze.

But the waves
came crashing,
down,
with intolerance and insensitivities,
ignorance and idiocy.
They bleached its skin and used files
to shred
and to scrape
and to scorch
the bleach into its skin,
making it so bright white.
Pain and agony,
"racism and hegemony"?

The paper was blank. My *mind* was blank. What a difficult task my fifth-grade teacher, Mrs. Goncalves, had assigned: to pick only one unique word to sum up all the thoughts and feelings, emotions and expressions that made me who

I was. *Hey, I'm smart enough. I can probably devote an entire typed page to myself. Or maybe an entire essay! Oh, I bet that essay could get published in a book!*

Mrs. Goncalves had red-orange shoulder-length hair complemented by her matching red-framed eyeglasses. She was considered to be the nicest teacher in the school because she supposedly treated her students more like adults than fifth-graders, rarely raised her voice, and often had us sing aloud to her cassette songs (anything beat memorizing the names of all 206 bones in our body). One song, the only one I remember from that class, is the one that goes

And I'm proud to be an American,
where at least I know I'm free
and I won't forget the men who died
who gave that right to me
and I gladly stand up,
next to you
something, something, blah, blah
God bless the U.S.A.

Typical grade school propaganda for breeding nationalism that leads to so-called patriotism that whitewashes minds into thinking "democracy" can be achieved by killing some poverty-stricken brown-skinned folk in a country whose name we can't pronounce right. I swallowed it faithfully with a happy smile. The power of the words caused my skin to freeze over me in shock, tightening like saran wrap. The feeling of acceptance and belonging sent chills lining down my spine, tickling me with the sensation of great awe.

"Try to pick a word that is unique to *you*," Mrs. Goncalves emphasized, "so that nobody else will have the same word." I began brainstorming a single word. Previous writing lessons had outlined the rules for the perfect paper: brainstorm, prewrite, first draft, revise, second draft, revise, final draft. *Surely the creation of a single word is no different!* I generated many possible words that I considered. First, I wrote down "fast." *I'm fast with math problems and homework assignments . . . but I'm definitely not a fast runner.* I scratched it out. Then egotistically, *Oh, I'm a lot smarter than everyone here!* I wrote "s-m-a," stopped, and realized it seemed too cocky. Scratched it out. Then another word popped into my mind, and it seemed to be that unique fit Mrs. Goncalves was looking for. I spelled out "d-i-f" and then hesitated for a bit. *It's too embarrassing, I can't write this*. I stared down at the paper, at my right hand, holding the number-2 pencil midair, midstroke, midword.

Mrs. Goncalves interrupted my dilemma. "Okay everyone, share with the person sitting next to you." My arm and my hand began to shake, feeling the weight of my nervousness bearing down upon the sheet of paper. My hands succumbed to the weight of my nerves and quickly penciled in the rest of the word: "f-e-r." *Differ.*

I knew that everyone had their own individual differences and realistically anyone else in the room could have actually picked the word "differ" or "different." The word still felt unique for me. I didn't understand it.

"What's your word?" I asked Brianna, my desk-neighbor.

"Pretty," she said. *Jeez, if I had known you hadn't put so much thought into yours, I wouldn't have put so much thought into mine! I can't share this! I don't even know if "differ" is a real word!* "What's yours?"

"Uh," I hesitated. "It's uh . . . differ."

She laughed. "Differ? Differ? Haha, that's funny. Differ."

I sank into my chair. *Differ.*

Mrs. Bynum's Lesson

Ludlow, Massachusetts: population approximately eighteen thousand; suburban; predominantly white, predominantly inhabited by Portuguese and Polish immigrants; infamous for pumping out amazing soccer stars for the high school team that always won the championship. Ludlow was the only home I knew.

My parents were immigrants from Hong Kong, China. I, like several of my other classmates, was second-generation American. I felt that I had as much claim as my fellow classmates to this wonderful home—*a place of equality created from a diverse melting pot.* I felt that I was *free* like my classmates. *I mean, come on, we can't forget the men who died, who gave that right to us. Aren't you glad to stand up, next to me?*

I was the social butterfly, always talking. I remember my teachers had discipline problems with me because I talked too much to my fellow classmates. I just couldn't stop; I didn't want to stop. Splitting the seating chart into a boy-girl-boy-girl setup actually backfired in my case—I talked more with my female friends than I did with my male friends.

Maybe it was my misbehavior that caused her to hate me, but maybe it was something else too. Mrs. Bynum, an old lady with short gray-white hair, was my second-grade teacher. She was maybe in her sixties. Perhaps "hate" might not be the most appropriate word, but I was definitely her least favorite student (put nicely). One time she stopped in the middle of her lesson and dragged me to the back of the room, irritated by my constant socializing and chatting in class, and gave me a lecture about discipline. The other students just watched the whole thing. On another occasion, she gave me a punitive assignment to do during recess—a sheet full of multiplication problems. That backfired: *Oh, I love these! Yes! This is actually more fun than going out to recess to swing on the monkey bars! Oooh, nine times five, my favorite! Forty-five!*

Mrs. Bynum was one of those teachers who supplemented the texts and the readymade lesson plans with her own lessons. One day Mrs. Bynum, in one of her supplemental lessons, made a comment that really confused me.

"Nobody has black hair," she said.

Thinking about the power that grade school teachers hold instills grave fear within me today. Sure, the texts and the readymade lesson plans had their major flaws, such as huge chunks of missing history like: What happened to those Chinese after they built that railroad? But what messed me up the most, aside from pledging allegiance to the flag every day, were those random "lessons" far worse than anything you could have ever learned, or didn't learn, from those texts. One of these "lessons" that Mrs. Bynum taught was very hands-on. She passed out blank sheets of paper and crayons to every student. An art lesson? No, a lesson in patriotism! Everyone in the class filled out a card to send to an American who was fighting in the Persian Gulf War.

I imagine classmates of mine returning to their nice suburban homes yelling, "Mommy! Today I wrote a card to a man who drives tanks and rolls over and crushes brown people's houses and dreams! I want to be just like him when I grow up!"

And Mommy says, "And you can! Just pursue your dreams, and you can be and do anything you want to! Even crush brown people's houses and dreams in Iraq! I'm sure when you're older, *your* Mr. President can make a special war playground just for you."

"Yay!"

Maybe this dialogue isn't so made up. Perhaps George W. Bush had a Mrs. Bynum equivalent in *his* second grade and ran home to have the same conversation with his mother? Did this Mrs. Bynum equivalent tell W. Bush that nobody has black hair?

Her statement reverberated through my head: *"Nobody* has black hair." *I thought my hair was black?* Even my classmates questioned Mrs. Bynum in disbelief.

"What about Paul?" one girl asked.

"His hair isn't black, it's dark brown."

Maybe my hair is dark brown too; maybe she is right. I was anxious and impatient for Mrs. Bynum to just skip to me and tell me if my hair was dark brown or black.

"What about Sarah?" another classmate asked.

"Hers is dark brown too."

"What about Felix?" asked a classmate. Finally, my answer would come. I was ready to accept whatever came from her mouth as the truth.

"Felix doesn't count." My breathing slowed to a brisk walk, then to a standstill. I was right about the color of my hair—but never had being right hurt so much.

She had said that *nobody* has black hair. I processed this "lesson" rationally. *Am I a nobody? Do I not count? If I have black hair, then the sentence "Nobody has black hair" should be thrown out because I have black hair. Right?* Rational thinking—I think I inherited this from my father. Maybe he passed it down through the black-hair genes. Because of these black-hair genes, does my father not count either? My mother has black hair. My brother and my sister have black hair, and my aunts and uncles and my cousins and my family's friends. Did Mrs. Bynum also mean that they don't count either? Count as who? Or what maybe? As real people? I had swallowed up everything that Mrs. Bynum taught through her lessons, because she was authority. Authority hated me, because I was a social butterfly? Because I talked too much? Or maybe because I have black hair and because I don't count.

Mrs. Bynum's lesson had a bigger impact on my classmates than it did on me, because from that point on, physical differences were slapped into my self-consciousness by them. Jeremy and Philip often stared at my nose and laughed, as if they were watching a circus show. "Why is your nose so flat?" they asked as they pushed their noses in, wide grins on their "normal" faces. I didn't know the answer.

"Your eyes are so thin!" others would exclaim. "How do you see things?" they asked as they pulled their "normal" eyes into tight slanted slits. "I can't see anything! How do you see anything?"

In fourth grade, our school got a flood of new students from another part of town, including two new bullies who taunted me. "Ching-chong-wong-chung!" The mocking words twanged from their lips as they pulled back their eyes into slits. Could it have been true? Their old school had Mrs. Bynum equivalents too? I didn't know what to say. Normally, if I were being taunted for any other reason, I would try to conjure up a comeback, no matter how unwitty or pathetic that comeback was, and countertaunt them. This situation was different. What could I say about them? I could not pick out any physical differences these two bullies had; they were the "normal" ones. Instead I decided to brush it off, smile it off, laugh it off, bottle it up.

One afternoon, after the school day had ended, I was sitting on the bench waiting for the bus along with many other students. "Look! He's Chinese!" A girl's yelling voice caught my attention. I looked in the direction from which the voice had come, noticing a finger pointing at me. She was a new student who had come along with the flood. She was shorter than me and had black hair—wait, nobody has black hair, she must have had dark brown hair then. Anyway, her dark brown hair that looked black was tied into a ponytail behind her head. Everyone's heads turned to look at me. I felt like a rare exotic zoo animal on display.

Another girl, who had witnessed this, stood up either to defend me or to point out the girl's stupidity. "So what? Stupid! Who cares what he is?" she exclaimed. I began to feel very awkward that two girls had entered into an argument over my identity as I sat idly by, not knowing what to say or how to act.

The girl who had pointed out my "Chinese-ness" was taken back in surprise, not sure how to defend her intelligence. Eventually she came back with the only retort she could think of: "You *like* him, don't you?"

"Ew! No, I don't!" the girl in my defense hastily exclaimed.

Caught in the middle, I said nothing because I didn't know how to respond to this show of stupidity. What was I to say?

I was beginning to realize that my black hair, my thin eyes, my flat nose, my different appearance as a Chinese American were truly making me not count. Not count as cool? As accepted? As white? I was beginning to realize that I was the object of humiliation not because I was fat, or wore glasses, or for any of the other reasons to be picked on, but because I am Chinese American. *What can I do to not be a bully target? To be accepted?* Nothing. I will always be that Chinese kid, but maybe that kid Eric, who was always picked on, went on a diet and is at a healthy weight now. Maybe that nerdy-looking kid Nick decided to get contact lenses so he wouldn't have to wear those big, thick, geeky glasses. Maybe those two are feeling that they are finally accepted, that they count. *What can I do to be accepted?*

A sense of belonging was unattainable for me. I was removed from the social picture, and I was too confused to know what to do about it. I was still very book-smart, but I became socially inept. I doubted that anyone would care to hear what I had to say, so I didn't say anything at all. I went from the most social kid in class to the quietest kid in class in just a couple years. I guess Mrs. Bynum's lessons on discipline really worked.

I am the child of immigrants, just like many of the Portuguese and Polish children in Ludlow who were children of immigrants. They were considered all-American, yet I was not. Many of my classmates at school could speak Portuguese. I often overheard the Portuguese American students teaching each other swear words. Even teachers often joined in celebrating this cultural difference by allowing Portuguese American students to teach a few words in class. One day, it was my turn. I was being asked to share some Chinese in my fifth-grade class. "How do you say 'mom' in Chinese?" one of my friends had asked. My friend sparked Mrs. Goncalves's curiosity.

"Yes, how do you say 'mom' in Chinese, Felix?" she asked. Within only a second, the attention of the twenty-or-so students in the class turned to me as they sharply gazed at me, quietly waiting. This was different from my Portuguese American classmates' experiences in that I had an expectation of exoticness to fulfill. My classmates had a preconceived notion of what they thought the Chinese language was—asking me what "ching-chong" meant, taunting me in the halls with "ching-chong-wong-chung." All I knew was that I called my mother "mommy" and that other Chinese Americans sometimes said "mama" or "ma." These words sounded nothing like the words "ching" or "chong" that they were expecting. I began to ask myself what children in China called their mothers. *Do they call their mothers what I also call my mother? I don't want to misrepresent them if I decide to tell my class that I say "mommy."* I felt as if I was the newly appointed spokesperson for all the billions of Chinese people around the world—imagining white men in dirty-brown suits with bulky cameras circling my desk cutting off my escape route; blinding white flashes; microphones decorated with "ethnonews" logos jabbing at my head. "Mr. Chinese Spokesboy! What do Chinese people call their mothers?!"

I remained silent; I didn't know what to say. "Is something wrong?" Mrs. Goncalves asked. "Is there some rule that you can't tell outsiders what the word 'mom' is?"

A rule? How dumb is this question? Her question furthered my confusion, and then I had no idea how to answer the class. And what did she mean by "outsiders"? I was proud to be an American, and I sang the song standing next to my classmates and I considered us *all* to be fellow Americans. *Why would my classmates be "outsiders"?*

I had to give them an answer to get out of the situation. "Mommy." I murmured the word, masking it behind awkwardness.

"What was that?" Mrs. Goncalves asked.

"He said—Moo-mmeeeeeeee." My friend Carlos, sitting next to me, had twisted my word for "mother" into a Bruce Lee–like shrieking cry.

"Well that's good, at least it's similar to *our* word for mother," my teacher commented. *Why look at it in that way? Why not look at it as the English word being similar to the Chinese word, and not vice versa?* They forced my word into being different when it was actually the same. The stereotypes that ganged up on me that day forced my Chinese language to be something extremely exotic—something more different than it actually was. I couldn't make sense of it at the time. I didn't realize the significance of the experience or the answer to the question "why?" Now I know why, however. They were not only forcing my language to be more different than it actually was—they were forcing *me* to be more different from *them* than I actually was.

Felix Poon is from Ludlow, Massachusetts, and studies sociology at the University of Massachusetts at Amherst.

4 A Place Where I Want to Be

Nupur Chaudhury

When I was younger, I used to forget that I was Indian. I used to think that being Indian never came up for me. I now realize that I didn't let it come up for me. I would never search for my Indian-ness. I realize now that what I would do was push it away. I never found my Indian-ness to be of any importance—even my parents didn't find it to be important. All they would tell me in their muddled English—a result of their Indian education, their temporary residence in England, and their twenty years in the United States—was that "my studies," my education, was the most important thing in my life and that my main concern in my life was to, in their words, "get through my studies."

And so, I studied. I studied for what seemed to be my entire life, beginning with my Jewish elementary school and then at my white upper-class private school. But in all the days spent "getting through my studies," I always found something distracting me, something pulling me away from "my studies" that I couldn't quite figure out. Something that made me different.

I remember always being frustrated in elementary school—not from "my studies," no, that wasn't it . . . My frustration lay in the fact that I was not Jewish like my classmates. We would always get the Jewish holidays off from school, along with an explanation of the holiday itself: Whether it was Passover, Rosh Hashanah, or Hanukkah, I knew all about the Jewish holidays and all about the Jewish culture. The Hindu holidays? They were rarely mentioned; neither at home nor at school was there ever a day off for any of them. I never knew as much about the Indian culture and the Hindu traditions as my Jewish classmates knew about their Jewish culture and their traditions. My constant frustration lay in the fact that I did not know as much about myself as my Jewish classmates knew about themselves. My frustration lay in the fact that I was not Jewish, so I could not know all about myself: my religion, my people. I often asked myself why it was that I wasn't Jewish, why it was that I didn't know about myself, about who I was. But I never did find the answers to my questions.

And so, I studied. Third grade . . . Fourth grade . . . Fifth grade . . . They all passed through my life with the same outcome on my report card: *Nupur is an excellent student.* I never did understand that comment, given to me every single year of my elementary life. I never did understand what they thought to be so excellent about me. I wanted so badly to be Jewish, to get my holidays off, to understand my culture and understand my heritage. I wanted so badly to trade all those good grades that I got in school, just to slip the skin that I was forced to wear off my body and wear the skin of another race. Another culture. A race that I knew about. A culture that I understood. But I knew that that was impossible.

And so, I studied. And it was in the fifth grade that my teacher realized that I was amazing at numbers. I was forced to join the town math league, where I was a year younger than everyone else in the competitions and without friends. Even the numbers weren't my friends. Math didn't have brown or white, Hindu or Jew, but math always forced me to be aware and methodical, things that I didn't want to do. I didn't want to be in a classroom after school, with thirty other kids that I didn't really know. What I wanted to do was read. To escape to far-off lands, to distant places. To places that didn't have little Hindu girls in Jewish schools. To places that were far away from the world in which I was living. But no matter how hard I tried, I could never remain in those far-off lands, in those distant places. I always had to return to the world in which I was living so that I could "get through my studies."

And so, I studied. So much so that my teachers at my Jewish elementary school had no other work to give me. Their comments about me being an *excellent student* got me into a white upper-class private school where I had plenty of schoolwork. When I entered this private school, I found that in the literature classes, all of us students were encouraged to draw upon what we knew, in terms of our lives and experiences, and apply it to the books we read. Our teachers thought that bringing in our personal experiences would help us analyze and decode the books that we read. I would often wonder what of my life, what of my experiences would help us analyze and decode the books we

read . . . A first-generation Indian, a confused Hindu . . . these had no relationship to either *Jane Eyre* or *Great Expectations,* either *The Odyssey* or *To
Kill a Mockingbird.* I loved all these books, they took me to those far off-lands
that I loved so dearly, but when it came time to sit in my freshman and sophomore English classes, I would have nothing to say. When the class talked
about a character's similarity to Christ, or a historical reference, I would
always be lost and I would always feel out of place. I always felt as though I
were in limbo when I was in class, never quite part of the discussion but never
quite far from it. As if I were just outside the room, looking in. I would be
able to hear everything that was discussed in the class, but not in its entirety.
I always would ask the teachers for explanations of the Trinity or what Moses
actually did, but after a while, I stopped asking. Because I never could open
the door to that room. Because I never could join the class. No matter how
hard I tried, I was always looking into the room, watching the class move on.
Without me. I often became frustrated, this time not at what I *didn't* know but
at what I *had* to know in order to do well in the class. *When would people be
forced to learn about my culture?* I would often think as I studied Christianity,
European history, and other such markers of white culture. *When would I
learn about me?* But it was still "my studies" that I had to be concerned about,
and "my studies" involved learning about white culture.

And so, I studied. I learned everything and anything that related to white
culture and nothing that had to do with my culture. Everything that had to do
with the white books that we were reading and nothing to do with me. I realized that the only way to do well in school was to deny what little I knew of
being Indian and Hindu and adopt white culture as if it were my own. Study
it as if it were my own.

And so, I studied. I buried myself in "my studies": in the Holocaust, in
European history, in the civil rights movement. I tried to please my parents
by doing well in school. But as I buried myself in "my studies," I denied an
important part of me. The part of me that says that I am not like everybody
else. The part that says that I am different. I denied a part of my soul, a part
of my being. I denied my very existence and filled it with everybody else:
blacks and whites, gays and straights, Jews and Christians. Everyone but me.
But the denial of myself and the acknowledgment of everyone else made me
hurt even more. *When would it be my turn?* I would think. *When would we talk
about me?*

Junior year came, and my future, according to my parents, was nonexistent. I stopped doing well in school. My frustration with "my studies" became a problem for me. No matter how hard I studied, I couldn't do well. I became what my parents feared most: average. It was with this frustration with "my studies" that I entered my expository writing class, a required class for all juniors. Expository writing was unlike any class I had ever taken in the sense that it gave me the freedom to write what I wanted to write. With each writing assignment I was taught the style of writing, but the subject matter was entirely up to me. Each paper gave me the chance to explore whatever I wanted about who I was. Each paper gave me the chance to be free.

And so, I wrote. I wrote about anything and everything that I cared about. As an Indian. As a Hindu. I wrote about the history of classical Indian dance. I wrote about affirmative action in the United States. I wrote about the death of my grandmother. I wrote about my trip to India. And for my final paper—the paper that counted for more than half of my grade, the paper that I spent a whole semester writing, my longest paper—I wrote about India. India and its struggle for independence. Why a country like India was ready for a leader like Gandhi and what Gandhi, "the Bapuji of India," did to make his movement so successful that it led to his country's independence. I spent four months of my life on that paper, researching, writing, and thinking about India. Four months on something that I had been waiting my whole life to do. And it was in that process that my soul awakened. It was in that process that I began to see who I was, where I came from. Things that I didn't get from school. Things that I didn't get from my parents. That paper was where I began.

I returned to my private school for my senior year with a different outlook. I threw out the school's required summer reading list, and in its place I invented my own. A summer reading list full of books that I could relate to. As an Indian. As a Hindu. Salman Rushdie's *Midnight's Children*, Rabindranath Tagore's *Gitanjali* . . . My self-imposed reading list was full of books that pertained to me. Full of books that *were* me. Gone were the white books, and in their place were the books that had my soul. That had my culture. That had my heritage. Books that had a part of me.

And so, I read. I read about everything Indian. Everything Hindu. Anything and everything I can get my hands on. I no longer deny my Indian-ness just to "get through my studies." I learn about it. I've embraced it. And the

5 Comings and Goings

Vinh Nguyen

Breast milk: It's the reason why I am here today, healthy and alive and able to share my experiences as an Asian American in this country. Aside from its nourishing attributes which encouraged my growth, breast milk is the essential reason why I am here—in the United States—and not in Vietnam, where I would have been, had it not been for that oh-so-tasty and enriching refreshment enjoyed by countless millions of screaming infants out there. Yeah, you're probably scratching your head right now, wondering if all this nonsense has a point to it . . . Well, it does; it just takes a while for that point to come into fruition. So read along! Smile! Shed a tear! *Relate!* You can do just about *anything*, so as long as you take a moment at the end to reflect upon your own experiences as Asian, and as American, in this country. Asian American: You. Me. *We.* (Extremely corny line, admittedly.)

Going

Year: 1981. *Setting:* Small village on outskirts of Hue, Vietnam. Rice paddies everywhere. No electricity. No running water. No nothing. Situation: People are running back and forth, grabbing things, dropping things, losing things. Many of them are getting ready to board fishing vessels and sail away from their homes, their families. To where? And why? Clouds and smoke pollute the sky.

[Enter my Mom, holding an infant of three weeks wrapped in a bundle of sweaters. Her three-year-old son, Phuoc, is by her side. The infant is crying.]

Mom [talking to the bundle of sweaters; well, actually, not to the sweaters necessarily but to me, the infant, who is buried within the sweaters—it just looks as though she's talking to the sweaters; whatever, you get my point]: Oh dear! Oh dear! How will I be able to go? I can't bring you along. You'll surely die out there in the open seas! But I can't leave you here. There will be no milk for you to drink. Oh dear! Oh dear!

[*Enter my Grandmother. She is also crying.*]

Grandmother: You must leave him here! There's no way he can survive a two-week voyage up the South China Sea. The winds are fierce, the monsoons are imminent. The poor baby will certainly die if you take him with you.

Mom: That's what I'm afraid of. But if I leave him here with you, how will he get his milk? Powdered formula is not available in this village and there isn't anyone who will wake up in the middle of the night and breastfeed a crying baby! I am his mother; that is my responsibility.

[*Grandmother thinking. Her hand is under her chin. She's thinking really hard.*]

Grandmother [shrugging her shoulders]: Ehh, you're right. Okay, take the little shit. Just make sure he's kept warm on the boat. But one thing: You have got to leave Phuoc behind. I am old. All of my children have left me or are leaving me, leaving this country. I have no one to take care of me once everybody's gone. This is all I ask of you.

Mom: But mother, I can't—

[*Seeing that Grandmother is heartbroken and realizing that, yeah, she would be all alone, Mom changes her mind.*]

Mom: Okay, I'll leave Phuoc behind. I don't know how I could abandon my firstborn, but at least I know he'll be in good hands.

[*Sound of boat motors heard in the distance.*]

Grandmother: They're beginning to leave now. Go, my dear. Your husband is waiting for you on the boat. [*She picks Phuoc up.*] I will take good care of this grandson and hopefully, you'll take good care of the one you're carrying. Go now, leave. Everybody's leaving.

[*Grandmother, carrying Phuoc, begins to cry. Phuoc also begins to cry. Mom, too, begins to cry. The infant, by default, due to his young age and maybe a couple of*

clumps in his pants, has been crying all through the dialogue. Kisses are
exchanged between everyone. People are running around everywhere. Confusion
overwhelms. Mom reaches boat, with infant in arms, and climbs aboard. Husband
is with her, along with many other people. Boat sails away. To where? To where?]

That is the account given to me by my mother of how I left Vietnam. She
often tells me that had there been powdered formula available, I would have
definitely been left behind with my grandma. Whenever I tell this story to
other people, I always tweak it a bit by saying, "Had there been a spare *breast*
anywhere . . ." I don't know; I just think it sounds funnier that way. But seriously: Breast milk (or the lack thereof) is the only reason why I was *not* left in
Vietnam and why my older brother, Phuoc, was. Rage and violence consume
his thoughts whenever I joke with him about this. He does not find it funny.

About a year after my parents and I sailed away from Vietnam, we came
to the United States. No, we didn't sail *straight* from Vietnam to America.
Who do you think we are? *Imperialists?* From Vietnam, we sailed to Hong
Kong. From Hong Kong, we sailed to the Philippines, where we spent several months living in a refugee camp. I don't remember any of it and I'm glad
I don't: The term "refugee camp" does not sound very appealing to me;
refugee *resort* maybe, but definitely not *camp*. Okay, whatever: I wound up in
the United States—that's all that matters, really.

Overcoming

Living in the United States was unlike anything my parents had ever experienced in Vietnam. They were from the countryside, where houses were
hand-built, sugarcane swayed in the breeze, and children ran around bare-
footed. In Stockton, California, we lived in a two-bedroom apartment with
about ten other people, most of them my aunts and uncles. Similar to my stay
in the Philippines, I don't remember any of it. I was too young to record any
of those moments in my head. Sure, we have pictures and stories and what-
not, but those are not as good as having the actual experiences in your head—
of which I have absolutely nada. In fact, I have no recollection of *any* events
that happened to me prior to 1986, when I was five years old. But I'm thinking most people are the same way, so . . .

September 1, 1988: I was turning seven years old. I did not know this.
Nobody had ever told me which month and day I was born on; or maybe they

had, but, as you've probably noticed, I have a crappy memory. So there I was, sitting in my second-grade classroom, doing copycat worksheets or looking at baseball cards or doodling stuff, when suddenly my teacher, Mrs. Religo, announced to the class that it was my birthday. This came as a surprise to me. *Could it be today?* I wondered. Maybe—I wasn't sure.

Mrs. Religo made me stand up in front of the class so that I could be sung to. As my dear teacher was leading the entire class in a "Happy Birthday to You" song, I got completely shy and embarrassed and wanted the whole celebration to stop. I interrupted that lovely song—that lovely song being sung to me, no less—and started shouting at Mrs. Religo: *"Today is my lie birthday! Today is my lie birthday!"* What I really wanted to say was that today was my *fake* birthday, that it *wasn't* my real birthday. Obviously, that was not the line that spewed out my mouth. *Lie birthday?* What the hell was that? My teacher stopped singing that spectacular rendition of that goddamned popular song and asked me, *"Lie* birthday? What do you mean?" I meant that today was not my real birthday, that it was on another day—I'm not sure which—but I definitely knew that it was not on this day. Of course, those were not the words that came out. No sir, nothing came out of me except for tears and whimpering. Yep, I was actually crying in front of my teacher and all my classmates, those lovely and thoughtful people who had been singing to me only seconds earlier.

I don't know the exact reason for my excessive display of emotion, but as I think about it now, I'm pretty sure it was due to my frustration with the English language. I knew the things I wanted to say, but I could only express them in my native Vietnamese. English was still a new language to me, and I did not have a firm grasp on it during the second grade. As stated before, my family and I had come as refugees to this country only a few years earlier, and none of us could speak English. That lack of language was apparent in me when I entered grade school. Honestly, I don't know how I ever passed kindergarten and first grade—I must have been good at cutting and pasting or something. I didn't know any English back then, except those usual words people first learn when they're in a new country. (Yes, motherfucker, I'm talking about profanity. Ahem, excuse me.)

My deficiency in English came to a head on that glorious day in second grade. That was the first time I spoke loud so that people could hear me and was also the first time that I was aware of people looking at me. While I was talking. In English. Yes! Yes! Now I'm definitely sure of the reason why I wept that day: It was because I wanted to express my thoughts in English but was unable to do so. Also, everybody was staring at me and so I got self-conscious about my broken speech. Crying was the only avenue that I could take, and so I went for it. And I remember crying for a really long time, so long that the school had to contact my mom so that she could pick me up—I was that uncontrollable. Mrs. Religo tried to explain the entire situation to my mom, who understood less English than I did, but it was all to no avail. On the drive home, my mom asked me why I had caused such a fuss, but I was too embarrassed to tell her. I just did that signature move used by all young kids and pretended not to hear her. I stayed silent all the way home. When I finally got home, I washed my face and probably picked my nose (both nostrils) and went to open the refrigerator and was greeted by a birthday cake. Birthday cake? Shit, I guess it had been my birthday after all. I felt so dumb, man . . . you just don't know.

Shortly after the events of my seventh birthday, I was placed into the ESL program at my school. I hated attending those ESL sessions because I had to leave Mrs. Religo's class each day and trek to a puny portable at the other end of the school where the ESL sessions took place. That tiny room was a nightmare for a kid like me: Workbooks, pencils, letters—learning-oriented stuff—filled every wall, cubbyhole, and desk inside that room. On top of that, there were teachers who could speak Vietnamese and communicate with my non-English speaking parents, if I were to ever mess around. It was horrible, but in hindsight, it was essential to the development of my speaking abilities. I endured ESL for nearly two years, and then when I entered fourth grade, my English was comparable to all the screaming and jumping kids around me. At about this time, my father made it a requirement that I read an hour a day, every day. This was so shitty.

When I was younger, maybe about five, I would always go to the library with my dad so that he could check out remedial, self-help English books. He was attending classes at a local junior college and had had difficulty understanding the things being taught. So we would go to the library, he and I, and look at all the amazing and wonderful books available for our choosing. I checked out a few books here and there, mostly ones that were big as a pillow and had bright, colorful pictures inside; if the pictures popped out, then even better. My dad borrowed mostly grammar and vocabulary books, each containing a million-billion pages and completely filled with words. I remember watching him sit by the lamplight and just *recite* the words, as if the more he recited, the more he would understand. Unfortunately, learning a new language is never that easy. In actuality, he didn't understand *anything* he read, and eventually, he gave up. He had four kids—all under the age of six—bills to pay, lives to improve, and so he stopped going to school and just worked as a gardener. As the years went on, my father gradually got the hang of English through listening to his kids, watching TV, reading newspapers, and such. I don't think he'll ever lose his heavy accent or conquer those moments when he can't find the right words to communicate his thoughts, but he has definitely struggled hard and come far from where he began. Okay, back to the required-reading part.

Around fourth grade, my father required all four of us kids to read an hour a day, every day. Yeah, I hated going to those ESL sessions, but this was pure fucking torture. I was young! Full of energy! I wanted to climb trees, smash bottles, ride bikes! Anything besides reading! But since I obeyed everything that my father said, I was stuck on the couch, an hour a day—*every fucking day*—scrolling my eyes across endless pages and secretly wishing they would conflagrate in my hands. Dude, I read so many books between fourth grade and tenth grade that I began to notice a difference between the way I spoke and wrote, and the way my friends spoke and wrote. I was much more refined, eloquent . . . um . . . *sophisticated* in my use of English, as compared to my friends. (Yes, you're probably saying, "Stop fucking lying, Vinh. You write like a piece of shit. You use simple, elementary words and you cuss over and over again. Shut the fuck up about being *refined* and *sophisticated* and all that nonsense. I don't believe you." Well, alls I can say is: I got a pretty good score on the verbal part of my SAT [*nodding my head*]. I'm not gonna give any numbers, but it's pretty *up there*. Okay, I'll stop inhaling helium now. Read on.)

Becoming

The ability to speak my mind and write my thoughts with the English language was very convenient. (Understatement.) I could confidently talk/argue/cuss-out/flirt with any person/teacher/prick/cute girl I pleased. There were no fears of lost words or heavy accents; as far as I could tell, my English was 100 percent understandable to any poor soul who had to listen to a ramble-mouth like me speak. But unfortunately (there's always an "unfortunately," for some reason) with this so-called convenience, there also came the inconvenience, which lurked behind at a distance and was visible in the rearview mirror, ready not only to make mush out of my bumper but to smash straight through the back windshield and plop right alongside me in the passenger seat. And the accident happened exactly like that. However, even though I was aware that this "accident" was happening in my life, I was completely apathetic toward it. You see, in gaining my new language and new culture, I was "accidentally" bleeding out my own.

Similar to how some people lose their religion ("That's me in the corner . . .") or their car keys (probably in the corner of the sofa), I was losing my Vietnamese culture, cornering it into a peripheral space in the distant parameters of my life and simply detaching myself from it. This "losing-of-culture" phenomenon flashed its fangs sometime around sixth grade, when I started becoming more self-conscious of who I was in relation to others. This self-conscious business was nothing unique or exclusive; every pimply-faced, squeaky-voiced kid in the beginning stages of puberty experiences the same thing. Sure, our bodies morph at different rates and our girl/boyfriends change every other Wednesday, but the one thing we all have in common around the age of twelve and thirteen is that we are all self-conscious. Besides worrying about the stiff-solid stance of my hairstyle and the "gangsta-ness" of my gang-bang slang, however, I was also preoccupied with many of the "abnormal" characteristics of my native culture.

We didn't celebrate any American holidays at home, but nobody at my school knew that. As far as they were concerned, I was a big flag-saluting, turkey-eating, Star Spangled-singing Asian boy. I never invited any of them over to my house anyway, for my house carried a stench of burning incense and Vietnamese food, smells I assumed other non-Vietnamese weren't accustomed to. I had mostly Vietnamese friends, but I didn't let them in my house either, mostly because we were poor and I was somewhat ashamed of it. Whatever. I dyed my hair, subscribed to *Rolling Stone*, wore my shoes around the house, and even changed my name: At school and elsewhere, I was no longer known as "Vinh"—"Vinny" had emerged and blossomed into this Asian American, oftentimes much more "American" than "Asian" and oftentimes satisfied that that was the case.

But was I making a concerted effort to reject my Asian roots? Was I making all those decisions with the thought "I want to be white, I want to be white" tagged in the back of my mind? No, of course I wasn't. I dyed my hair because my friends dyed theirs. I became "Vinny" because a few people started calling me "Vinny" and after a while, it stuck. I started wearing shoes around the house because . . . well . . . I don't know why, really—I just did. But none of those things were done with the intent of "becoming white." They were done because they felt white—I mean, *right*—at the moment. I was a teenager; I didn't know what the hell I was doing half the time any-ways. Then one day, one of my cousins accused me of being "whitewashed." This bothered the shit out of me.

What's the definition of "whitewash"? I can't provide you with an exact, *Webster's*-quality answer, but it's something to the effect of: "Trying to be white when you're not fucking white." Was that me? Did I really, truly, *con-sciously* want to become white? I don't know, but that accusation plagued my head similar to the way girls did: Both made me utterly confused and uncer-tain of myself. I mean sure, I didn't walk around with "Asian Pride!" scrawled on my backpack, nor did I wear a necklace with a fat Buddha dan-gling freely off the chain. But was I "whitewashed" because of that? I didn't think so. Who cares if my favorite band was Oasis and if I was known to sport a few "skater" shirts now and then? I wasn't "whitewashed." I had a lot of white friends, but all of my close ones were Asian. And all the girls I had ever gone out with were Asian as well. (By ninth grade, I'd only had two girl-friends—not many, but enough as to allow me to write "girls" in plural. Lucky me. What a stud I am.) That "whitewashed" claim clung to me for some time, and then in the summer of 1996, when I was fourteen years old, I went back to the place I had abruptly abandoned during my infancy: I was making my return to Vietnam.

I'm Coming

The humidity was unbearable as my family and I touched down in Saigon. I had never inhaled air that was so warm and moist in my life. It was like breathing with a Ziploc bag sealed around my head, less all that CO_2, of course. That was the first adjustment I had to make in Vietnam. The second adjustment was the mosquitoes. They loitered around in the air—*every-where!*—and pillaged innocent victims such as myself and kept us in constant motion, scratching god-forbidden places using the most god-awful things.

Our family was from Hue, a city centered in the center of central Vietnam. (Redundant, you say?) At the time, the one airport in Hue was under repair, so the only way we could reach Hue from Saigon was by van. Upon first thought, this didn't seem that bad: The distance between Hue and Saigon is similar to the distance between San Francisco and Los Angeles—around four hundred miles. Okay then, I thought. I could sit through a drive of that distance. No problem. But then we had to factor in the two drivers, bringing the total number of people up to nine. And then the suitcases, which we had overpacked to the extreme. And then the boxes—there were so many fucking boxes. Goddamn. In an instant, that "oversized" van filled to the brim and that option of "sitting" through the drive was no longer on the table; it was replaced by "contorting." And contort I did, for the entire duration of the twenty-two-hour drive, save the three bathroom/food breaks.

Normally—as in *"Normally, in the United States . . ."*—it usually takes about five or six hours to cover a four-hundred-mile distance. We're lucky. We have paved roads, many of them going to certain destinations. For the most part, we avoid mountainous or "hilly" terrain if we can because we have many options. On our "dirt-road trip" in Vietnam, we literally traveled on that: a dirt road. It was modest in size and appearance (just dirt; a few pebbles here and there, but mostly dirt) and was indifferent to scenery: It stretched up the countryside, curled along the coast; it rolled right through the rice fields and hung off the hills. I'm no expert on relationships, but from my assessment and experience on riding that road, I can certainly say that that road was infatuated with hills; that's why it took so long to reach Hue! We had to drive up, down, around, and through so many hills, and *up some more*—it was nauseating.

The only comfort I had during the hellish ride was the stars: Nighttime in Vietnam brought forth a flurry of stars, more alive and vibrant in those skies than anywhere in California. There was no illumination from streetlamps, electric signs, or billboards. Everything around us was black except for the heavens above (and yeah, the stupid headlights of the van below, but that was necessary). My head was fixed to the sky during the evening, with my eyes staring off into space and my mind wishing I could be there. In that van, at night, I was a dreamer, but I wasn't asleep; it's amazing how clear your thoughts become when the blanket above you is a brilliant night sky, wrapping you in and comforting your entire being. (Okay, that's enough of this "artsy" crap. I was just experimenting. You know how it is.)

When we finally—*finally!*—got to Hue, we didn't stop. We drove some more. Apparently, our family wasn't from the actual city of Hue, but from a small village, An Duong, located on a tiny strip of island off the central coast.

My heart was broken, and I felt that if we continued any further, my back would be in the same condition. Thankfully, our village wasn't too far from Hue, and so I was able to endure the pains of a few more miles. As the van traveled over a bridge and onto a road that grew increasingly more uneven, my parents recalled stories from their youth and pointed to places/things they recognized. Their voices carried a tune of excitement and nostalgia; I knew that we were close. But was I ready to see my grandmother, that lovely and powerful woman who had insisted that I be left behind when my parents made their escape? (Breast milk, remember?) What about my brother, Phuoc, the one who *was* left behind? I had never spoken to him in my life, and the last time I saw him was through my infant eyes. What would our initial encounter be like? Joyous? Awkward? Tearful? I didn't know. Suddenly, waves of butterflies winged in my stomach and nervous energy spilled throughout my body. I was having doubts. I wasn't so sure of wanting to be there anymore; I wanted to be elsewhere. But then, I had no option: We were there. Literally. The van was parked in front of my grandmother's house and there were so many people standing in her front yard.

As each person slowly climbed out of the van, I just lay there. I could hear the ecstatic cries of the villagers—many of them related to me in one way or another—as they commented on the appearance of my parents and younger siblings. "My, look how big/tall/handsome/pretty/healthy/blah-blah you are," followed by more commotion. I was still supine in the van; I did not want to come out. I could feel emotions brewing inside of me, and they had a propensity to escape through my eyes and trickle down my cheeks in the form of tears; however, I did not want to cry in front of all those people. I was a teenage boy: Crying was not something I did in front of strangers. So I continued to lie there, like a stowaway or fugitive or cripple, and then I heard my mom calling for me from the outside: "Vinh, what are you doing in there? Get out here right now! Everybody wants to see you." Fucking hell. So with the utmost lethargy and reluctance, I urged myself up and slid out the side door. Immediately, hands were upon me.

"Is this him? Is this actually him? That tiny little baby that left me so many years ago? God, look how big he has become!" My grandmother was crying as she said those words to me. She was hugging me. My aunts were hugging me. Everyone was hugging me. I felt like a pop star. The levee was weakening and I could feel an onrush of tears at any moment . . . then I saw my brother. *Man, he looked just like me.* I could feel my eyes getting heavy, watery. All I

could do was stare at him as he came closer and closer. I didn't know what to do, say, or feel when he stood right in front of me. All I could come up with was, "Hey, whatsup?" How fucking pathetic of me. We were brothers—same mom, same dad—separated shortly after my birth. I was raised here, he was raised there. This was the first time I had seen him in nearly fifteen years, and my greeting to him was, *"Hey, whatsup?"* He didn't even know English, forgodsake! I wanted to suck those words back as soon as they flew from my mouth. We embraced for a quick (really quick) moment and then I fled to the bathroom. I was surprised to discover that the bathroom was actually that: a *bathroom*, complete with a sink, toilet, showerhead—the whole bit. I had always assumed that it was a big hole in the ground, but this was pleasant. In the bathroom, nothing was expelled from my body except for tears. Yeah, yeah, I came in the bathroom to cry. I let the shower run (so that I could not be heard) and sat on the toilet (with my pants still on) and cried. (Like I said before: I have a problem crying in front of other people, especially strangers. I don't know. Maybe it's a "guy" thing. I'll work on it.)

At first, I had a difficult time adjusting to life in An Duong. Aside from the aforementioned humidity and mosquito problem of Vietnam, there was the monotony, simplicity, and plain ol' boredom of Vietnam. There was nothing to do. Sure, you could saunter about and visit all the aunts whose names you didn't know and see their kids whose faces somewhat resembled yours. Cousins. Distant cousins. Great uncles, aunts, people, so many people. Yeah, it's cool to see and meet them all, but I had already done that within my first three days of being there. After that, there was nothing to do. Not even TV. Dang, I thought, it's gonna be a helluva long month staying here. I wish I had a Gameboy or something. Of course, my quick-to-prejudge attitude came to crumble once I finally got past the superficial reasons as to why I was in Vietnam and what it was *supposed* to mean to me. I was not there to ride towering Ferris wheels or browse through super-mega-hyper-shopping malls. I was there to experience the place of my birth, my homeland. I was there to spend time with my relatives, whose presence I had lived without for all my life. I needed to live as they lived, talk as they talked, and find comfort and connection in the things they cherished. I relinquished my "poor sport" attitude and embraced what was in front of me: Home. Culture. Family. The rest of my stay in Vietnam was as memorable as anything I have ever experienced.

It's amazing how brief and fleeting time becomes when you're engaged in experiences that you will remember forever. When I was in Vietnam, I saw how "whitewashed," or "Americanized," or whatever it is you want to call it, I had become, only because everything there was so different from how it was in the U.S. I spoke Vietnamese with an "American" accent and I looked differently, dressed differently, walked differently, and even rationalized differently: I became aware of the distinct difference between Western thought and Eastern thought. When the day for our departure came on the calendar, I regretted not being able to stay longer and cried as I hugged my grandmother, brother, aunts, cousins—everyone. This time, it wasn't isolated, but out in the open where everyone could see me. I tried to stop, but it was uncontrollable. The tears kept on streaming as we lifted off and I watched the airport shrink away in the distance.

When I came back to the United States, I tried to "reacquaint" myself with the Vietnamese culture I had shoveled aside, but it was very difficult. I attempted to speak Vietnamese with my friends who were Vietnamese, but my vocabulary was extremely limited. I wanted to learn how to read and write in Vietnamese, but impatience got the better of me. I was curious to know more about the history of Vietnam, but was sidetracked by something else I thought to be more interesting, but I forget what it was. I dabbled with the teachings of Buddha but quickly discovered that they were not for me. I tried so hard to keep the will of "becoming more Vietnamese" alive, but I couldn't. I was still, after all, a teenager and was undisciplined in many aspects of my life. I spent the rest of high school in a state of ambivalence, conflicted in my intent of "becoming more Vietnamese" and what I was actually doing to achieve that. I wasn't sure about anything I did and was confused by everything I tried, so eventually I stopped caring. *Apathy: A longtime friend of mine/ So fine, So fine/ With Apathy, I can deal with problems of any kind/ Any kind.*

Here. Now.

Currently, as I am writing this, I am a changed and changing person, whatever that means. I am at the point in my life where I need to decide which paths I want to take and how far I want to endeavor down those paths. I am not sure; I am still searching. But in the effort to find those roads, I encountered again the feelings I harbored shortly after my trip to Vietnam: I wanted to become more Vietnamese. This time, however, my head is not caught in a crisis and I am less critical of the things I do. I have come to realize that it's too hard to determine whether an action I take is more "Vietnamese" or more "American." Who knows? They don't have charts for those kinda things. Sure, you could tally one up for the "American side" because I bought a Nirvana CD last week, but you could easily equalize that with one for the "Vietnamese side" because I own a Honda Civic. Essentially, all this adding and judging and pondering leads you nowhere but to a place of little resolution and shitloads of confusion. It brought me a pile of that gloppy stuff. But now, with three years of college crossed off my list and invaluable lessons instilled in me, I move through life with more direction—and less confusion—proud to be Asian and American, divergent roots from which I sprang to appear before you in the form of these words.

Just as our many Asian cultures are plentiful and unique, so are our individual experiences in this country. Some of us are immigrants, others are fifth-generation. Some are affluent, others are still clawing. Some find themselves the only one, others are just *"another one,"* lost in a swarm of black hair and brown eyes. The degree of difference in our respective lives is vast, but it is those differences that mold us into the individuals we are today. I have been to ESL classes, Asian American conferences, and Tet festivals, all of which have led me to this book—a book by Asian Americans and for Asian Americans—authoring this extensively long, corny, sometimes-funny-though-usually-not essay. Your experiences also led you to this book, compelling you to pick it up and graze through its contents. But you know, it's only fitting and proper and necessary that you—that *we*—"stumbled" upon this book: It's a marker telling us that we're on the right path and we're on our way to make a difference. *What's gonna change?* Who in the hell knows. Sure, we're still young, and sometimes we get detoured from our path. Nevertheless, we continue to forge ahead, still strong, still determined; soon we'll be uplifting, inspiring, ideal. Soon, our dreams will come into bloom, the world will heal, and we will love immensely. But for now—*for now*—we will just remain proud: Proud to be Asian. Proud to be American. Us.

Vinh Nguyen is from Stockton, California, and graduated from the University of California, Berkeley, with degrees in English and Southeast Asian studies. He currently teaches and writes.

6 Seoul Searching

Rebecca J. Kinney

Usually the metal bars lining the ceilings of a commuter train exhaust me. Whether in San Francisco or in Paris, I always find my arm stretched out like a human Gumby when faced with the uncomfortable reality of a full train. In Korea, however, the subway trains are better suited to fit my compact build. My arm reaches easily above to secure myself against the jarring of the train.

As I ride the subway around Seoul I find myself an "invisible foreigner" until I open my mouth. People turn to see the "American," speaking English with a bit of Detroit twang. No "American" is detected, all they see is me. I traveled halfway around the world and I am still faced with a second round of questions after I tell people I am American. "But aren't you Korean?" "What are you?" How is that for irony? The dominant way that people think about identity is constrictive but is still able to transcend borders, moving fluidly over place and time. I struggle to claim and create a space representative of my multiple identities, but my international status only seems to complicate things.

I began my life, transnational garbage—thrown out, abandoned. Picked up thousands of miles away and loved. I am one of thousands of Korean children who were adopted by United States citizens. This is where my traditional narrative begins, six months old and on a flight from Seoul bound for Detroit to a family already comprised of a mom and dad, both descendants of poor white sharecroppers, and a three-year-old sister who had been adopted from Korea three years earlier. However, I have begun this piece on "Asian American identity" where I am right now, at a PC bang in Seoul.[1]

So here I am in this smoke-filled room surrounded by the click-clacking of people playing Star Craft as others chat online with friends all over the world. And I ask myself, What am I doing here? Partly, I am here based on me as a commodity, a Korean American college graduate who speaks English with an "American accent" and *"can offer insight to my students about what it means to be Korean American."* If my boss only knew that there is not a singular definition of "Korean American." More important, the economic pull and my own personal curiosity about this foreign biological motherland landed me on a flight to Seoul, twenty-one years and twenty-one days after taking the same flight, only with opposite points of embarkation and destination. It is almost like my own personal coming-of-age narrative, as if suddenly I were a heroine in one of the novels I had to read in my freshman-year English class. This heroine is on a search for answers. I'm seeking an alternative way to think about identity and give voice to my own personal story. I have spent a lot of time looking for the archetypal version of my immigration story. But for all my searching, I have not found one.

Growing up in a post–World War II suburb created from the first waves of white flight, I was vaguely aware of my racial "otherness" (I recall one second-generation Chinese American girl and another Korean adoptee in my high school of about one thousand students), but more often than not it was not talked about. I did not know how to define myself; there were not any representations of Asians readily available to me. This meant that usually I tried to blend into my vanilla suburb as best I could. When friends told me that they thought of me as white, or as *"the same as them,"* I recall feelings of discomfort, although at the time, I did not know how to articulate what I was feeling. My physical features set me apart, but in most ways my family was typical of suburban Detroit—my grandparents came from the South to work in Detroit's auto factories, and my family was more likely to eat meatloaf than *bulgogi.* It was clear that the difference between my family and those of my friends was a result of my physical difference. When I was very young one of my favorite bedtime books was *Why Was I Adopted?* My parents would explain to me why I looked different from them and help me understand this difference (one thing they would tell me was that while other kids were just had, I was picked). They also tried to give my sister and me outlets into Korean culture. The local Korean Presbyterian church worked with many Korean adoptees, providing cultural classes, and my mom still cooks Korean food as a special treat. But these forays were "special" and not an everyday occurrence. In a way, learning about Korea was like learning about any other foreign place, not necessarily the place where I was born.

In the United States when people ask me where I am from my stock answer is Detroit. And when they question that with a "No, for real, where are you from?" I follow up with, "Okay, I won't front. I am really from the suburbs." That usually quiets them for a little while. Here in Korea it is different. With popular culture spinning trends like webs across the globe, it is difficult to discern where someone is from based on style or dress. While I feel like my mannerisms and appearance scream "AMERICAN!" perhaps it is more of a soft whisper. In the first three weeks of my three-month sojourn to Korea, I have been asked for directions multiple times, and shopkeepers, waiters, and bus drivers speak to me in Korean. To their confusion, and my personal shame, I stare blankly in return and say (with an appalling accent): "Han-guk maul mol-la-yo."[2] Fortunately I have been taking a Korean class at night, and now I am able to converse on the most basic of levels so that when people ask me where I am from I can understand their question and reply appropriately, "Mi-guk sa-ram."[3] So here I am in a place where I am functionally illiterate, and not even conversational in terms of speaking ability, but I am treated as a native. Well, until I open my mouth and massacre the Korean language. It is only then that the where-are-you-from comes into play. This is a complicated, confusing, and difficult reality for me to live within.

On one hand, I kind of enjoy being an invisible foreigner. Countless times I have thought to myself: "Is being Korean in Korea the same experience as being white in the United States?" It is strange how I move with ease in Seoul despite my cultural ignorance. If I am riding on the subway or the bus or sitting in a café or PC bang (or any other activity that requires no linguistic interaction), I feel as if I receive no more notice than any other young woman. I'm not automatically pinned as a tourist when I browse in the stores. Other foreigners don't always realize I too am a native English speaker when they size up Korea and Koreans.

On the other hand, many Koreans have a hard time understanding how one can be Asian and American, especially when the Asian American is adopted. Explaining my situation is doubly complicated, not only by the cultural and social difficulty but by the linguistic difficulty. I keep meaning to ask a bilingual friend or coworker how to say "adoption" in Korean. For now it is all in my hands, so to speak. I am left with body motions to accompany the words: "Ae-gi. Pi-haeng-gi. Mi-guk. Eom-ma Mi-guk sa-ram. Appa Mi-guk sa-ram." This literally translates to: "Baby. Airplane. America. My mom American. My dad American." While these linguistic charades are alternately amusing and shameful, they are also indicative of the restrictive way we think about racial identity—even in Korea. This interaction more often than not comes in response to questions such as: "Why can't you speak Korean?" "Are you Korean?" So my response is an attempt to validate my Korean identity while at the same time making excuses for my Korean cultural foibles. I also know that when I say my parents are "Mi-guk sa-ram" this will be translated by my audience as "My parents are white Americans." But the questions I am not able to ask or am never offered an answer to are the questions of the larger picture. Why is it so hard to comprehend being Korean and American in the way that I am? What created the historical circumstances that led Koreans to give up their children to the U.S.? What does my presence both as a Korean adoptee in America and as an American in Korea teaching Korean youth say about American imperialism?

Peel back another layer and I know deep inside that while I feel like I am able to blend in while I roam around Seoul, the reality of my situation is, I am sure, that most Koreans feel uncomfortable with me when I tell them that I am adopted. On some level I feel as if I am seen as "not good enough" or "inferior" since this is the culture, the people, the land that tossed me out and sold me on the international market with as much thought as one would give to a Samsung cell phone.

For a long time I felt embarrassed or did not want to talk about my adoption history. I just wanted to be able to fade into the scenery . . . In high school maybe that could have happened by having that look of stereotypical Midwestern beauty (dirty blond hair, light eyes, the "all-American" girl next door), rather than East Asian otherness. Early in college, I simply had a deep desire for my last name to be Kim, or Park, or Lee, and have "strict Asian parents" who would never be my confidants. But now, I am at a stage where I am challenging the rules society places upon us. I am a self-identified woman of color who takes pride in her claim to Asian American identity. I often look toward the wisdom W. E. B. DuBois set down one hundred years ago, in his own personal reflections on race, for inspiration to continue my struggle:

The history of the American Negro is the history of this strife [double consciousness],—this longing to attain self-conscious manhood, to merge his double self into a better and truer self. In this merging he wishes neither of the older selves to be lost. He would not Africanize

America, for America has too much to teach the world and Africa. He would not bleach his Negro soul in a flood of white Americanism, for he knows that Negro blood has a message for the world. He simply wishes to make it possible for a man to be both a Negro and an American. . . .[4]

I too want to rid our world of hyphenated and competing identities. Not in a color-blind, raceless way, for our five-century-long history of oppression in the land we currently know as America is too long and complicated for us to simply stand and say today: WE ARE ALL AMERICANS! WE ALL HAVE EQUAL OPPORTUNITIES! (The resounding echo of bullshit, from sea to shining sea.)

But the more I grow and stretch, the more I feel myself confined by the term "Asian American" because I feel as if my story is still not a readily recognized piece of that Asian American story. Other Asian Americans have also asked me how an Asian girl got a last name like Kinney, or expect that I am *hapa* or white when they know me only via telephone or email.

Whereas before I allowed myself to be silenced, I now feel as if I am a Pandora's box, opened and ready with endless questions, accusations, and stories to be shared. In college my ethnic studies and sociology classes opened my eyes and gave me the histories that enabled me to understand and feel proud. Before this, my racial identity served as a site of difference, of confusion, of the unknown. My classes and "world as a classroom" experiences of my first two years of college gave me the foundation to see that although the identity labels "Asian American" and "people of color" are responses to oppression, they also serve as sites of pride.

I am left with a couple personal conundrums. I know that race is a social construction. However, the more I learn, the harder it is for me to forget. I cannot afford to be color-blind. And the further I take this argument, the more I realize how confining the ideas of "ethnic studies" and "Asian American" (and "Korean American") are. Even within the small safe space that I have found and molded into my own, I am still placed in the margins. I am questioning who gets to write the "authentic" version of history or identity. I am questioning the current dialogues and frameworks from which we approach these topics. I am questioning the way we talk about race and ethnicity. I am SCREAMING out loud in hopes that someone will hear me and we can collaborate together and find new words and new ways.

For now I search for another perspective in Seoul. Like so many of my ancestors who sojourned to foreign lands, maybe my three months will turn into a lifetime. As is evidenced by my click-clacking on the keyboard, I have many more questions to ask. As I zoom around Seoul on the subway trains I will focus on my musings and open myself to answers, maybe finding them on the walls of the PC bangs or in the faces of my Korean sistas. Meanwhile, I find satisfaction in the knowledge that I can reach skyward on a full train and grasp a handful of metal within arm's reach.

Notes

1. A PC bang is an Internet café.
2. I don't know Korean.
3. American person
4. W. E. B. DuBois, *The Souls of Black Folk* (New York: Bantam Books, 1989), 3.

Bibliography

DuBois, W. E. B. *The Souls of Black Folk*. New York: Bantam Books, 1989.

Rebecca J. Kinney is from Royal Oak, Michigan, and graduated from the University of Michigan, Ann Arbor, with degrees in American culture and sociology. She currently works for Resource Development Associates for Asian Neighborhood Design, a San Francisco–based nonprofit.

7 Chinese Again

Yijing Yang

I'm sitting here writing the truth, the whole truth, and nothing but the truth. MY truth. This is a new experience for me. I'm not used to seeing myself squarely, straight in the eye.

I'm not a writer. I hate writing and frankly, I stink at it. In fact, my computer is telling me right now that this is 6.5-grade material. So much for an expensive private school education. I couldn't care less about grammar right now because I hope that this will be known more for its honesty than for its writing mechanics. And I know this may not be the most eloquent essay either, but so far, this has made me feel better than any grade-A history paper I will ever write. After bottling everything up for so long, it feels so good to let it all flow. I feel like I'm telling, not writing, because that is what this is, the telling of a story. My story, my life, is typical of many other Asian teens growing up in America, but it is the similarity between our stories that gives it power.

I am Chinese. Until very recently I would've been ashamed to say that simple sentence. I believed that if I denied my roots I could grow afresh as a Caucasian. Now I know I've been lying to myself for so long. You can dig a plant up and plant it somewhere else but it will never grow as well as before you dug it up. More important, though, no matter where you plant it again it will not become another plant, another species. It took me eight years to learn this. All eight years I tried so hard to fit in with "the American crowd." I didn't succeed, and my failure to become American left me wondering why I was cursed to be different. I resented being Chinese so much. I would often ask God, the Western god, why I had been stuck with being Chinese, why I had such bad luck.

I don't know exactly when and where I started hating all things Chinese, but I think many things had built up to create this loathing over many years. They had built up inside of me like toxins, and I had never known how to expel them. Right from the beginning, when I moved here at the age of five, I was an outsider. Not just kept outside by a language barrier but by ignorance and hostility between the two cultures. I was all new, like an alien to the other kids. How I spoke, what I ate, my attitude toward things—it was all new to them and therefore unwelcome. I knew prejudice firsthand at an early age, and it made me afraid of American culture. I didn't notice anything fundamentally different between me and them so I didn't understand the basis of their prejudice, but unconsciously I distanced myself from them. Of course, this didn't exactly help their understanding of me. As I grew up, I started to notice my ethnic differences for the first time and for the first time, I saw myself as the other kids saw me. Chink. Gook. I also learned what popularity was. As a child, I hadn't minded too much the fact that I was an outsider, but as one grows older, acceptance from peers becomes increasingly important. I blamed my inability to fit in on my ethnicity and my parents (the two were perpetually linked in my mind). For me, my parents were embodiments of ethnicity. They were the ones who didn't let me watch the popular TV shows, go to the movies, talk about boys, so they were the ones that I resented on an immediate level. Although there are still things about my parents I haven't learned to accept, I have at least begun to understand their reasons for being that way. And over the last several years, I've established several "ties" back to Chinese culture that have helped me understand myself.

Last year, I began doing Chinese dancing in Chinatown. These dance classes, together with Chinese school, made me think anew about myself as an Asian growing up in America. By comparing these two environments I discovered that there were two different kinds of uprooted plants. The ones from Chinatown were fiercely proud to be Asian. They defied the stereotype that all Chinese are book-smart, but they had enough street smarts to know how to take care of themselves. They were always so confident. Their confidence amazed me. What amazed me more was that they didn't ask for acceptance from their American peers and therefore they were accepted anyway, despite their yellow skin and flat noses. On the other hand, many of the kids at Chinese school tried to be American and forgot they were Chinese. They were smart in a nerdy, school way but didn't have social smarts. And they never seemed confident despite their smart-aleck comments. It was hard to believe these two groups came from the same place.

The last several years I went to China a couple of times to visit during summer vacation, once by myself. The minute I stepped off the plane on both trips, I felt like I *couldn't* speak English anymore. I just couldn't get it out. It was like I was reunited with the little Chinese girl I used to be before moving here, like she had reclaimed me. I had so much fun those two summers. I went everywhere, ate everything, and everyone made a fuss over me. Even more than that though, for the first time, I felt like I totally belonged, every bit of me. I was accepted without question and I never had to pretend to like something or do something to get people to like me. When I came back the second time, the changes in me were so obvious that my parents noticed immediately. They told me that I seemed much more confident and assured. It makes sense. When you spend a lot of time in a place where everyone loves you, of course your morale is boosted.

When I was little, the first few years living in America I always felt like I was missing some vital body part. It was so weird. I would constantly check myself to make sure I had all my parts. Now I realize that I was right. I didn't have all my parts. Something important was missing. I still don't know what it is and I don't think there is a name for it anyway. But I realize now that that little piece will always remain in China and that the only times when I will feel completely whole are when I go to China and that little part makes its way back into my body. This little piece will always anchor me to China. I will never escape it and I can never cut it free. This knowledge has helped me on the project of accepting my heritage. A while ago, I would've seen this as a curse, but now, I simply accept it.

Last year, I read the most amazing book ever, and no, it was not *Harry Potter*. It was called *Paper Daughter,* by Elaine Mar. I read it as a part of my little phase of reading every English book written by a Chinese author on being Chinese. These books included *Wild Swans* and books by Amy Tan and Anchee Min. They were all helpful in educating me about Chinese history and culture, but *Paper Daughter* alone achieved a special distinction. It made me cry. Positively bawl. Not even Amy Tan had previously managed to induce a single tear. What was so different about *Paper Daughter?* It was painful how truthful it was. It was told through the eyes of a Chinese teen. A girl like me. What's more, it was real. *Paper Daughter* was Elaine Mar's own autobiography. And she was so like me it was frightening. She too struggled with generation gaps and fitting in. She shoved the ugliest, rawest moments in your face. The early poverty and fight to survive in this "land of opportunity." The hardships that wore away at a family structure until its bonds snapped from strain. The way a Chinese kid felt every time her parents told her "try harder," "always be the best," or "still not good enough." Yes, especially that last one. Elaine Mar hid nothing, and her truths made me see for the first time that nothing I was going through was limited to me alone. It hit me that so many other kids were feeling it too. I had always felt like I was the only one being punished. I had always felt so lonely because of this. After reading this book, I was consoled that other kids were just as lonely. This book made me grieve not only for myself but for all of us. When I was done with it, I felt a thousand times wiser. I want to say that I found myself in the book, but I don't know how that would make sense. That's just the only phrase that comes to mind. I think maybe a better description would be that I saw my own life reflected in the book. My past is in there, but I sincerely hope that my future won't be. Elaine Mar didn't learn survival skills in time to use them in life, so she put them to use by putting them in a book. To me that book is a guide for generations of Chinese kids like us to come. I have learned from it, and if I use it well, I will share no more of her pain and our paths will diverge from here on.

All these recent connections to my culture taught me two essential things. The first is that confidence and acceptance of yourself are the absolute most important things you can own. Once you have mastered these two you will master the world. Money, clothes, ethnicity—none of these make a difference in society if you have confidence and acceptance of yourself. The second is that you can be American without giving up being Chinese. If you accept yourself both worlds are open to you. This idea was what had eluded me for eight years. I had tried to jump from one world to another too quickly and fallen short, which left me suspended in the chasm between the two, belonging to neither. Once armed with these truths I tried immediately to use them. Having once been self-conscious and afraid of others' opinions, I now told myself that their acceptance didn't matter, it was *me* that mattered. I tried to go about doing everything confidently, not caring what others would say. Having once been afraid to speak Chinese when American friends showed interest and asked me to say something, I now no longer hold back from speaking in Chinese. I've stopped trying to hide my ethnicity, and as a result, I have felt increasingly better about myself and I no longer care about being popular. I've learned that popularity doesn't mean anything and that in most cases, popularity is not determined by what kind of person you are but by petty things like money or boys. The changes in self have not been easy to make. I don't think I've reached my full self-esteem level yet. After all, there are still painful differences between my family and American families that I have not yet learned to accept. Further acceptance and clairvoyance is another reason why I'm writing this. Sometimes all you need to do to find out the truth is put down what you know already on paper. Then you realize that you subconsciously already knew everything you needed to know. You just needed some prodding to get it to the surface.

As a result of my late discoveries about myself and my ethnicity, lately I've been feeling like I'm "becoming more Chinese," if that's possible. I don't understand how this is happening, but it amuses me in a way, because my English has actually gotten worse lately. Believe it or not, I don't read nearly as fast as I used to and sometimes I have trouble thinking of certain words or voicing my ideas. I can also hear an accent in some words I say. I don't know if all this is my imagination or if I'm simply noticing for the first time what has been there all along. To me, it feels a bit like the time that I met these two American men in a restaurant in China. When I tried to talk to them, it was hard to get the English out because I had not spoken it at all for the two months I had been in China. The only difference is that I'm not worried or embarrassed about it this time. The times that I spent in China were the happiest times of my life, and if my mind and my mouth think that I'm in China, it's fine with me. More important, it's like I'm making up for lost time. I had adopted English so quickly and rushed to become American so fast that the Chinese inside me got covered up. Now it feels like a little bit of me is returning to those days when I first moved here as a naive little five-year-old, so happy, and very much Chinese.

Yijing Yang is from Nanjing, China, and currently lives in Boston, Massachusetts.

8 Being Oil

May Chang

In fifth grade, I remember experimenting with the density of different liquids. My teacher had us pour cooking oil, rubbing alcohol, and colored water into a large beaker and observe as the different liquids separated themselves, as if they knew their differences and their place of belonging. The water found its way to the bottom of the beaker, the oil to the middle, and the alcohol to the top.

I have always been the oil.

I slumped on a wooden bench in the middle of Oakwood Mall, unaware of the rushing people and the gushing of the globe water fountain next to me. The hands of my watch slid into the six o'clock spot as my parents and older brother appeared in the distance. I could see their black heads bobbing among the crowd of shoppers. A sudden feeling of apprehension vaulted into the pit of my stomach. I could already envision my father's stern face and hear my brother's taunting voice. My mother would be relieved, glad I was safe. But I knew they all shared the same immense disappointment.

Only a week ago, I had quietly crept out of my bedroom window into the early spring air with a backpack slung over my shoulder. Two blocks away, I climbed into a blue Camry with people I thought of as friends and sped off into the crisp golden picture of a sinking sun. A song called "Insensitive" blared off the radio at me, but I could not think of what the name of the singer was. It bothered me immensely for some strange reason. Five minutes later, however, all I could think was how odd it was to be doing this, knowing that running away didn't solve a single thing.

No matter what I did, I would always be oil. My parents are the water on the bottom, representing a conservative culture that, in this country, is slowly fading out against the high-tech fashionable world of America. The layer of alcohol on top, of course, is American society. As a second-generation Hmong American, I felt I was living in a trapped world, spilling back and forth between two different cultures. In the mornings, I went to school and became "American." I spoke English, ate hamburgers for lunch, and hung out with friends, all the while pretending I came from the same sort of family background as my American friends did. In the afternoons, I returned home to be "Hmong." I spoke Green Hmong, made rice with our Tiger rice cooker, which we put to use before every meal, and meticulously sewed purple cloth bookmarks with *pajntaub*, or delicate embroidered designs, which my mother would bring to be sold to Americans for a little extra cash to support our family of ten.

Being born in America, I will never fully understand the Hmong culture. Although since college I have become more aware of the importance of keeping and remembering my own cultural roots, there are still things I'll never fully understand, not the way my parents and the other elders do. I remember thinking of some of the traditions as being silly. Some were even stupid in my American-accustomed eyes. For example, I could never understand why a sick person's soul or spirit had to be called back by a shaman. Why not just take that person to the doctor? After all, that's what hospitals are for. I didn't understand that in my culture, when a person is sick, his or her soul has wandered off and has to be called back by means of a special ceremony.

Not until I was eighteen did I know how to put on a Hmong costume by myself. The many colorful pieces were odd, something I didn't particularly care for and was unfamiliar with. My parents, however, urged me to learn. Every year, my mother and my aunt dressed my sisters and me in our Hmong costumes to attend the Hmong New Year celebration in our city. The dressing itself took well over two hours for all of us. After complaining throughout the duration while I was being layered with pieces of the costume, I would finally be ready. While I waited for the rest of my sisters to be dressed, I would look in the full-length mirror we had in the hallway between the kitchen and the bedrooms. I looked almost five months pregnant with all the layers around my waist (plumpness was more attractive than slenderness). I would then grab my backpack and toss a pair of jeans and a T-shirt inside so I could change later. When my sisters and I were all dressed and ready, we would cram into our maroon Toyota van to attend the Hmong New Year.

At the celebration, there were Hmong dance shows, singing, speeches, and the dreaded ball-tossing. My parents always persuaded me to ball-toss with men I didn't know and didn't like, simply because it was "fun" and was the polite thing to do if I was asked. Tossing the green tennis ball back and forth was a way of courting in the traditional Hmong culture (in Laos, it was a ball made of cloth). To me, though, the tradition was ludicrous. Why should I have to *pov pob* when courting in America consisted of calling each other on the phone and going on dates? Sometimes, if it was a particularly unlucky day for me, I would be asked to ball-toss with a much older Hmong man who would even sing a *kwv txhiaj* song. I just about wanted to die during instances like those. The ball-tossing I had no appreciation for, and the meaning of the *kwv txhiaj* songs I had no understanding of. But I attended and participated, with grunts and complaints, because my parents wanted me to follow the traditional Hmong customs. After all, I'm Hmong and should *think* as they do, as they were accustomed to thinking back in the days of the Laos mountaintops and the small farming villages.

I have often thought that many of the older Hmong people in America are only physically here. Their minds and their true selves are still back in Laos, back before the Vietnam War, before they were forced to leave their peaceful homes to endure a journey treading by foot through the jungle to Thailand's refugee camps, eventually to be flown halfway across the world to the United States. No matter how hard I tried as a fifteen-year-old, I couldn't think the way they thought; I wasn't the one who had lived in Laos, and I wasn't the one who went through all the havoc they did. Because of this, I knew I could never be the person my parents wanted me to be.

I also knew I could never be the average American girl. Living in a small city with little cultural diversity, my black hair, slanted eyes, and slightly darker complexion leaped out almost everywhere I went. In a classroom of thirty students, I was usually the only "different" one. Some students thought I was Chinese and would ask, "How do you say hello in Chinese?" I would tell them I wasn't Chinese and they would say, "Don't all you Asians speak the same anyway?" They didn't understand anything about me.

I had a small group of American school friends though, whom I had known since elementary school. When they invited me to go places with them, they didn't know (and I was too embarrassed to tell them) that in the Hmong culture, girls are generally not allowed to go out. A female's responsibility, even at a young age, is to stay home and do the house chores, mainly cooking, cleaning, and caring for the younger ones. So when my school friends realized that I could rarely go to the mall or the movies with them, or that I couldn't even hang out at their houses for a couple of hours, I was only less able to fit in.

In the local community of our town, I especially did not feel accepted. It was evident from the racist comments that I sometimes received from people when I was at the store or even walking home from school. I once tried explaining to an old man at a grocery store, who had told me to go back to my own country, that Hmongs were now living in America not by choice but because we had served in an alliance with the United States during the Vietnam War. Once the war was lost, we had no choice but to flee our mountaintop farms and our self-governing society or be killed for helping America fight against Communism. Our houses, our villages, our farms, all had been destroyed, burned to the ground. In addition, many of our Hmong men had been killed during the war, while they tried to rescue downed American pilots and soldiers and while they aided the Americans by scouting the Laos jungles and blocking the Ho Chi Minh Trail. But it was no use explaining to the old man at the grocery store. He only smirked and called me a gook.

Eventually, I felt more and more like I was being dumped out of the American world, like the deep-frying oil at McDonald's that has been used too many times and needs to be discarded. And because I wasn't exactly Hmong either, at least in my parents' eyes, I found myself stuck.

When I ran away at fifteen, I was sick of being stuck, sick of not fitting in with either culture. The fire underneath me was beginning to feel awfully hot and I was sizzling, ready to burn, to produce a fire that I was certain would only be worsened by water. I'm not sure what I thought running away would achieve; all I knew was that perhaps if I got away, I could at least be my own person, even if I didn't quite fit in anywhere. My thought was that at least I wouldn't have to hear my parents' constant lectures about what I should be like as a Hmong person.

That evening, after a half an hour's drive slouched in the backseat of the run-away Camry, an intense feeling of uncertainty crept in. I began to seriously wonder about my decision in running away. What would happen to me? What would my parents think when they found out I'd run away? In addition, I knew what I had done would be damaging to my father's reputation as a leader of the Hmong community in our city. Reputation was extremely important. To have a daughter run away meant that you could not control your own children, so how could you possibly be in charge of a Hmong community? My father was going to lose face because of me.

I knew that running away would damage my reputation as well. There was a chance I would not be able to find a suitable husband in the future, one my parents and others would approve of, because I would now be known as a girl who had been a runaway, or a *menyuam laib,* as the Hmong parents would call it. I thought about everything that was wrong about running away, but at the same time, I was determined to find myself as a person, not as a Hmong or an American. Just simply as a person.

An hour later, I arrived at the house of a stranger, someone who was a friend of the people I was with. The house looked ancient, with peeling paint the color of pea green. The rooms inside were dimly lit and crowded with teenagers, most of whom were Hmong. The place had the stench of heavy cigarette smoking. After I had been introduced to everyone, I was offered a cigarette. I had never tried smoking before because the smell of cigarettes always repulsed me. I shook my head and waved the cigarette away. Looking around, I wondered what all these teenagers were doing there.

Soon I learned that most of the teenagers were from around the area. They liked to come there to hang out. In a sense, I felt the majority of them were also there to get away from their homes and their parents. Some of the other teenagers in the place were like me; they were runaways who had left for reasons of all sorts.

There was a girl I remember in particular. She was sixteen years old and had run away from home because her parents were going to marry her to a thirty-year-old man who was related to her mother's side of the family.

"I don't wanna marry him! He's old and ugly!" she exclaimed as we sat at a kitchen table that looked as though it would soon collapse. "But you know how parents are."

I nodded my head. "They don't listen. They just think you're supposed to do everything they say."

"Yeah. I know I'm supposed to respect my mom and dad's decision, but I'm only sixteen! Some of my cousins got married real young and their life sucks! They have two kids by the time they're eighteen and they don't get to have any fun. I don't wanna be like that," she said. "Besides, we're not in Laos anymore. We're in America. A lot of people here don't get married till they're twenty-something. I wish my parents would realize that."

I listened to her and recognized her opinions as my own. I felt empathy for her because her parents were obviously very old-fashioned. In Laos, it was common for Hmong girls to get married as young as thirteen years old, and parents sometimes arranged marriages to ensure that their children would marry into a decent family and lead a good life. At least I knew my parents would never arrange a marriage for me. I had asked them once, and they had assured me they would never force me to marry someone I didn't want to.

Time at my new home went by very slowly. Those of us who were runaways were told we shouldn't go out very much because we were on runaway lists and could be captured by the police if we were seen around the area. In fact, the house was often watched because it was known for housing runaways.

On the fourth evening, an American lady came knocking on the door and asked to come in. She was a dark-haired lady with a stocky build, and she had a police badge clipped to her belt and a notepad in hand. I heard someone say to her that there were no runaways here. She only nodded slightly and went around to everyone. The faces she didn't recognize, she asked for their names. When she got to me, I felt a twinge of panic.

"What's your name?" she asked me.

A minute ago, someone had whispered to me in Hmong that if I was asked for my name, I should give a false one.

"Jessica Thao," I replied as I glanced at the floor.

The lady cringed her eyebrows together, looking as if she doubted me. "Let me see your ID please."

"I don't have an ID," I told her. And I really didn't. I wasn't old enough to drive yet, and my school, which was a seventh- through ninth-grade junior high, didn't issue school identification cards until we got into high school.

"How old are you?"

"Fifteen."

"What are you doing here? Where are your parents?"

Panic started to grip me. The more questions she asked, the more I felt certain that I was going to be found out.

"Um, my parents are here . . . but they're not *here* here."

The lady stared at me, her hazel eyes searching for something that signified I was a runaway.

I scrambled for something to say. "I mean, they're . . . somewhere visiting relatives here in this city. We're visiting from out of town."

I felt my face growing hot. I was sure she was going to handcuff me and haul me into the police station. Perhaps she was even going to lock me up in jail until my parents could come pick me up, and I was certain my parents would let me rot in jail for a few days first before they came.

The lady looked at me carefully and then asked for my name again. She jotted something down on her notepad and walked away. That evening, she left without taking anyone.

Not long after, a feeling of restlessness began to sneak in. I was no closer to finding my own identity than I had been before. Slowly, I realized something. Although I tried to ignore it at first, it kept butting into my thoughts. Who was I without parents? Who was I without a home? I was an even bigger nobody on my own, sleeping at the house of a stranger and eating food that tasted nothing like my mother's home-cooked meals. Sometimes I didn't even have food to eat at all. Finally, I came to the conclusion that running away was foolish, only the act of a frustrated self. I had known it all along.

Now I needed to go home.

So in that shopping mall where I had made a collect call home an hour ago, I stood up and waited for my parents and brother to reach me by the bench. And just as I had quietly snuck out a week earlier, I quietly snuck back in, to resume the role of oil.

May Chang is from Wisconsin Rapids, Wisconsin, and graduated from the University of Wisconsin, Stevens Point, with degrees in English education and writing. She currently teaches high school English.

9 Double-A

Mai Anh Huynh

"So are you Japanese or Chinese?" she asked, as if those were the only two labels possible for a black-haired, brown-eyed Asian girl.

"Neither," I replied, having deja vu of past conversations that had started along this line.

"Korean then?"

"Nope," I patiently responded, gearing myself to expound on the fine differences within the generic category "Asian."

"WELL?!? What else is there?"

My childhood experiences were peppered with similar conversations. Because my last name was strange to the ear, I was often asked, "Where are you from?" If I, who was born in this country, am not considered "American," then who is an American?

In my search for an answer, I looked to different sources. My history book tells me that the stereotypical American is a self-made man—a Horatio Alger hero rising to success through hard work, thrift, honesty, and luck.

Certainly many new immigrants coming to America—from the Puritans to those arriving at Ellis Island—believed in this perception. However, while my history book gives me one definition, newspapers and television convey an entirely different meaning. If newspaper stories are an accurate reflection of social conditions, then Americans are a violent, gun-toting, lawsuit-crazed people. With the spate of shootings committed by my own peers, is there a grain of truth to the perception that an American is simply a Canadian with a gun? Rich or poor, violent or peace-loving, self-made or profit-driven—I believe that superficial generalizations about "the" American fail to capture the essence of what it means to *be* an American.

Though my childhood experiences intimated that the typical American would be "white," that would not be an accurate statement. An American cannot be classified by race, for the true archetype of the United States is part white, part black, part Hispanic, part Asian, part Indian, and, of course, part Tiger Woods. But this diversity among Americans has not always been appreciated. New initiatives to make English the official language, fights over bilingual education policy, and pitched battles over affirmative action manifest the struggle to define our nation's identity. Without a common heritage, what shared ideal characterizes the American experience or defines what being an American is all about?

My family has its own interpretation of what it means to be an American. Listening to my parents' stories of their struggle in Vietnam and escape from Communism, I understand that for my parents being an American is synonymous with being free. But as a native-born citizen of democracy, I have never experienced a life which has *not* been free. My experience of being American was more like that of a juggler. Life was a fine balancing act between maintaining the values and beliefs that I had grown up embracing, and adapting them to an environment in which cultural differences were not exactly celebrated. In the classroom, I was shocked to find young children daring to contradict the "infallible" teacher, while the cafeteria held a rude awakening that duck eggs and chicken feet were not considered American delicacies. For me, and probably many other first-generation immigrants, being an American is being a juggler of different identities.

I now realize that though I am certainly not the quintessential symbol of Americana, my experiences contribute to what being an American is all about. As English has been shaped by myriad accents, America is the rich product of all her citizens. An American is no one person, yet every individual is a typical American. Understood as a collective rather than personal expression, the American culture can permit anyone to claim it as their own.

It is with the added wisdom of a few extra years that I look back, yearning for the chance to answer my schoolmate properly:

"So are you Japanese or Chinese?" *she would ask.*

"No, I'm American," *I would reply,* *"but my parents came from Vietnam."*

Four years have passed since I originally wrote that essay for entrance into Harvard College. Four years during which my life and my focus changed from figuring out what it means to be an American to simply trying to figure out what it means to be me. Born and raised in Indiana, I went from being the lone Asian in a sea of white faces to melting into a pool of brown.

Oddly enough, now that I'm thrust into an environment that is 20.2 percent Asian, I find myself suddenly self-conscious about how I look and how well I fit into ye olde Asian stereotypes, which I had never heard of until coming here. Ironically, everyone still assumes that I'm Chinese—even my Chinese friends. "You don't look Vietnamese," they say hopefully. As though at any moment, I'll tell them I was pulling their leg the whole time.

You would think I would be happy. That just as I used to try and stake my claim as an American, I would be eager to be considered part of another large ethnic group. But I am not.

Why should it matter if people make false assumptions about me based on how I look—try to classify me as "sex kitten," nerd, or FOB (fresh off the boat) by how I dress or speak? It doesn't change the individual I am inside. Yet a part of me remains indignant that if I am smart or hardworking, it was preordained in the model minority myth. That since I choose to pursue medicine, I must be one of those obedient Asian premeds. That if someone thinks I'm pretty, it is because they have an Asian fetish.

More important, these generalizations, which seem to circulate as much within the Asian community as outside of it, obscure many of the real, tangible tensions I face struggling to be both Asian and American.

I grew up the youngest of three overachievers. When my eldest sister graduated from high school, the local newspapers trumpeted the story of a girl's rise from nothing to achieve the "American Dream." Then my brother graduated—also valedictorian, also peppered with numerous awards, and also honored with a coveted full ride to Indiana University. Then came me. As the years progressed, the admiration at an "American success story" faded until by the time I was through, I felt stifled by a sense of resentment from the local community at seeing my family succeed. The newspapers fell silent, the admiring smiles of peers' parents faltered as they seemed to take each achievement as a personal stab against the "American" way of life. It was as though they had done something wrong raising their children—encouraging them to date, go to parties, work for their money—while somehow my parents had done something right by sheltering me so that all I could do was study . . . or of course it was just because I was Asian.

Grouping all Asians as one, society proclaims Asians are emblematic of how minorities can overcome past instances of prejudice and discrimination in their quest for success without resorting to political or violent confrontation. Citing statistics that show Asians have the highest college-degree attainment rate and median family income, Asians are collectively used to refute the need for affirmative action, to gloss over potential inequalities in America, and to prove that America is indeed a golden land of equal opportunity. These same numbers show that Vietnamese Americans only have a quarter the rate of college graduates (16 percent), Laotians and Cambodians even fewer than that. The numbers indicate that on average Asians—along with most minorities—must achieve a higher level of education in order to earn the same salary as their white counterparts.[1] Despite these perceived inequities, when I consider what my life could have been like had my family not escaped Vietnam, I feel blessed to have opportunities which far too many take for granted.

That does not mean I don't feel pain every time someone mutters "Chinese" jibberish at me and gives me a mocking bow. Each time someone patronizingly says "Welcome to our country!" is a wounding reminder that in their eyes I will never be 100 percent American. My bittersweet memories of trying to convince my friends that my barbecue pork sandwiches were actually a pink form of peanut butter have been replaced by a false sense of security now that I find I have inadvertently cushioned myself in college by acquiring a circle of friends comprised mostly of Asians . . . like me.

Here I navigate murkier waters. I don't want to be a pro-Asian activist. To promote the cause would be to concede the existence of a problem. I have been raised in a culture of passive resistance, where you beat the system by finding better routes. Recently, a miniature uproar (at least among the Asian American associations) emerged on my campus over Abercrombie & Fitch Laundromat T-shirts advertising "Two Wongs Can Make It White." I can't remember if my first impulse was to laugh or to just be happy that it wasn't my last name. My peers argued that it was time for Asian Americans to stand up against prejudice, pointing out that in today's politically correct world one could never crack jokes like that about black people or Jewish people. I instead wondered why people would laugh at someone's willingness to do whatever it took to make a living. Was my immediate "Asian" impulse to take the passive, nonconfrontational approach driving my desire to pursue medicine, where I knew I wouldn't need any "old-boy" connections to succeed?

So now I waver between "me against them" mentalities, alternately substituting Asians versus society, Vietnamese versus Asian, me versus Vietnamese, me versus family. Can there be a protagonist in such a struggle for identity? It used to be easy for me to juggle two cultures. My mother, who is relatively liberal for a Vietnamese woman, would always very logically say, "Who cares more about your future than we do?" when I had to forego the all-American teenage life in favor of a date with my books on a Saturday night. I learned through experience that it was generally better to yield and agree that the Vietnamese way is the best way.

My parents never spared any expense when it came to my education. "Study hard," my father would say when he came home late from work, "so you can have a better life." "Don't do anything to jeopardize your future," my mother reminds me, which generally equates to "no serious boyfriend." My older sister, a pioneer for both academic and romantic success, paved uncharted territory by getting my mother to allow her Caucasian fiancé to progress from being "best-friend-that-is-a-boy" to his current status over the course of four years. My sister tells me that she thinks he would have been "perfect" in my mom's eyes had he been Vietnamese; sometimes I wonder if she means in her own.

In my heart, I know my parents love me enough to accept whoever I decide will make me happy. My dilemma is attempting to sort out what exactly I am looking for. I am not going to marry someone to make a statement, nor marry someone just because he is Vietnamese. I don't want to marry someone Asian just because that is relatively close to my culture, nor do I want to get trapped in a relationship where my husband thinks I will be the traditional Asian wife. All this from someone who has never even had a boyfriend! You see how difficult it is when East meets West? I've grown up with such a traditional background that I don't know how it's possible for me to get an American kind of marriage based on love without going through the American style of dating. I want to have the traditional Asian values of filial respect and family but refuse to be the subservient Asian wife. I know my life isn't a two-toned deck of cards in which I can pick and choose what customs to keep or discard. Nevertheless, fearing that I will lose part of myself by marrying someone incompatible with my family and culture, I fear that I will unknowingly sacrifice my own happiness without being able to tell the difference.

W. E. B. DuBois once wrote, "It is a peculiar sensation, this double-consciousness, this sense of always looking at one's self through the eyes of others, of measuring one's soul by the tape of a world that looks on in an amused contempt and pity."[2] How do I construct an identity when I don't even completely understand myself? Glibly stating my status as an American with Vietnamese heritage only affirms in words that I'm Asian American—not that I've fully adjusted to living as a double-A.

In time, I suspect I'll be more amused than irritated at the mistaken attempts to guess the identity of the five-foot-six-inch, black-haired, brown-eyed "giant" striding through Chinatown. In retrospect, I will laugh at the stereotypes that come along with looking different. Maybe I will even celebrate the commonalities I can find in the experiences of others—the warm feeling I got from reading *The Joy Luck Club,* a shared appreciation of Coca-Cola and pepperoni pizza. At the same time, I will revel in all of the unique qualities that define me as a person.

Then I will say with confidence—more for myself than anyone else:

"I'm American, but my parents came from Vietnam."

Notes

1. Statistics are from <http://www.asian-nation.org/issues2.html>.

2. W. E. B. Du Bois, *The Souls of Black Folk* (New York: Signet Classic New American Library, 1982), 45.

Bibliography

Du Bois, W. E. B. *The Souls of Black Folk.* New York: Signet Classic New American Library, 1982.

Mai Anh Huynh is from Evansville, Indiana, and studies biochemistry at Harvard University.

10 ABC for Life

Katie Leung

Katie Leung is a girl with long, black, straight hair and slanted eyes. She is short, petite, and has small feet. She loves to play volleyball and enjoys being active, although she has never learned karate like everyone assumes she has. Nor has she eaten dog. She does, however, use chopsticks when she eats dinner, and yes, she always has white rice. She wears T-shirts, jeans, and sneakers, but to her homecoming dance, she wore a genuine Chinese *chi-pao*. She loves to read and write, but can't read or write a bit of Chinese so please don't ask her to decipher anything. Also, that "two 'Wongs' don't make a right" joke really doesn't amuse her at all. She loved *The Joy Luck Club,* but *Forrest Gump* is also one of her favorites. Sometimes she watches Chinese television stations with her father via satellite, but she rarely misses Thursday nights on NBC either. Katie Leung is a Chinese girl who was born in Fort Lauderdale, Florida, and this is her identity crisis.

Our plane loudly cranked and strained its machinery, announcing its landing at Beijing International Airport. After twenty-some long and hellish hours on the plane, I groggily looked out of my window at the foreign land and thought to myself, "We're here." Despite my exhaustion, I was able to summon up a bit of excitement at the thought of being in China. China had fostered the roots of my heritage, and my family and I would be spending the next two weeks exploring its various wonders. We gathered up our carry-on luggage and followed the rest of the passengers off the plane. A blast of hot, dry air welcomed our arrival onto Chinese soil, and we were immediately bombarded by crowds of people. I suddenly got the feeling that the term "minority" no longer applied to me. "Geng wo lai, geng wo lai." Our tour guide quickly beckoned us to follow her to where the rest of our group was and my mom also worked full-time, so my share of sleepovers and pool parties was quite limited. How could I explain to my seven- and eight-year-old friends that my dad was a cook by day and a bartender by night, that my "home" constantly smelled like fried rice and was divided into a smoking and a nonsmoking section? It had gotten to the point where I would stop asking my parents to do things, fully aware that a somber "no, I'm sorry" would follow my plea. I stopped questioning why and made a habit of throwing out the invitations I received, convinced that it was useless to bring them home.

However, during my teen years, "no" was getting obsolete. All I wanted to do was be like my American peers. I didn't like the feeling of isolation anymore. I didn't think it was fair that I was being left out of so many "ordinary" childhood activities. I wanted to wear "cool" clothes and go out every Friday and Saturday night. I wanted to date boys and talk on the phone and sleep over at my friends' houses. But my parents would not have any of that. "Ni ying gai zai jia duo nian yi dian shu." According to my father, I should have been sitting at home reading more books. I was already an avid reader and had been for years, and for him to make this request was ridiculous. As for my new fashion sense, I refused to let my mother pick out my clothes. I had had enough of the frilly dresses and big clothes that I was supposed to eventually grow into. I wanted to be popular, not practical. (Of course, in the meantime, I was swimming in my shirts and constantly pulling up my pants.)

I started saving up the money I earned helping out at the restaurant and desperately began to imitate the latest styles. And it wasn't enough to just fit in with the rest of the round-eyed kids. Being a child of great aspirations, I didn't just want to be an American; I wanted to be a "cool" American as well. I don't think I was ever quite there though. Maybe it was because I was missing the beautiful blond hair and sky blue eyes. Or perhaps it was just that Chinese girls never looked quite right in such Western styles. American girls my age were perming their hair, spraying it in all kinds of waves, curls, and bobs, and my straight, black, lifeless hair could and would not even come close to their creations. They wore these huge, thick socks called EGs in all different colors, and every day, I sat at my desk trying to poof up my clean, white, pathetic crew socks. I hated wearing all of my imitation clothes and the jelly shoes I had once loved, while everyone else was wearing real Z. Cavaricci's and designer shoes instead. I didn't want to be different anymore, but the more I tried to conform, the more isolated I felt. My fraudulent outfits didn't fool the cool crowd, and if they didn't sneer at me, they looked at me sympathetically as if they were thinking, "We should just be nice to her since she's trying so hard to be like us." I tried so hard, yet I still didn't fit in.

Halfway around the world, I wasn't fitting in with the thousands of Chinese people in Beijing either. The crowded streets allowed our tour bus to become closely acquainted with many of the local cars, buses, cyclists, and cab drivers, and they all peered inside to get a glimpse at the American tourists. I felt like I was in some sort of freak show. Sitting near the back, I was able to tune out the tour guide and her broken English to observe all of this commotion. It seemed unfair to a country that was already suffering from pollution and the rays of a burning sun to be so overcrowded. The cars in both lanes seemed to have no concept of staying within them, and even though the bus was quite roomy, I felt claustrophobic. I watched dozens of people cycle by, and suddenly, a couple caught my attention as they walked along the sidewalk. They were barely even holding hands, but the woman, about my age, looked admiringly at her companion, and I could tell that they were dating and perhaps had been dating for a long time. This was quite different from the openly affectionate American couples I was used to seeing.

Dating was quite an issue in my house. The boys I wanted to date didn't want to take out a girl with such an early curfew, and the long-term relationship I was in often involved arguments as to why I couldn't stay out later or why I couldn't do something or go somewhere. At sixteen and seventeen years old, I felt an incredible, cramping pain in my chest, the weight of having to choose between my parents and the boys I was infatuated with. I was suffocating. My parents could not understand why I needed to be so "American," why I needed to go to every party, or what I wanted to do while out so late. They were always very protective, and I was getting fed up with being treated like I was still ten years old. I couldn't understand why they didn't trust my judgment or respect that I had my own life. Eventually, I stopped respecting their rules because I didn't feel like their rules respected me, and pretty soon, the tight reign they pulled encouraged me to rebel against them. I angrily peeled off their overprotective blanket, ready to take in huge gulps of air. If I didn't really like the boy I was seeing at the time, the mere fact that my parents didn't accept him in my life encouraged me, convinced me that I possessed stronger feelings. I learned to fall in love fast in order to spite my parents, and I chose to depend on my boyfriends in order to prove that I didn't need my parents either.

When I was sixteen, I told my mother I was ready to see a gynecologist to start birth control, and we didn't talk for a whole week. I was scared to ask and even more scared to admit that I was having sex before marriage for fear of disappointing her. My mom had always tried to convey that sex should be reserved for married women. While many of my American girlfriends were already taking the Pill and had open relationships about sex with their mothers, it wasn't that way in my house. Sex was never really spoken of; it was assumed that if we didn't talk about it, it wouldn't happen. My mom assumed that I knew enough to make the right decision. When I got my first period, she gave me a book about the way my body was changing and where babies came from. And while I knew about the dangers of sex and had read about my body parts, I still engaged in sex and stood by my decision. I felt it was a reasonable one, and in a way, it was like I had gained this power over my mother, who had always overpowered me. For so long, she had tried to preserve her perfect Chinese daughter and prevented me from dating and going out with friends; she made it clear that she did not approve of my boyfriend or his American influences. By having sex with him, I conformed to the American way of intimacy among teenagers my age and proved to her she couldn't control my life.

It must have been a great shock to my mom, considering that she and my dad had never so much as held hands in front of me. It was unfathomable to a woman who had not engaged in such intimacy until marriage to hear such requests from a daughter she thought was perfect. And I no longer wanted to be her perfect daughter. It haunted me that I was no longer perfect. It hurt me to know that I was the cause of her pain, that I disappointed the young mother who had once gazed adoringly at me with the highest of hopes. I was breathing in my American life and convinced myself I didn't care. There was a time when my mother was my world, and there was nothing in my mind that separated us. I used to sit on the toilet seat and admire the way she put on makeup, desperately wishing that one day I would possess her porcelain skin and natural beauty. I thought she was the most beautiful woman I'd ever seen. With time, our world divided, and the bang of our culture clash was almost too much to bear for the both of us. She caught me at my boyfriend's house once when I told her I would be somewhere else. I heard the doorbell ring, and she stood there crying when I opened the door. I could only think to myself, "What are you doing in *my* world?" My urge to be like all the other girls with their American boyfriends caused a great strain between my Chinese mother and me.

Sitting in a restaurant in Shanghai, I felt a different kind of strain. My stomach was so full, I felt on the verge of nausea. Our tour group had just finished a full dinner, and we were picking at the rest of the dishes placed on the lazy Susan. More than a week had already gone by, and my stomach had surrendered to the attack of sweet and sour dishes and Kung Pao chicken. I felt as though I was about to burst when the waitress asked if I would like some beer. I looked at my father, and since I was of legal drinking age while we were staying in China, he nodded his approval. For the first time in my life, I drank a glass of beer in front of my parents, and although it was warm and bitter, it was quite liberating. However, I still couldn't shake the twinge of guilt I felt. Indulging in alcohol was not acceptable behavior in my house.

My parents had always preached against the abuse of marijuana and alcohol. Unlike sex, the topic was open for discussion at home, and my family often talked about their dangers and their own personal experiences with them. It was almost like they brainwashed me into thinking that both substances would eventually be the death of me if I ever tried either of them. I grew up thinking that all people who drank were bad and all people who smoked or used drugs were worse. To this day, I have never smoked pot or taken a drag off a cigarette, and in high school, I prided myself on being a junior who'd never had a drink. As I got older, my dad started offering me beer or wine on special occasions, and I would still refuse. When I got accepted to the University of Florida, my father found out that it was one of the top-ten party schools in the nation. He warned me against getting too carried away with alcohol. "Zue yao jin, shu yao du hao. He jiu bu yao he tai duo. Katie-ah, qian wan bu yao luan lai." The most important thing for me to do was to concentrate on school and not on the alcohol that thrived there. I MUST behave myself.

At the time, it was ironic of him to be telling me this. I was a senior in high school with two months left before graduating, a time when celebrating was an essential weekend activity. I finally caved during a trip to Tallahassee, when one of my friends went to visit a college there. I drank and discovered that it was actually kind of fun, and the silly, giggly feeling I got from it was like a cure from the moody, introverted Katie. I wanted to drink again because it gave me access to conforming without inhibitions. But with such an early curfew, it was easy for my father to wait up for me until I came home. I always told him, "Dad, you don't have to wait up for me," but he did anyway. "Jiu shi ying wei wo hui dan xing." He waited up, for even if he tried to sleep, he would still worry. One night, I went to a party, and due to the Chinese trait of high *in*tolerance, and to this being only my second time drinking, I had a cup of vodka and cranberry juice and quickly found myself drunk. I came home that night and found him sitting quietly in his chair, watching a blank television screen. Shit. "Katie, don't you think it's a little late . . . tai wan la ba?" I muttered an apology and tried to keep my distance. I hurriedly said good night and escaped to my room, where I lay in bed in a drunken, swirling daze. I knew I had done something wrong. In my mind, I tried to contemplate whether I was a bad person or if I had opened the door to acceptance. In a matter of an hour, my proud streak of sobriety was over, and I had to admit that I was a bit disappointed with myself. But I also felt too liberated and too intoxicated to care.

Of course, I didn't get away with anything. The next day, he told my mom he smelled liquor on my breath. I denied everything for fear of disappointing my parents again, but they never said anything to me. They had preached and lectured enough. They only told me that I was old enough to make my own decisions whether they were right or wrong and stood strongly by their philosophy. "Hao de shi ni de, huai de ye shi ni de." Good decisions were mine, as well as the weight of bad ones. After that, I never came home drunk again just to avoid the mere guilt of a bad decision. That time, Chinese teachings prevailed over American temptations.

My family had just arrived in Shenzhen, and my grandmother walked into the room. I immediately stood to acknowledge her. She had lost so much weight, and the gray of her hair had become streaked with white. I was shocked at the transformation. She smiled widely at me, exposing her gold crowns and deepening the wrinkles around her face. "Katie-ah, ni pang le," she exclaimed. I had to admit that after my first year of college, I *had* gained a few pounds. I nodded and smiled back at her. Our lines of communication were limited. I did not speak Mandarin as well as I used to, and it was difficult for me to find the words that encompassed my true feelings. Throughout our trip in China, my mother explained to others that I understood Chinese, but I just wouldn't speak it. It made me angry and ashamed to hear the hint of disappointment in her tone. Yet I couldn't defend myself. It was now a frustrating task, and it seemed that the Mandarin that came out of my mouth never sounded as fluent as when I said it in my head. I thought about how my parents had hired a woman to teach Mandarin to my brother and me. We did not enjoy the weekly visitations. As far as I was concerned, I didn't care about expanding my language abilities past the conversational level. Besides, learning Chinese would be like surrendering to my parents and to a culture I resented. My dad always said that one day I would regret not learning to speak Mandarin fluently, but I never believed him. He always asked me, "What kind of Chinese person does not speak Chinese?" I refused to believe that I would ever need to learn perfect Mandarin. And then, standing in front of my frail grandmother, who probably would not be living much longer, I knew and understood why. Lately, I've started feeling that not knowing my language as well as I should has cheated me from allowing myself to believe I am Chinese. Today, I am a nineteen-year-old political science major who must fulfill a foreign-language requirement. I am currently registered for Chinese 1102.

We had climbed the steep steps of the Great Wall of China, stood in the center of Tiananmen Square, ooh-ed and ahh-ed at the wonders of the actual Forbidden City, gazed at the unique mountains of Guilin, and strolled along the busy neon streets of Shanghai and Hong Kong. I was back on the plane, sleep deprived and ready to go home to America. I sat awake thinking about my parents and the happiness we had shared while on the trip, and it was hard for me to believe that I had been having such difficulties with them only a year before. Shaping my identity while my parents controlled my thinking and my friends controlled my behavior was not easy. It was like living two lives. I was an American by day, going to school and socializing with friends. But at night, sitting with my family around our kitchen table, I was a dutiful Chinese daughter. My desire to conform pushed and pulled against the overbearing urge to please my parents. I hated disappointing them, and by conforming, I knew that many of the things I did saddened them greatly. It is just recently that I've become disappointed in some of the things I did during my time of rebellion, and I now wish that I was always comfortable with just being different. I wish that I had braved it out and worn my Chinese label as proudly as my parents wore theirs. I wish I had been secure enough with my own identity to listen to myself when I knew I wasn't being true to my convictions. My parents tried their best to mold me into what they believed was right, and although I still don't agree with some of the philosophies they chose to preach, I have to admit that their expectations did at least steer me in the right direction.

Sometimes, I wonder what I would be like if my parents weren't so adamant about me living up to their Chinese standards, if they hadn't chastised what they deemed "American inappropriateness." Perhaps I would have realized earlier that my boyfriend at the time wasn't the "one"; perhaps I would have refused to participate in the race to lose my virginity. Perhaps my hair could have been saved from an awful perm, and I would have realized that "EG" actually stood for "extremely gaudy." Perhaps I would have been more confident and comfortable with myself. Looking back, a lot of my identity has been shaped outside of my house. Once I was given the chance to embrace my Chinese identity without the pressure of maintaining it, I really appreciated my heritage. I am proud now. There are still times when I'm around friends that I forget my hair is straight and black, and my eyes are slanted, and I speak a different language. But certainly, there are more times when I admire those things about myself and wouldn't change them for the world. My world has grown to include my parents instead of resenting them. I've learned to thank them for their efforts and to absorb what I choose from their teachings to make myself the best person I can be. I have grown to be Katie (or even Kai Lee) Leung, a Chinese girl who enjoys being American but absolutely loves being Chinese.

Currently, I am teaching five-year-olds at a summer camp, and one of my students innocently asked, "Ms. Katie, why don't your eyes open all the way?" I chuckled heartily to myself and proudly but gently explained, "Because I'm Chinese," and walked away . . . sand free.

Katie Leung is from Fort Lauderdale, Florida, and studies political science at the University of Florida.

11 How Not to Eat *Pho:* Me and Asia America

Michael Sue

> I'm the Goong Hay Kid, hope you understand.
> Don't do no kowtowing or no rickshaw. So don't be talking
> no dragons or the Great Wall. I ain't good in math,
> don't know kung fu. Ditto for Confucius or Fu Manchu.
> So don't mess with me or call me Bruce Lee.
> 'Cause ain't no one badder than Kid Goong Hay.
> —Alvin Eng, *Rock Me, Goong Hay*

I was brought up as a kid on a daily helping of good ol' American hot dogs and beans, so one can imagine how different a bowl of Vietnamese *pho* would have tasted to a college kid who had been taught all his life that "it was okay to like Asian food, but just not to let other people see you eat it." As a third-generation Chinese American on my mom's side and as a fourth-generation on my dad's side, I grew up in a world where I was discouraged to reveal or express my Asian identity. I was taught that if I brought any Chinese food to lunch, the other kids would look at my food, laugh and point their finger at me, and say that I was strange, different, was not a real American but "Chinese." Accordingly, I grew up believing that eating Asian food meant you were a foreigner and un-American. Foreigner or not, when I had my first taste of *pho* my sophomore year, it was love at first taste. For those unfortunate souls who have not experienced *pho*, it's a Vietnamese rice-noodle soup in a beef or chicken broth, served with bean sprouts, green onion and cilantro, basil leaves, and different meat strips and meatballs. To enjoy *pho* fully, most people flavor the taste of its broth, kinda sweet and salty, by adding lemon, hoisin sauce, and red chili sauce. In fact, it's exactly this sweet and salty taste that everybody strives for when they're adding their different ingredients. Everybody wants to get the *pho* just right. Unfortunately, I never do and always seem "to be looking for *pho* in all the wrong places." Rather than my *pho* "hitting the spot," my bowl almost kills me. Strangely enough, though, it is from these "*pho* fiascos" that I have gained a better understanding of who I am as an Asian American.

It starts simply enough. I have the big bowl of *pho* in front of me, and as soon as I sit down, I instantly put some hoisin sauce into the bowl without even thinking. I don't put too much in, however, just enough to make the soup look black. Then I add the red chili sauce to give it that extra kick, and that's when things start to turn dark. Thinking that the soup could use more hoisin, I add some more. Then I add more red chili. Then I add hoisin. Before I know it, my tongue starts to burn and my eyes tears up. Moreover, I'm only about five minutes into it; I practically have a full bowl left. But like any good American schmo, I think to myself that I just can't leave the bowl right there; I have to finish that baby up. So, thinking that I can somehow beat the "*pho* game," I add more hoisin sauce in the hopes that the hoisin will somehow overpower the chili sauce, but that only worsens it. I am in tremendous pain, both mentally and physically, not only because of the extreme heat from the sauce but because of the humiliation of the situation. I'm literally crying over a bowl of *pho*.

It is usually at this point that I acknowledge defeat. By now, I am all red in the face and staring at the big bowl in front of me that is still three-fourths full. More important, it is also at this point that I begin to question my cultural identity as an Asian American and think about what defines a real Asian American and how real Asian Americans should think and behave. Although I myself am Asian and grew up being exposed to the culture, obviously I have not yet even come close to mastering how to eat *pho*. I'm kind of like that "ugly American" who enters a Chinese restaurant and fumbles with his chopsticks as he chuckles to his wife, "Hey honey, look at these." Or I'm like that guy who enters a Chinese restaurant and is given an American menu, eventually ordering himself an egg roll and fried rice, while all the "Asian" customers around him are given "Chinese menus" and are eating authentic Chinese dishes, i.e., the "good stuff." Sometimes I feel almost as if even though I look Asian, I somehow am not Asian enough and I should be. Then again, what is being "Asian" enough in the first place? Or, sometimes I feel that even though I, my father, and his father were all born here, I somehow am not "American" enough. Thus comes the question, just what is being "American" enough anyway? It is exactly this dichotomy between the "Asian" and "American" in Asian American that I have struggled with since childhood. This is the story of me and my Asia America.

Growing up as a kid in a primarily white suburban neighborhood, I've had to live in two worlds. In one world I had to be "American," where I grew up watching *Leave It to Beaver,* the essence of the American Dream and the model for how all "real Americans" aspire to live their lives like. I grew up waving my American flag every July 4 and watching the fireworks and parade. Like other kids on vacation with their families, I grew up sitting in the backseat of my dad's car listening to the oldies station, eventually memorizing the lyrics to "American Pie." And like any good American, my dad told me the importance of always buying American-manufactured cars. However, in the other world, I had to be "Asian," where I went to Chinatown, ate the food, played the piano and cello, had the "Moe"-style haircut, etc. I grew up listening to stories from my older relatives about the village where my great-grandfather on my mom's side of the family came from, seeing my relatives play mahjongg and watch Chinese videotapes instead of American television, and hearing the banter and gossip of my relatives speaking Chinese and not understanding a word of it.

This dichotomy between the two worlds is nowhere more apparent than within my own family. In fact, it helped me define myself as an Asian American. My dad's side of the family are the "assimilated Americans"; I suppose that's because of their early immigration. Immigrating to Canada in 1889, my great-grandfather, for some reason still unknown to our family, quickly moved south to Minnesota, where he set up a motel in a mining camp, which is now Hibbing, Minnesota. The fact that he actually moved to Minnesota, while most other Chinese immigrants at the time were settling in New York or California, is simply amazing to me, and I can only wonder why he did so. After my grandfather was born, the Sue clan moved from Minnesota mining camp to mining camp, but my grandfather eventually moved out of Minnesota and settled in Evanston, Illinois, where he set up a Chinese restaurant with my grandmother in Park Ridge. If you're interested, the restaurant is still around and is called Chinese Dragon. Make sure you try the egg foo young; it's the best in town. When World War II came about my grandfather was the first guy in the neighborhood to sign up. Like many Chinese and Japanese Americans at the time wanting to prove their loyalty to Uncle Sam, my grandfather threw himself at the Germans, waving the American flag with one hand and mowing down the Germans with the other.

After the war, my grandparents had my father, two uncles, and my aunt. Both of my uncles ended up becoming hippies. One became a photographer and rode across America on a Harley just like in *Easy Rider.* With his long black hair, headband, and his dark skin, one time a couple of locals from a small town in the South thought he was a Native American and chased him in their pickup truck as he was passing through. He had to hide in the woods with his Harley that night so that he could escape. My other uncle was the ultimate greaser when he was a kid, kind of like a Chinese John Travolta, except that he couldn't sing or dance, just act tough. Once, when he was sixteen or seventeen, my uncle went down to the basement with my dad, who was twenty-one or twenty-two at the time, and told him that he was going to quit high school. My grandfather had died when my dad was a small boy, so my dad ended up acting as head of the family since he was the oldest of his siblings. Upon hearing that my uncle planned on quitting school, my dad told my uncle that he could only do so if he could beat up him up. Losing the fight, with bruises all over his body, my uncle finished high school and eventually became a computer programmer. Accordingly, my uncle was definitely not what one would consider a "model minority." As for my aunt, she married a cheesehead from Wisconsin, who hands down is the best fisherman in the Midwest.

Consequently, my dad's side of the family is more or less a perfect example of the Americanization process. In fact, my grandfather's brother, whom I called Uncle Frank, absolutely hated Chinese food, not because of its taste but because he felt that eating it would show that he was un-American. He was so intent on being "Americanized" that he even refused to talk to his wife in Chinese, even though she was from China and only spoke Chinese. My mom and dad, while in college, even used to avert their eyes or look down any time they saw another Asian American coming their way because they didn't want to be associated or connected with being Asian. To be Asian or to give any hint of being Asian would mean that you were un-American.

My mom's side of the family, on the other hand, are the Asian extremes. My grandfather came to the U.S. during the 1930s and ended up taking over his uncle's Chinese laundry in Chicago, where he worked till the day he retired at age seventy. He then worked for ten years bagging groceries—talk about the Asian work ethic. As a result, my mom and my uncle Larry ended up growing up in the laundry business and speaking Chinese, contrary to my dad's side of the family, though my dad speaks a little.

Consequently, whenever I get together with my mom's side, the whole family speaks Chinese, and since I don't understand a word of it, I just sit there and twiddle my thumbs. With my dad's side, however, there is only English. While my uncle from my dad's side of the family brags about the latest deer he bagged with his hunting bow, my cousin from my mom's side of the family talks about how well her kid plays the violin. While my dad's side of the family talks about *Rambo II* and how good or bad it was, my mom's side of the family talks about a Chinese movie that they have seen. The two were and still are complete opposites. Whereas my dad's side of the family rejects anything Asian, my mom's side embraces it.

A perfect illustration of this difference would be if a white guy asked one of my uncles where he was from. If he was an uncle from my mom's side, that uncle would smile and say Chicago. Then if the white guy said, "No, where are you really from?" my uncle would realize what the guy was getting at and would respond with, "Oh, China." My dad's side, however, is a completely different story. An uncle from my dad's side would fold his arms and say Chicago. "No, you know what I mean, where are you from?" the white guy would ask again. But my uncle would not budge and would still say Chicago, even though he too would realize what the guy was getting at. But to him, to give in and say China would mean that he wasn't as American as everybody else.

As Asian Americans, we thus grow up having to live in two dual worlds and to learn to adjust to the two realms. On the one hand, you have to be just Asian enough to fit in with the Asian community or the Asian American community will call you a sellout, or *gi-lo,* Chinese (Cantonese) for white person. On the other hand, you have to be just American enough to fit in with the "American community" or "Americans" will think of you as being too Asian and being a foreigner. It's the catch-22. It's almost as if we have to be "super Asians and Americans." We have to be more American so that "America" accepts us, and we have to be more "Asian" so that the Asian community accepts us. This is a very difficult task, and many Asian Americans end up going to the extreme, either becoming completely "Asian" and identifying themselves as such or becoming completely "American."

Given the extreme backgrounds between my mom's and dad's sides of the family, I too had to learn how to balance the two in my struggle to become "Asian American." But that was not an overnight process, and even today, usually whenever I have *pho*, I still find myself grappling with my identity. I, just like my parents before me, grew up rejecting my cultural identity, yearning to be accepted as an "American." When kids asked me whether I knew kung fu or made Bruce Lee jokes, I laughed right along with them. When I was called a chink, jap, nip, or a couple times a gook, I laughed right along with them. One time when I was a boy in Florida with my family, a street performer pulled me into his act and asked me, in front of about twenty people watching him, where I was from. I said Chicago. He said, "No, what part of the Orient are you from?" Then I said, "Actually, I'm Asian American; I'm from Chicago." He then said, "Whatever, you people all look the same anyway." This was followed by laughter from the audience, and both my family and I grinned right along with them.

It was only after my junior/senior year in high school, and particularly when I first entered college, that I began exploring more my cultural identity and learned to accept more my Asian heritage, but maybe to an extreme. I no longer felt the need to put on a show for everybody else. And boy, did I become militant. If somebody made reference to a racial slur, even if it wasn't directed at me, I asserted myself and fought back. If I heard somebody say "Oriental," I pounced on the person and started waving my "Asian American" flag. I would even get on the cases of other Asian Americans who saw nothing wrong with the term "Oriental." They would look at me confused and say, "What are you talking about, Mike? Stop being so radical." And I would then lecture them and talk about Asian this and Asian that, scream out Vincent Chin, how white people were racist, and how any other Asians who didn't hold the same political views as I did were all sellouts. I even got myself an Asian car ornament to hang in my car, very much like people sometimes hang fuzzy dice. As college progressed, however, I eventually realized that I too had become the Asian extreme and that all of my pro-Asian ranting and raving didn't necessarily mean that I was "more Asian" than the next guy.

Thus, I came full circle. As a young boy, I was the absolute assimilated American, rejecting my cultural heritage altogether. As I got older, I embraced my Asian identity and became the militant extremist, actively assuming and looking for racism against Asian Americans, even where there really was none. Eventually, I learned to balance the two extremes, though even today I still periodically question my identity and the proper role of Asian Americans. However, in doing so, I'm slowly learning to accept the fact that maybe in the end there is no proper approach or right/wrong way of being and expressing oneself as an Asian American because there is no absolute mold of what constitutes an Asian American. While Little Johnny might grow up learning to speak both English and Chinese and going to MIT as an engineer, Little Mary might grow up speaking just English and becoming a cop. While Tim might grow up and consciously avoid the company of other Asian Americans, Gina might grow up and do the opposite. In fact, maybe when it comes to identifying and respecting one's Asian culture, killing oneself over a bowl of *pho* is what being Asian American is all about. Then again. . . . maybe not.

Bibliography

Rock Me, Goong Hay. From the punk-rap musical *The Goong Hay Kid*, dir. Shelton Ito and Alvin Eng. Third World Newsreel, 1992.

Michael Sue is from Naperville, Illinois, and graduated from the University of Illinois, Urbana-Champaign, with a degree in health administration. He currently is a student at the Northern Illinois University College of Law.

12 A Little Too Asian and Not Enough White

Matthew Noerper

Like most adopted Koreans, Matthew grew up in a predominantly white Jewish/Christian suburb. Along with his German American parents, he lives with three adopted Korean sisters and one adopted Korean brother. Two of his siblings are African American adoptees, and he has one adopted Caucasian brother. His two eldest brothers are his parents' only two biological children.

I hesitate to even call myself Asian American. No, I am not an ideologue blindly devoted to the oftentimes suffocating sense of political correctness that seems to have found its way into even the darkest conservative corners. As far as I'm concerned I am 100 percent white—that is, if you ignore my eyes and skin tone. I possess no claim to any sort of traditional Asian or Asian American heritage and history. My grandfather was not an exploited railroad worker who was barred from citizenship and the right to own land due to his race. Nor was my grandmother forced from her home only to live out World War II in guarded camps. Politically and socially I cannot claim that my parents were victims of systematic discrimination—and I cannot say that economic disparities caused by cultural and ethnic barriers have limited my opportunities while growing up. Yet because I was born into this world looking a little too Asian and not enough white I am compelled to check "Asian American" in the race category of all sorts of applications and documents—because society says so. It's ludicrous, but in the context of an American society in which even the word "race" carries with it scores of politically charged and even emotional implications stemming from primarily sociopolitical origins, race, defined, is usually no more than phenotype. It's amusing and somewhat disturbing how it is only my face that implies my identification with Asian America, but over the years it has been only my face that has forced me to appreciate the advantages, drawbacks, and prejudgments that come with having this face. Ironically even in this individualistic democratic society one has less say about who one is than the surrounding masses do. As an adopted Korean I am too ignorant to be legitimately yellow and too realistic to be satisfied as just white. I reside in a cream-colored state that quickly becomes a contradiction if I venture too far in either direction.

My family strongly influenced my early Eurocentric definition of America. While my parents would sometimes take my Korean siblings and me to Korean cultural events and sign us up for tae kwon do lessons, my America was absolutely color-blind. I really had no idea that I was different from 99 percent of my peers or parish, and culturally I wasn't. I was raised with traditional, conservative, common-sense American values and even speaking with a middle-class light Chicago accent, and Asian America simply did not exist. In fact, various influences within my family further distanced me from ever even wanting to identify myself with other Asians. Unfortunately and perhaps naturally, my family made me very aware of their and the rest of America's negative perceptions of Asian Americans—which did not even necessarily stem from malicious intent. My mother, who grew up in a very conservative part of America, would oftentimes speak of "ruthless little Korean women" who had the annoying knack of literally running her over in crowded markets, malls, and streets. Her perception of Asian men conjured a picture of selfish, amoral, and sexist jerks—prime examples of guys that she preferred her three adopted Korean daughters not date. Her default perception of Korean business owners (including my tae kwon do masters) depicted them as dishonest con men—as if somehow their business practices and promises were worth less than a Caucasian's. Perhaps most puzzling to me was my mother's constant portrayal of Korean women in the context of traditional Korean culture. I relive the times she joked that I should find some "little submissive Korean housewife who is there to cook, clean, and follow ten paces behind me wherever I go." Regardless of whether or not there was any truth to the implications of her statements, the ambiguous messages combined with the fact that I am Korean no doubt led to a degree of self-hate.

One of my parents' biological sons does not keep secret his belief that Asians (especially the men) are inferior to whites. He believes that Asian men are doted upon to such an extent by their relatives that they end up "weak" and detached from reality—with no expectations for themselves due to massive doses of compliments and attention. Their lack of regard for others limits their ability to work together, and many have never experienced working for what they receive while growing up. He believes that this "prince mentality" with which Asian families oftentimes raise their sons accounts for the "glass-ceiling" phenomenon. In short, when Asian men reach a certain level on the corporate ladder they simply lack a unique brand of American competitive spirit needed to win over their white rivals. He thinks that I am stronger somehow because I was fortunate enough to have been raised in a white family.

Similarly, my two older adopted Korean sisters seem to have accepted my family's general perception of Asian males. One of my sisters despises Korean males—not only are they short sexist wife beaters, but they also lack aesthetic attractiveness. She describes them as ugly and dopey-looking, to be exact.

What made these messages so insidious was not so much their content as my belief that they stemmed not from raw racist frustration but rather from rational deductions and years of observations and experience interacting with Asian Americans. Not only was I young and impressionable, but I respected the elder members of my family and thus their opinions.

I quickly internalized this conglomeration of negativity toward Asian America. Influenced by my mother, I became overly suspicious when I discussed money matters with my tae kwon do masters—automatic distrust appeared when it otherwise would have been nonexistent. I became hypersensitive to any forms of possible deception and was especially put off when my masters wanted me to call them *hyung* (older brother). Here were these Koreans who were essentially asking me to neatly transform into a pseudo-Korean simply because I could qualify for the part. Didn't they know I was white? There were other Koreans who chastised me for not speaking the language and those who pitied me for my circumstances. "I'm sorry (that you were adopted)!" was an all too common response in my interactions with some Koreans. Perhaps these Asians were as bad as my family had said they were. While I internalized these messages I found an easy way to distance myself as much as possible from Asian America. I convinced myself wholesale that I was different—that my entire family was different because we were fortunate enough to live comfortably within a more enlightened white America. I had no difficulty persuading myself, since outside opinions claimed that I do not even look Korean. I look "Chinese," "Japanese," "half-Asian half-white," and in any case "too good-looking to be an ugly Korean," according to many of my white peers. In my later years, when I started to explore my Korean identity, I became demoralized when I realized that there were shreds of truth to these stereotypes. Many times I joined my family and friends in condemning Koreans.

Other than within my family I had very little exposure to issues regarding race while growing up. I attended a very white Catholic school from kindergarten to eighth grade. Except for one incident in which a peer of mine mistook me for an African American, I was never really aware of any racial differences with my peers. My peers were not even aware that I was different. All of my junior high football, basketball, and volleyball teammates and friends treated me just as any normal child. Like most, I had my share of best friends, fights, and crushes (on white girls of course). It's funny how children do not possess inherent notions of race—it is society that emphasizes the differences and brings out prejudices. As I progressed into high school, I gradually became more aware of the fact that I did not physically resemble any of my peers. I initially hung out with a white group of friends because there were very few Asian Americans at my high school and I had negative perceptions of Asians. I got along more with the people and lifestyle that I had grown up with than with the Asians, who always seemed to be outside of mainstream culture. As the stereotype goes, the Asians I encountered were reclusive bookworms or pseudo-Asian gangsters. I remember spending time with an Asian gang after one of my Korean friends glorified the lifestyle, and I left after I witnessed how they shot out car windows and stabbed people for no apparent reason other than machismo posturing. In any case, the few Asians who were at my school all sat at the same table. The ones who were exceptions to this rule were females who played completely into the "China doll" mold that white America found nonthreatening, cute, and desirable—and the ones who tried so desperately to distance themselves from Asian America that their demeanor bordered on self-hatred.

As much as I resented most of the Asian Americans at my school, I could not help but identify with them on a certain level. By the time I was a junior in high school I was very aware that I was racially Korean. Many white students at my school had a very Hollywood-enhanced, Westernized view of Asians, and I began to resent being part of a community that was so utterly ignorant. As much as I saw Asians to be out of the mainstream picture, I paradoxically became angry when white students would exclaim, "Why do all you Asians sit together, walk around together, study together, etc.?" Ensuring that my phenotype would not be reduced to a tissue box-sized definition, I would quiet them by retorting, "Funny, I was wondering the same thing about you Jewish kids!"

Nothing made me sicker than when an ignorant white peer of mine would ask, almost sincerely, "Hey, Jackie Chan, have you ever killed anyone?" or when younger students would look at me and pull up the sides of their eyes to create "Asian eyes." When I became the first nonwhite to win a male talent/beauty contest that held with it a tradition of social prestige for the winner, it seemed to upset the school consciousness. Victory was usually all but assured for popular white jocks, but what did this mean that an Asian, whose talent was a tae kwon do demonstration, had won? The satisfaction of the title was tainted by accusations that I had won by some fluke, or that the judges were attempting to make a particular political statement—a threat to the safe and established order for most of the school's student body. It was a bittersweet event soured by comments such as, "That Jackie Chink routine was really something, wasn't it?" Even my closest friends made me sick sometimes. They seemed to be attracted to all things Asian, especially Japanese. To them Asian women were exotic sexual objects, and bland whiteness was repulsive. While I may have to an extent naively admired their relative openness, I realized that their fascination with Asians was almost unhealthy. I remember one evening, after some drinking, how about half a dozen of my white friends ranted on about how Asians were superior to whites, how I was extremely lucky to be Asian, and how they wished with all the marrow in their bones that they were Asian. This disturbed me, as their understanding of Asian and being Asian did not get much further than watching anime and Asian porn, as well as obtaining kanji tattoos.

At times, when I was simply bored or sick of being white, I complained with my yellow peers about the lack of Asians at the high school, sat at their usually all-Asian tables, and even traded in my middle-class speech for a horrible imitation of a Korean American accent to fit in. The Asian Americans accepted me, if only because I looked liked them—but I was always on the periphery and could never relate to them as well as to whites. The Asian American culture centered on Christian praise sessions, Asian pop culture, video arcades, *norebang*, pool halls, and—well, more pool halls. There was also a sense of Korean pride evident within the stances of all of my Korean friends. In my mind this was almost preposterous—if they were so proud of being Korean, why were they in the States? Shouldn't they try their best to assimilate, as I had—wasn't that what the American Dream was all about? At this time in my life their sense of pride seemed false to me; it wasn't until I entered college that my perceptions of Asian America gradually transformed.

As I progressed beyond high school, I involved myself more with Asian Americans and Asian American–related issues. Infuriated by the rampant ignorance on what was supposedly one of the more liberal campuses in the country, I made more Asian American friends. Despite much of the student body's perceptions and wishes that we should or do live in a color-blind society, anti-Asian graffiti has been placed in public forums, and some organizations have even advertised themselves by capitalizing on Asian stereotypes. "More fun than a raging hoard of mongrels" (alongside a picture of a Mongol warrior) appeared on one flyer advertising an event. In another incident, students were disturbed to see a large and clear message that called for the deaths of all Asians. After joining one activist and educational organization as an Asian American mentor, I was bombarded by negative sentiment from many white students who saw such organizations as alienating, exclusive, and most of all unnecessary. Many white students saw the program not as an institution meant to assist Asian students in their adjustment to a majority white community (many Asian American students come from predominantly minority communities while the majority of white students come from privileged middle- and upper-class backgrounds) but as an institutionalized version of "Asians once again simply sitting at their own exclusive table." Letters to the school newspaper frequently criticized our mentor program for not providing enough cultural events such as sushi making—reflecting a gross misunderstanding of our purpose.

One of the worst experiences I had at college was living in a hallway meant for students with an interest in speaking Japanese on a daily basis and understanding Japanese culture on a deeper level. Unfortunately the hallway was populated primarily by students with, as I bluntly put it, "Asian fever." The novelty with which they viewed Asian culture was enough to make it a passively hostile environment to live in. Pictures of naked Asian women and *hentai* were frequently posted in the hallway, suggesting that a very large part of their interest in Japan was due to what I call "an unhealthy obsession with Asian women and culture"—aka, a fetish. Events such as these drew me even closer to Asian America.

Any efforts the activist and outreach organizations made to dispel this "white ignorance" that I have discussed were typically countered with comments such as, "Why can't we all just forget about color?" "All you Asians do is complain," and "I don't need to know this stuff, it doesn't affect me." I perceived the white community in general as unwilling to even try to understand what people mean when they refer to Asian stereotypes—only three white students attended our mentor program's workshop on Asian stereotypes that semester. I realized that even on a liberal campus much of the white population, and even many minorities, remain blissfully ignorant of issues surrounding ethnic and racial identity—issues that minorities are forced to deal with because of phenotype-driven prejudices and biases placed against them by the majority culture.

For the first time in my life I felt truly disgusted with white America. After growing up in and supporting its institutions, educational systems, and culture, I felt tossed aside simply because of my appearance (I don't think that the authors of the "Asians die" message in the college's public forum meant to differentiate between nonadopted and adopted Asians). I latched onto the Asian American community to reassemble the scattered pieces of my identity. I actively involved myself in fighting against stereotypes and supporting the goals of activist groups on the school campus. The majority of my friends were individuals who looked like me. Unfortunately this story does not have a happy ending.

Despite my newfound connection with the Asian American community, at times I was torn between what would seem to be a logical view and my default responsibility to act consciously with regards to race. Many times it seemed that Asian Americans were perpetuating and embodying many of the stereotypes that they were trying to eliminate. On top of that I found many Asian students to be just as unwilling to understand Anglo American culture as white students were to understand Asian Americans. Many Korean Americans I have met are eloquent when they describe their frustrations in their struggle to gain acceptance within America, while at the same time hypocritically holding adamantly intolerant views toward homosexuals, interracial marriages, and other races. I even had some distasteful run-ins with peers who epitomized the "Asian prince syndrome."

A single incident perhaps summarizes some frustrating experiences I had with the Asian American community. Going back to my brother's beliefs, I cannot help but observe that Asian American families often hold their males in much higher regard than their females relative to the dynamic within white families—to the eventual disadvantage of the males as soon as they enter the "real world." I once took it upon myself to vacuum after an Asian American cabin retreat, and you would have thought I had cursed out the Lord himself—the guys were absolutely shocked that I would voluntarily perform such a chore, especially given that there were so many females in the room who no doubt had comprehensive experience in this area. (My parents had me carry out such chores regularly, and to me this was more a matter of simply cleaning up my own mess—an attitude that I *thought* was more or less universal.) They even joked about my masculinity. Were these guys fortunate enough to have never had to perform routine housework? Worse yet, was this notion of civic consciousness—cleaning up after yourself—not in line with the attitudes of Asian American guys? Did their reaction toward me stem from an insecurity that I was somehow different or just from a cushy upbringing? This episode, while minor in itself, ignited a metaphorical powder keg made flammable by years of contradictory messages from Asians and whites. For the first time in my life I was disgusted to be an Asian American male.

As dismayed as I am with some aspects of Asian America, I am just as sick of the seemingly inherent racism within white America. If my parents (whom I view as being extremely accepting and liberal) are any indication of the average American, then we definitely have a long way to go. I have developed extremely complex feelings toward Asian America. A lifetime of growing up with these influences, interestingly enough, has caused me to resent many Asians but not myself. I was proud to be different—to be what my white peers described as a "good-looking Asian"—and of my "enlightened" white upbringing that condemned the sexist and seemingly nonprogressive nature of Asian American society. At the same time I empathize with Asian Americans' struggle to gain acceptance within American society and their fight against the usual malicious stereotypes, if for no other reason than because I look like them. Unfortunately, because race has become the conceptual equivalent of phenotype, it seems for the time being that I cannot afford to be either white or Asian.

Matthew Noerper is from Deerfield, Illinois, and studies economics and theater at Pomona College.

13 Half and Half

Jenny Chen

"Hi. My name is Jenny Chen."

Sometimes I wonder what this introduction means to the other end. More often, though, I wonder what it means to myself. Just as the generic name reflects, I consider myself half-Taiwanese and half-American—culturally, that is. However, Taiwanese and American cultures are in many ways incompatible with each other, so how does one reconcile these two? I confess that I have yet to find a harmonious solution within myself.

"Flakey" is how my ex-girlfriend described me—in terms of my sexual orientation. Maybe so. Then again, it is a fitting description of me as a person because maybe I am just confused in general. Having been raised in Taiwan until my eleventh birthday and spending the time since in the States has been an enriching experience. But it has had its side effects.

I was taught throughout elementary school to respect my elders, be they parents, teachers, or just a random old man walking down the street. Societal hierarchy must be respected: I had to be humble before those above me but was allowed to be arrogant in front of those who were younger. Gendered roles dictated what I was allowed to do or not do: I was allowed to stay behind after dinner to watch my mother wash dishes while my brothers were told to go study. Countless dresses hung in my wardrobe, and my hair was permed until my forehead burned. Until I entered the ninth grade, I was wearing shorts made to look like skirts. More interestingly, though, as a child growing up in Taiwan, I never thought to define myself along racial lines because everyone I had contact with had black hair, black eyes, and yellow skin.

The world I had constructed in Taiwan was greatly challenged when I entered junior high in the States. Well, "challenged" may be the wrong word to use in this case. Because aside from the language and the cookery—both of which forced me to adapt quickly—everything else crept up on me so slowly that I didn't even realize it.

When my parents first sent my brothers and me to the States, they had an ideal situation in mind: We were to receive American educations, and once we had received our medical degrees, we'd return to Taiwan and become successful doctors. The potential for cultural gap seems to have never entered their minds, as they were, and still are, in shock at how my brothers and I have turned out. My mother even asked me once whether I was possessed by the devil. As far as they understand it, smoking cigarettes and dyeing my hair (once!) reflect an immoral self.

I once had to, for class, make a list of ten things that my parents had taught me. My list looked something like this:

WHAT THEY TAUGHT ME
1. Work hard and I will succeed.
2. Respect my elders and any form of authority
3. Respect societal norms
4. Family comes first
5. Be realistic and think in practical terms
6. Money buys everything, even happiness
7. Be humble
8. Be disciplined
9. Education is important
10. Persistence goes a long way

The list didn't look all that bad, and in fact, I agreed with most of it. So how did I turn out so different from my parents' expectation? The following list may help:

WHAT THEY DIDN'T TEACH ME
1. Working hard is not enough because it's solitary—in a word, networking
2. Respecting elders/authority doesn't mean following blindly

3. Societal norms aren't always "right"
4. Family comes first, but friends are especially important when the family is not around
5. Be idealistic
6. Money buys as much as we think it buys
7. Being humble is not equivalent to being bashful
8. Play
9. Education is not limited to textbooks
10. There is a fine line between being persistent and being stubborn

As I thought it over, I realized that it wasn't a matter of who was right or wrong, nor was it a matter of—as I liked to believe during my rebellious teenage years—good versus evil. It was just a matter of modification and moderation. I guess this is where "flakey" comes in.

Being Asian American for me is not a mere juxtaposition between being Asian and being American. It is not like putting together pieces of a puzzle, with different pieces labeled "Asian" or "American." Rather, it is creating a new identity that is neither Asian nor American. Whenever I receive chain letters that ask a million questions like "Where do you live?" and "What's your favorite color?" I always fill in "None" for the question "Where is home?" I am not trying to be a smart-ass, but that's how I feel. I can say that my current residence is in New York. I can say that I visit Taipei, where my parents live and where I grew up for eleven years. But when it comes to "home," I am at a loss. A home is what one misses when one is traveling abroad, the place one thinks of when one is homesick. I am constantly homesick.

Language determines how one thinks and how one approaches the world. So how do I approach the world when my native language is both English and Mandarin? When I think in Mandarin, I think in terms of family obligation, societal expectations; in short, I think along the lines of the list under what my parents taught me. When I think in English, I think in terms of my choices as an individual. I have realized to my dismay that with these two polar opposites, I can only communicate fully with those who speak the same language.

Inevitably, as I am sure many Asian Americans have experienced, one falls into some sort of subcategory under the overarching term "Asian American." Allow me to be politically incorrect for a second here. As my brother and I are constantly discussing what it means to be Asian American, here is the conclusion we came to during one of our discussions. There are essentially three broad categories of Asian Americans: the FOBs, the Twinkies, and the Floaters. Under the "FOB" category, you have the stereotypical clubbing Asians who have a ganglike dress code and speak only Mandarin or whatever their native language is. They commit the crime of Asian snobbery and only associate with other Asians. In milder form, they are exclusive because they simply find their American counterparts uninteresting. The extreme opposite are the "Twinkies," who deny their own Asian culture and heritage. They are desperate to shed their yellow skin and would only be seen with Caucasians. Then, there are the "Floaters," who fit into neither of these two categories. It is indeed horrible that I or anyone should fit all Asian Americans into one of these three categories, but stereotypes are not made without generalizations, and generalizations cannot be made without some empirical data. I am not defending these stereotypes but am simply pointing out what is in the back of most, if not all, Asian Americans' minds. I, like everyone else, would hate to be grouped into any of these categories, but I am also aware that were I to categorize myself, I would be a Floater.

In general, I do find my Caucasian counterparts uninteresting, and I end up having friends who share my last name and/or some sort of variation of my first name. "Uninteresting" does not mean that I have a fundamental distrust of or judgment against my Caucasian peers. Rather, there is a cultural gap similar to that between my Taiwanese peers and myself. How can I explain to someone who has lived in the same house, has had the same friends, dating back to when he or she was born that I am always homesick and that I feel uneasy whether in the States or in Taiwan? How can I explain to them that I like U2, can't stand Mariah Carey, but like A-Mei, who is the equivalent of Mariah Carey in Taiwanese music? While communication helps, it helps only to a certain extent. And more often than not, I become impatient. It's not impossible to have close non-Asian friends, but it is harder.

On the other hand, my identity does not consist only of my migrating experience. Sometimes, I find that while I blend in physically with other Asian Americans, mentally I don't. While it is comforting to talk about problems with my parents with those who can immediately understand, there are interests that I don't share with the same people. I don't like putting on makeup and dressing up to go clubbing. Yet getting together to cook or going on shopping sprees is not my idea of fun either. My brother says that this is more of a personal problem, not an East versus West problem. And I think he may be right. In any case, I stay away from group activities, whether they be for Asian Awareness month or simply social. After having turned down a couple of invitations to cook/eat/shop with the Asian Americans at school, I am aware that I have been ostracized and have probably been labeled a "Twinkie."

For all these reasons, I float, depending on my need, from one tiny group of two or three to another, whether the group be Asian, Caucasian, or another minority.

I realize that someone who has never met me and has read this far may think that I am either bitter or arrogant. And I admit I am kind of laughing at myself as I read over what I have written. Maybe my ex was right when she described me as flakey. Just as I physically don't belong here or there, psychologically and socially I am roaming in no-man's-land.

During the presidential election of 2000, I failed to vote. I wouldn't have voted anyway, but this time I didn't vote because I couldn't decide where my allegiance lay. As my brother said, as an American, I would have voted for Al Gore, but as a Taiwanese, I would have voted for George W. Bush. Why? Because Gore would have been a better candidate for the States, but Bush had a stronger international platform and he would have been more willing to protect Taiwan should China have decided to attack it. One of my friends asked jokingly what I would do if there was a war between Taiwan and the States. Honestly, I don't know. This hypothetical question is equivalent to asking whether I would rather kill my father or my mother. I guess I would just have to go hide out in Europe until the imaginary war ended.

The way I think about being Asian American reminds me of a story I read when I was little. The story goes that one day, the birds and the mammals got into a war over which was superior. When the mammals won, the bat flew to their side and claimed that it was a mammal. The mammals accepted the bat and allowed it freedom and all the privileges of being a mammal. However, another war between the birds and the mammals broke out again a couple of weeks later, and the birds won. The bat then flew over to the birds and showed them its wings and asked to be accepted as a bird. The birds said to the bat, "You cannot get the best of two worlds. If you can't even decide whether you are a bird or a mammal, then you are neither." So the bat was sent into the cave and was not allowed to show itself during the day. When I first read the story, I remember muttering to myself that it served the bat right for having been so greedy and unwilling to stick to one side or the other through good and bad times. But after having spent half of my life in Taiwan and half of it in the States, I am beginning to understand the bat's plight. While it can be quite lonely sometimes, it is overall a worthwhile learning experience. The most important thing, I think, is not whether other animals think of the bat as a mammal or a bird. It is whether the bat can reconcile within itself that it *is* a bat.

So what does it mean to me to be Jenny Chen? I think it means just that. I am Asian American, but I am not limited to being Asian American. I have just as many universal experiences as other twenty-some-year-olds experience, regardless of their race/ethnicity. True, I find myself constantly being pulled by two different "oughts" because of my background, and I end up, in many cases, acting inconsistently, at least outwardly. However, it is not for lack of moral awareness that I act as I do. I simply judge case by case how I should act, and like everyone else, I make mistakes and I learn. In fact, being Jenny Chen has made me more aware of my own decisions and actions as well as more tolerant of differences. Being Asian American is no longer the focus of my life. It has, undoubtedly, forced me to open my mind before I was ready to, and it has definitely played an important role in shaping me into who I am today. However, I now think of my Asian American experience as only one of the many learning experiences in my life. In a way, to reduce my personal struggle to an Asian American question would be to belittle a complex personal rite of passage into life.

Jenny Chen is from Taipei, Taiwan, and Scarsdale, New York, and graduated from Williams College with degrees in philosophy and psychology. She currently works at Advocates for Children in New York as an Americorps VISTA.

14 China Pearl

Julie Jia-Yi Greene

I look at my grandparents across the pink tablecloth and try to think of something to say to these relatives whom I haven't seen in nearly a decade. My Cantonese is pretty much limited to "I have this," "I want that," "I eat this." I am silent, nervous. I am thankful for the loud chatter from the other tables in the restaurant that fills the silence at ours.

Kau-mo picks up the blue and white teapot.[1] She stands and reaches across the table to pour for my grandmother, my grandfather, my other aunt, me, and finally herself. I mentally scold myself for not paying attention to the state of everyone's tea. I am the youngest at the table and should have poured.

Yi-ma breaks the silence with a burst of uncontrollable giggles.[2] She gestures in my direction. "How can it be that someone who looks like this could have come from people who look like that?!" she says, motioning toward my grandparents.

My grandparents are the picture of a diminutive elderly Chinese couple. Next to them, I must look like a bumbling foreign giant. Restaurant patrons at other tables are staring at our party. I imagine that they are wondering what sort of a lunch gathering ours is. We aren't dressed for a business lunch, and our ages are too disparate to make it likely that we are colleagues or friends. So how did a *gweimui* like me end up the sole pink face at this table of Chinese?[3]

In Cantonese, Yi-ma asks my grandparents, "Who does she look like? Doesn't she look like her father?" My grandmother absently fiddles with her teacup, which lingers in front of her lips. She nods. I wonder if she remembers what my father looks like, since she hasn't seen him in eight years.

She drinks in the fragrant swirls of jasmine tea and sets the cup down. This time my hand is on the teapot, ready to pour.

First grade: The bathroom was on the other side of the blacktop. I had to pee. I ran and ran. Chris and Bryan jumped in front of me. I couldn't get around them. They pulled the corners of their eyes up and down. "I am Chinese, I am Japanese, I am Chinese, I am Japanese." My eyes were stinging with tears. I still had to pee.

Third grade: It was three-thirty. I sat on the big concrete sign in front of the school and waited for my mom with Kristen and Sarah. They asked, "Is your mommy going to pick you up? Ching chong, ching chong!" I tried to protest, "No, it doesn't sound like that at all!" I tried to prove it with a sentence in real Chinese. All I could think of was "I'm hungry," so that's what I said. "See?" they squealed. "You're saying 'ching chong, ching chong'!"

Fifth grade: The little redheaded boy called me "nip." I was angry; I was sure he was saying something mean. I told him I'd beat him up. "Nip!" he said. I wanted to rip out that red hair. When I got home, I asked my dad what a nip was.

My stomach is gladly massaging my lunch as we walk out of the restaurant. I love dim sum, with all the delicate rolls and steamed dumplings and juicy shrimp. My mother calls it "Chinese junk food," but I don't feel guilty. I drink lots of tea to compensate. My mother says, "Tea cuts the grease."

Gung-gung shuffles along, each foot advancing only a few inches before he shifts his weight and moves the other foot forward.[4] He is about ninety but refuses to use more than a cane. When we visited Yosemite eight years ago, he held his cane above his head with both hands and trotted up the hills with vim, his smooth cheeks pulled back in a mischievous grin.

We are inching down a narrow back road. There are men wheeling boxes in and out of glass doors all up and down the street. Gung-gung leads me through one of the doors into a tobacco store. A couple of graying men emerge and greet him. My grandmother and I sit down near the window. Po-po doesn't pay attention to Gung-gung, or anyone else for that matter, except the lady with fuchsia lipstick who offers us tea.[5] I want some, if only to occupy my hands, but Po-po says no, thanks.

Gung-gung disappears with his friends into some back room. Smoke lingers in the air and floats in wispy tendrils from the cigarette of a man who looks pensively through the sooty glass. I wonder if this is the tobacco company that my grandfather worked with after the war when he first immigrated to Hong Kong from Taiwan.

Gung-gung brings a middle-aged couple out to meet me. They speak in rapid-fire Cantonese and I just smile brightly. The woman tells me that she has known my grandparents for many years. They peer at me approvingly, examining my hair, commenting on my skin. The woman nods, satisfied, and proclaims, "You look like your dad!"

I call my mom that evening and tell her about the trip to the tobacco distributor. She says, Ah, yes, Gung-gung goes there sometimes. He is so old that all his friends have died, so occasionally he likes to visit the shop because a few people still know him there. I ask Mom about the woman, and she says she remembers that they met years ago. She says that woman has actually never seen my dad—but of course the woman knows that he is white.

Whitewashed. Half my high school was Asian, and they called me whitewashed. Whitewashed meant stupid, whitewashed meant inferior, whitewashed meant I had betrayed my culture and was giving in to Them.

I wanted to be Chinese enough for my classmates, Chinese enough for my Chinese boyfriend, Chinese enough to be smart. People told me my dark eyes were the only thing that hinted that I'm not all white, so I drew them in darker. The beauty magazines recommend cool hues for Asians, so I bought tight gray shirts and silver eyeshadow, which disguised the creases of my eyelids. Maybe I could pull it off, I thought, just like that Nancy Drew book where she enters her friend's beauty parlor as a fair strawberry-blond and emerges a black woman.

I guess it's hard to not be whitewashed when you're half-white.

I bring Etienne to a pub after a long day spent walking around open-air markets in search of a street opera that we never found. He is the nephew of Yima's friend and is en route to London after a three-month sojourn in southern China. I promised Yi-ma that I would show him around.

Etienne squints at me through a pint of amber brew. "Soooo . . ." He traces the logo on his glass. "How do you like Hong Kong?"

I take a sip of Tsing Tao to stall. Outside we hear a commotion on the wet streets of Lan Kwai Fong, a popular nightlife area. A black car drives slowly down the hill, followed by mobs of excited people wielding cameras, vying for space next to the car, trying to peer through the tinted glass. The car stops in front of the bar, facing us, and we can no longer distinguish it from the black suits swarming around it. We bring our attention back to our beers and the dark wood table.

How do I like Hong Kong? I am glad to have discovered family that I hardly knew existed. I am glad to have this chance to see the land and the culture and the people who helped shape my mother. I am full of questions about what could have been, what friends I could have had, and what things I might have studied had my parents decided to live here in my mother's land rather than in California, where my father is from. But this is not my land.

Face is really what it is all about. I don't mean "face" in the Chinese sense, where it refers to your image and the respect people give you. I mean "face" in the purely physical sense. What do people assume when they look at me? Do they see a long face, wavy hair, freckles, and heavy hips? Or do they see black eyes, yellow skin, straight lashes, and small wrists?

I think of my college nestled in the young New Hampshire forests. As I walk around that isolated campus, I sometimes notice the rare Asian holding me in her gaze just a little too long. I try to send a conspiratorial look back, hoping that I am sharing a hidden understanding with this stranger. I like to imagine that she sees my black eyes and knows we are of the same blood.

One November night in college, while eating at the local hamburger joint with a hallmate and her brother, the question arose: "Do you people—do you—do you actually use those sticks?!"

"I—you mean chopsticks? Y-yeah . . ." Back home in California, everyone I knew used chopsticks with ease.

"But that's so primitive!" Clear green eyes stared back at me. "Barbaric!"

James starts the whole conversation. We've been at this table in the Seung Wan district for an hour, enjoying a little camaraderie now that our seminar has finally concluded. I think a few swallows of beer have loosened everyone up.

James says that he shouldn't have avoided breaking up with his girlfriend of the last seven years just to save her feelings. Chun-Yin tells us about all the things he wishes he had done with his brother, who recently died. Yao reveals that she has always wanted to be a singer but has been giving herself excuses to avoid auditions because she is so scared of rejection.

My classmates look relieved to share their stories, as though revealing their feelings and ambitions will motivate them to follow through with their dreams.

Silence. Everyone has spoken except for me. I look into the clear yellow liquid in my glass for help, but it is flat and uninspiring.

Dennis softly nudges me and says, "I think someone hasn't shared their story yet . . . ?" It isn't a question.

All eyes are on me. What can I tell my new friends? Can I tell them that I am uncomfortable because I know how different I look to them? It is my turn and I have to be honest, just as they were.

I tell them I want my family to see me as one of them and to truly believe and accept that half my blood is also theirs. I tell them I just want to have a conversation with someone who is not conscious of race or the superficial differences between us. I tell them I want to walk around for a day and not be stared at, not be treated with more respect or with less respect or with awe or with curiosity because of the way I look. I tell them I just want to be, be me, be the same as everyone else.

I tell them I want this to be my land too, but I know it is not.

I am reminded of that every time I am introduced to a friend or family member who examines me like a new addition to the zoo and makes some all-encompassing proclamation about how white I look, driving it in that I am not one of them. I am reminded of that with every shopkeeper who acts as though I am Mr. Ed, the talking horse, each time I speak in Cantonese. I am reminded of that with every auntie who says, "Oh, we shouldn't order chicken's feet—Julie, the *gweimui,* wouldn't eat that."

I stop and look around apprehensively. A circle of welcoming faces looks back at me; pairs of eyes just as black as my own take me in. Yao, sitting beside me, taps my knee. "Look at me," she says, locking me in her intense gaze. "When I look at you, I don't see white or Chinese. I see another person, just like me."

Notes

1. "Kau-mo" is an aunt, specifically, the wife of the mother's older brother.
2. "Yi-ma" is an aunt, specifically, the mother's older sister.
3. A *gweimui* is a female foreigner. A male foreigner would be called a *gweilo.* Both terms are commonly used to refer to white people, whether they are actually foreign nationals or not.

4. "Gung-gung" is the familiar term for "Grandfather" on the mother's side.
5. "Po-po" is the familiar term for "Grandmother" on the mother's side.

Julie Jia-Yi Greene is from Cupertino, California, and graduated from Dartmouth College with a degree in environmental studies. She currently works at the National Council for Science and the Environment in Washington, D.C.

15 Roots and Wings

Joann Yi Jung Huh

No, my soul is not asleep.
It is awake, wide awake.
It neither sleeps nor dreams, but watches,
its eyes wide open,
far off things, and listens
at the shores of the great silence.
—Antonio Machado, "Last Night"
Times Alone: Selected Poems of Antonio Machado

For a long time, a period of eighteen years, my soul slept. It remained dormant, giving no thought to one of the most important questions we can ask ourselves: Who am I? From birth to emigration from my homeland, from my entry into America to entry into college, I never seriously asked myself who I was. It never occurred to me to inquire about it. Until age seven, my world was Korea. My parents were Korean. It was simple: I was Korean. And then we moved to the United States, greeted by a note in our mailbox telling us to "go back where [we] came from." The note did not bother me—I was seven and carefree. I would have gladly gone back to Korea.

My parents still desire to return. Such longing is natural: They spent their formative years in Korea. They have deep roots and attachments to our homeland. My father was born three years before the civil war, and tells me bits and pieces of his childhood during that indigent era. He recollects funny, sad, and tragic stories of those years. It was his world, and still is. Whenever he summons up the past, my father tenderly speaks of his mother. And he blinks back the heavy tears that threaten to fall or breaks out in joyous laughter. Both reveal a deep sense of loss and longing. I think my grandmother represents Korea to him: someone he loves so profoundly but can never see again. My grandmother has passed away, and so has the Korea that he experienced. Now all he has are memories.

I do not possess many memories of my first seven years in Korea. But those years and my parents' influence have been: I have an indescribable love for Korea. It blossomed further when I learned its history, and all the tragedies that my homeland weathered and overcame. I was deeply touched by the hardships that Korea endured, almost as if they had happened to me personally. In a sense, they had. I realized that I was never meant to survive—not as an ethnic Korean. Japanese colonialism, during its third and final mobilization phase, attempted to eradicate everything and anything Korean. Every word I read of the colonial period struck my heart, and I bled. I bled over the "comfort women." I bled over the countless executions of independence fighters. I bled over the murder of Yu Guan Soon. And the stream of blood became a torrential river as I learned of the division into north and south, the civil war, and the authoritarian regimes of several past leaders: I wept over the horrors that Koreans had committed against one another. I still weep.

Korean history came to me in college. My parents encouraged me to read about it, but they gave me books in the Korean language. Because I came to the United States at such a young age, I could not and still cannot understand sophisticated Korean books: I can read the words, but understanding the vocabulary is a different matter. And Korean history was not offered in high school. Nor was history of any other part of the world except Europe. I cannot, of course, expect high schools to create such classes when they have to offer classes on subjects like ancient Roman civilization or home economics. The only thing I learned about Korea from the second to the twelfth grade was the Korean War. Which was actually a civil war. Civil. Fratricidal. I do not know if a nation warring against itself is "worse" than two different nations fighting, but a fratricidal war just seems to carry so much more gravity. My class spent fewer than twenty minutes on that war, and I initially learned about it as it was taught: Americans saving foreign lives in some war in some other part of the world. It never hit me that some of my loved ones had survived that horrific war. That it represents the greatest thorn in the Korean psyche: The country was divided on the whim of another nation, and this preemptive division made the ensuing developments possible, and perhaps impossible to circumvent.

Knowledge of the civil war, and all the other events in modern Korean history, informed my mind and identity. I realized that my existence was a result of the combination of all those circumstances. I was not just Korean, but the descendant of Koreans who had witnessed the Sino-Japanese War and the Russo-Japanese War ravage their home. I was living proof that someone had endured and survived the degrading violence of occupation and the horrors of civil war. I had the stamp of thousands of lives on my soul: my father and mother, their parents, and their parents, and forever on. I was the result, the fruit, of thousands of years of existence and struggle. Heritage is a more serious reality than it is often viewed to be. It is not simply knowledge of culture, custom, and history; it is how these aspects impact your heart and soul. Heritage is not a, b, and c; it is how you internalize these things and make them come alive through your existence. Such is the way it is bequeathed to future generations: by living and love.

After discovering my heritage, I struggled with the idea of my own division into two: my "American" and "Korean" halves. I struggled with the civil war that was supposedly being waged in my heart. This was what being "Korean American" or "Asian American" seemed to mean. My parents said, "That is harmful American influence," whenever a show portrayed sexually explicit scenes. My friends complained, "That is so Korean," whenever my curfew conflicted with our plans. Each side looked down on the other side. I was to believe that Korean television never portrayed those kinds of scenes and that "Americans" did not have restrictive curfews. That Korea was everything America was not, and vice versa. That I was in the middle of these two opposing poles and had to choose by virtue of the inherent difference between the two.

But the idea that Korea, or the "East," is the opposite of America, or the "West," is flawed. People would have me believe that Korea, as part of the "East," is mired in outdated and sexist traditions, bound by restrictive social norms that negate individuality. Those same people would ask me to believe that America, as the forefront of the "West," is the epitome of a society that values individualism, equality, and freedom. Others would say that Korea has respect for the elderly, exemplifies a cohesive society made possible by the five basic Confucian relationships, and still retains morality. They would also characterize America as disrespectful to society's seniors, chaotic because society is not bound by reciprocal custom and obligation, and shockingly lascivious. Both sides are wrong. Korea is not completely conservative and restrictive, and America is not entirely free and liberated. Koreans are not all sexist, and all Americans do not support equality. There is portrayal of physical love on Korean television, and American parents also set curfews.

I am not being "Korean" by weaving my parents into the fabric of my life and respecting them, and I am not being "American" by believing that women are equal to men. I am not being "Asian" when I choose to keep quiet in class, and I am not being "American" when I decide to speak up. These are constructed categories, as arbitrary today as when they were first formulated by Europeans as they "opened" China. I am not half-"East" and half-"West"; those categories are as outdated as Kipling's famed "white man's burden." And because they do not exist, I do not have to choose. I never did. Others told me I had to make the choice, but they were wrong. I never fought a civil war between my "Eastern" and "Western" halves.

The more I thought, the more I began to see that it was misguided to turn to others as experts on my own identity. My identity was under nobody else's control and direction other than my own. The greatest and most empowering lesson I learned was to consider what others had to say but to never let them define my world. Some individuals may have words of wisdom, but ultimately it was my identity. I could chart my own course, separate from others if necessary. Such is the essence of identity and self-awareness: The challenge lies in discovering for oneself what identity comprises and ethnicity means, and living according to one's own unique formulation. It was my right and responsibility to determine my identity for myself. And so I took up that responsibility.

After much contemplation, I realized that attempting to define my identity is like trying to capture all the clouds in the sky in one bottle. Even if it were possible, the clouds would intermix in that one bottle and be completely amorphous to the observer. Such is the fluid, complex, and enigmatic nature of identity. However, I know that part of me lies in Korea. It never left. The clouds of my identity span both Korea and America. I may have been partially socialized into the different sociocultural reality of the United States. I may have lost fluent knowledge of my mother tongue. But I have never forgotten my heritage, my longing to look back. And I have not neglected to look to the present either. Analyzing the 1992 Los Angeles riots made sure of that.

I was only eleven when 4/29/1992 happened. I knew something had gone terribly wrong; my parents became deeply upset and said that Koreatown was now a war zone. When I revisited the riots in Asian American studies classes, I analyzed the model minority myth and how things had indeed gone terribly wrong. It was a grave injustice to many Koreans incited by a grave injustice done to the African American community by the Rodney King verdict. And everything became gray; the riots were not a solely black versus Korean incident. African Americans had not been the only rioters, and Koreans had not been the only victims (although they incurred the majority of the damages). Being Korean did not mean one was anti–African American, and vice versa. That was how the media constructed the event by showing selective images and juicy sound bites. Becoming engrossed in the riots made me realize that although I had been looking back at Korea, my present was in America. I was not just Korean and not just American. I was Korean American, and I could define for myself what that meant and did not mean. What others supposedly said was Korean or American need not apply to me. Other Korean Americans might not agree with my formulation of Korean American-ness. And that is to be expected because everyone has the right to frame her- or himself. This is the beauty of being an in-between: the capacity to pierce through blinding ethno-nationalism, to examine *and* critique both (or all) cultures, and then choose or reject certain aspects of them. The fact that my reality spans two different cultures is a blessing in that I have both roots and wings. Individuals with the intimate knowledge of just one culture will have roots but may not recognize their wings.

And I am not yet done flying. Perhaps I will forever discover and redefine myself. Perhaps identity is not meant to be defined in detail and cemented as such. Because after realizing that Korean American-ness is a self-defined identity over which I have control, I drew back from the tunnel vision of "American" versus "Korean" and "Korean American." I pulled back because at my innermost core, I am a human being. More so than anything else. Sometimes ethnicity and nationality, and the search for them, obscure the most basic and intuitive understanding: that we may act or look differently but that we are same at the core. The rejection of this intuition is exemplified by the experience of the "comfort women" under the institutionalized system of sexual slavery perpetuated by the Japanese Imperial Army. The violence between Israel and Palestine also serves as a harsh example. Many have let their wings atrophy and their roots mire them in hatred. And so, life reveals another lesson: We do have the right to formulate our identity, but with it comes the responsibility of being just toward others. An identity that thrives on the degradation of others is fundamentally unjust, attempting to fly above everyone else to keep them down. And our world has had enough of this brutality and violence. So we must change it, beginning with our own identities. We must look within ourselves and be awake, wide-awake. We must watch, not sleep or dream, but watch, with our eyes wide open, far-off things. And listen at the shores of the great silence and peace.

Joann Yi Jung Huh is from Seoul, Republic of Korea, and graduated from the University of California, Berkeley, with a degree in political science. She is currently studying at the University of California, Berkeley, Boalt School of Law.

16 Creating Myself

Curtis Steuber

This essay about my Asian American identity will not always seem to make sense or present clear ideas. But I myself don't have a clear sense or idea of what my identity is yet. In terms of age, I'm only twenty-one, which is fairly young. I haven't had all the experiences or situations other people have had, but I want to share what I have learned and who I am.

My name is Curt, and I am who I have made myself to be. I don't like the idea of having an identity based on skin color or race, so I have decided to make my own identity. Forming my own identity was, and is, not an easy task, but I have made a conscious decision to identify myself by my own actions, thoughts, and relationships. I don't blame others for my faults, and I accept responsibility for every action I take. Everything I do, I try to take a lesson from it. This helps me to learn more about myself and helps prepare me for my future.

It's too bad that there is so much emphasis placed on ethnicity and race. There shouldn't be any emphasis placed on ethnicity or race because they do not really matter. Stereotypes are needlessly placed on people and can hurt reputations and stifle personal growth. This is part of why I choose not to be South Korean, American, or be labeled by anyone. I am a person, and that is the only thing people should see.

To me ethnicity is unnecessary, a crutch that I have purposely striven not to have. I don't know if that is good or bad. By limiting myself like this, I might be missing out on some good friendships, but I'm okay with that. I understand the consequences and I still choose not to join ethnic organizations. I don't know if that is right for everyone, but it's right for me.

My twin sister and I are both South Korean, but the rest of my family is not. My parents adopted my sister Christen and me more than twenty-one years ago. We were born in Seoul, South Korea, but I have no memory of that land. I was adopted after I was only a few months old—how could I truly know it?

Although I have a twin sister, we are two distinct persons. Even though my sister and I are roughly the same physical size, I'm amazed at how different we are emotionally. Our thought processes and reactions are so different that sometimes it doesn't seem like we are twins at all. My twin is very conscious of being Asian, and she takes pride in being South Korean. I'm not sure if this is because she truly is proud of her South Korean heritage or because she feels alone in "white America" and that is her way of feeling like she's part of something. That possibility is awkward because I don't think she should be proud of having been born into an ethnic group, and this creates conflicts between us. I haven't asked her about it; I'm scared of her answer because I wouldn't know how to deal with it. I, as stated earlier, don't like to consider myself Asian. I'm not saying that being or feeling Asian is bad, but I don't feel like it's something I need to identify with. Why should I feel or be Asian when I don't know what being Asian actually is?

Our interaction with my family can also be difficult sometimes. Christen and I have two younger sisters who were born to my adoptive parents. And I know they mean well, and try to understand our situation, but they can't because they don't know what it's like to be a minority. They are white in a society that is predominantly white. It's tough to be different from everyone else, but I know they love us like family, because we are.

I think of myself as being more logical and reasonable than Christen. Christen is guided more by her emotions and feelings. Because of this, our reactions to similar situations are different. Since she's more emotional, she reacts more readily to situations that are racially sensitive. I try not to let my emotions influence my judgment.

Other people compare our personalities too, and they notice our differences and often point them out. I don't mind being compared at all, but Christen can take it very personally at times. These comparisons are magnified because we are so different from almost everyone else in our community. Christen is more social, and I think she interacts with people sometimes for the purpose of being popular and accepted. But I try to remain independent and don't seek the approval of other people. I think Christen is looking for something, I think she's looking for herself. Through popularity, race, friends, or whatever it may be, I think she's trying to form her own identity. I think I have made my own identity, but it continues to evolve on a daily basis as I live and learn. My identity is founded upon the idea that I am me; I can be whoever I want to be. That identity might not be enough for some people, but it's simple and easy for me. Not identifying myself with too many outside factors makes it easier for me to adapt to change while knowing who I really am as a person. My morals, thoughts, and ideology form my identity. Thus, my identity is my own creation.

My earliest memory is of living in Muskegon, Michigan. The only thing I remember is that the neighborhood I grew up in had no kids my age, and everyone living there was white. We moved from Muskegon when I was about five years old to Holland, Michigan. Holland is on the coast of Lake Michigan and is predominantly conservative and white. To be honest, I didn't even know I wasn't white until I was in first grade. I didn't know what being white, black, Asian, or Hispanic meant. All I knew was that there were kids my age around, and they liked to play with toys. Sometimes I wish I could have those days of ignorance back, when kids didn't know what race or ethnicity was. However, as nice as it was to be naive, it's hard to maintain that innocence as you grow older and learn more about life.

When I was in elementary school, our family would take trips to Florida to visit my grandma for Christmas. I remember once stopping at a truck stop in Tennessee and everyone was staring at my sister and me. I don't know if the looks were malicious, or out of mere curiosity. It's not as if what happened over ten years ago doesn't happen even now. Four or five years ago, my family took a trip out West. In every state we went to west of Illinois, every time my sister or I stepped out of our camper, we were stared at and sized up. But now, I feel like I have grown up and matured to the point that strange looks don't really matter to me. They don't matter because I won't let them. They don't know me, I don't know them, and that's why they don't matter. This has made it easier for me to be different and feel good about myself. It's not that I don't care about other people, but I don't try to please other people.

I honestly don't know how I could feel like I am South Korean. I do not speak, read, or write in Korean, and apart from being born there, I have never seen the country except on a map. Sometimes I wish I knew the language. But I can't think of a good reason why I would need to know it. I don't personally think it would make me feel better, or part of that culture, or more South Korean. I don't have a desire to learn about South Korea for any reason.

Growing up in a predominantly white community has given me a unique insight on "blending" into my town. I have come to think that no one is more important than anyone else. This has made me more independent because I do not rely on others; I know who I am and what I want to do. The events that have happened and the people I've met have all influenced who I've become and will develop into through the life lessons I learn. I am an independent person who just wants to succeed in life, not for others but for myself. I need to make myself happy and be satisfied with who I am before I can try and make anyone else happy.

Curtis Steuber is from Holland, Michigan, and studies international relations at Michigan State University.

17 Drawing the Boundaries

Priscilla Chan

When I was student-teaching, a white student told me that several black and Latino students had called him racist names. I wondered if this was a case of "getting a taste of your own medicine"—a white person experiencing the discrimination which has shaped so much of my life. Yet, horrified that I might have taken any satisfaction in my student's crisis, I questioned strongly my own beliefs about this new four-letter word: "race."

Here before me, a young person was asking how to deal with his own racial identity crisis, but as his teacher, I had no answers for him. I did, however, have a story to tell about a young girl who dreamed of "Asian America" . . .

Freshman Year and the Crisis of Identity . . .

I grew up in Chinatown, New York, in a tiny apartment roughly the same size as my freshman-year room. Everywhere I looked as a child, I was reminded of the monumental stereotypes of and pressure from my neighborhood and culture: poor, passive, non-English-speaking, reclusive, foreign. A significant portion of my adolescence revolved around the discomforting and awkward acceptance that I was Asian, from Chinatown, and that I would always be seen as such.

So I came to college with more baggage—and I do not mean just my suitcases—than a normal eighteen-year-old should hopefully have. Seeing my entryway-mates unpack their state-of-the-art computers, I quietly unpacked my own model, a rickety PC still running Windows 3.1. It was the first and only computer my family had ever purchased.

A friend, forgetting his tact, scoffed at my hardware. I came back with a line about how I appreciated its antique charm, but I was deeply embarrassed. What I really wanted to explain was how I was lucky to have a computer at all. But somehow, surrounded by hardware that put mine to shame, I just could not find the words.

Yet how did I even get there? From the Asian ghetto to the Ivy League— it is the road less taken. The journey began when I was given the opportunity to transfer into a more prestigious (and more white) middle school. This was the first time I had regularly left Chinatown, and saying that I had culture shock would be an understatement. I could not believe that some people who lived only minutes away from me by train could live such remarkably different lives.

Some kids took private charter buses to school; my family considered my free subway pass a godsend. Some kids blew ten dollars every day on lunch outside school grounds; most days, I made sure I had my tickets for school lunch. These were very hard times for me. My Chinatown had seemed so comfortable just a few weeks ago, yet traveling a little outside its boundaries, I quickly understood that being Asian in Chinatown meant climbing over more hurdles to even get to the same starting point as my new friends. No one likes to be told that their lives are not entirely in their control; imagine what it's like to realize this when you're starting middle school.

In this world, my issues with race blended with my issues with economics. I could not differentiate the discomfort that came from being Asian from that which came from being poor. The few other Asian students in the school did not go back to their own versions of Chinatown, so relating to them had its own difficulties. Awkwardness came therefore from the realization that not only was I in a subcategory within the school by being Asian but, by being from Chinatown, I was in a subset of a subcategory.

I often found myself remaining quiet when everyone spoke about their new CDs, or shows they watched on cable, or the latest movies, because I wasn't lucky enough to see or hear them. A naive belief that money would make me fit in characterized many of my middle and high school experiences. I hoped that upon entering college, this belief would take a backseat. I was so sure that here, in this wonderful world of higher education, intellectualism would always surpass materialism.

Unfortunately, I found myself only a few months after high school in another new world, far removed from Chinatown, at another moment of silence. I had become a person who allowed others to talk down to her—an Asian American who feared the outside, a less well-off individual who was ashamed of her means. Though disappointed, I did not come down too harshly on myself, thankfully. Freshman. So much to learn . . .

Sophomore Year and Preparing for the Enemy . . .

As I eased past the discomfort of freshman year on my journey to Asian America, I realized that helplessness was a pit stop where I did not want to rest long. Slowly, I discovered that the control that I had started losing in middle school was not lost forever. I felt confident that once I grasped why I had become *powerless* in the first place, I would be halfway to becoming *powerful*.

The path to regaining control was not easy; to understand the "enemy" was a skill. To hone my skills, like a boxer preparing for a championship bout, I mapped out some workout tips. I pictured the enemy as the all-encompassing "Ignorance"—another one of those words that would have incredible influence on my life.

REGIMEN TIP ONE: Ignorance comes in many forms, so be ready for any opponent. It never fails to irritate me when Asian "elements" are thrown upon an object for the sole reason of fashion. In a magazine, I once saw an outfit adorned with images of Mao Zedong. I immediately wondered if it came with matching Hitler and Castro accessories. Surprisingly, I didn't see them anywhere. In another magazine, a stylist described an exquisitely dressed Michelle Yeoh like so: "Forget Taiwan. How about Tai-wow!" First, Michelle Yeoh is from Malaysia. Second, imagine the parallel: A Mexican artist walks down the red carpet to similar commentary: "Forget Puerto Rico. How about Pretty Rico!" The comment's silliness was glaring.

Once, a friend of mine asked me to translate her Chinese-character tattoo. The cynic in me wanted to make up my own translation, but the human being in me conjured up my knowledge of characters. It wasn't too hard to spout off a rough translation, since there are only a few characters that have made it into the "Foreigners Guide to Things Asian." This handful will appear on various T-shirts, bracelets, slippers, and other trendy items (apparently including tattoos) and will say "love," "friendship," "success," or "strength" . . . Exoticism has hit an all-time high.

The objectification of a culture's traditions as marketable products allows someone to selectively choose what they see when viewing Asian America, a choice that is unacceptable to me. It offends me that modern-day "riches of the Orient" are embraced as a suitable substitute for a real exchange of culture, that racism is masked by dollars in the eyes of the Ignorant. It is as if the wearing of good-luck bracelets with Chinese characters means that the very arms wearing them are outstretched in a warm welcome. The hypocrisy makes me cringe.

REGIMEN TIP TWO: Know your weaknesses, and use them to your advantage. Recently, I learned the startling fact that Asian American youth have the highest rate of suicide in the country. I used to believe that as an Asian American, I knew better than anyone the issues affecting us as a group. Yet I soon realized that I knew little of the issues affecting Indian Americans, Filipino Americans, etc., and that I had a broad but shallow perspective on Asian America.

Knowing the disadvantages in the lumpy term "Asian American," however, does little justice to the benefits it also offers. I await eagerly the day when we will have the luxury of making distinctions between the various ethnicities covered under the term, but currently, our basic needs, hopes, struggles are too similar. But if I choose to fall under the "Asian American" category, I am expected to be a representative. But then we go full circle: How much can I claim to represent? It is a hard thing to know your weaknesses while at the same time using them to your advantage.

I fear that I appear to be hypocritical. While it is nearly impossible to know all of "Asian America," I refer to it as if somewhere a comprehensive list of components exists—as if it *were* indeed possible. "We." "Us." These words sprinkled throughout the essay refer to the "first-person plural," to something more than "me," but they are only words of hope. I could easily write "I" or "me," but there is an idealized community to which I envision belonging . . . *my* version of "Asian America," *my* concept of "we" and "us." My weakness and advantage lie in this hope. They have to.

REGIMEN TIP THREE: Stay on guard; the match isn't over until the opponent is dead. In other words, be wary of small concessions. During my sophomore year, a report entitled "Reaching the Top" concluded that since Asian Americans outperform other minority groups, they have less need for the numerous "affirmative action"–type programs offered under the College Board, like private scholarships, government aid, and job assistance. For many, the report signified the "success" of Asian Americans—the long-awaited stamp of approval that they had reached the academic levels of whites. For others, the report was rather a stamp of death, the epitome of embracing the tragic "model minority" stereotype. How better to lose than to accept your opponent's false congratulations? How better to let down your guard than to blindly believe that "we have made it"? What about our headway in other areas? Recently Asian American candidates have been turning up on local ballots in record numbers, rallying "their own" to the polls. Yet, with so many names to choose from, even optimists fear that minority votes will cancel each other out and split voting strength. Similarly, the recent campaign finance scandal involving Asian donors also signified future Asian American participation in politics. Even on the rare occasion that politicians actively court our votes, they usually hold their promises until the checks clear. Our community is indeed making progress on the American political front, but we are far from victory.

Undoubtedly, it is a major effort to actively incorporate all these tips into our lives. But there is the reward of knowing that you will hopefully be equipped to make an impact with your words and actions, and that is no small achievement. No pain, no gain.

Junior Year and Avoiding the Superficial . . .

Ask anyone to name the first thing that comes to mind when they think of Chinatown, and they will probably think of something along the lines of food, restaurants, etc. There's no shame in that. The shame lies in *only* seeing those things.

Chinatown is an expert at facades. What other community could lure hundreds of visitors every week into its boundaries without ever suggesting that people actually live in those tiny rooms above the restaurants? That factories (sweatshops) actually operate in those nondescript buildings?

The enemy, therefore, cannot just be Ignorance (not knowing). It must also be Facades (that which makes seeking the truth much harder).

I am reminded of an article in which a white student questioned why many negatively viewed her decision to consider herself ethnically Chinese. I admit to being part of this wary contingent. On the one hand, I was entirely a fan of allowing all people to choose their own "labels." (I would hardly be one to fixedly advocate being lumped into a category on the sole basis of your looks.) On the other hand, I was cynical about the fact that she had the luxury of *choosing* for herself what had *been chosen* for me. (I do not teach English, but I still know the difference between the active and passive tenses.) At the time, what I wanted to say to her was this: You cannot fully know what it means to be Chinese until you have walked one day in yellow skin.

But I was wrong. Perhaps the greatest progress I have made in my views on race is in considering this: If it is only possible to know what it means to be me by walking in my colored skin, then how deep is that reality? The most unique thing about what I imagine to be the Asian American community is its diversity. For every rich Asian American, there is a poor Asian American (if not more). For every Republican, there is a Democrat. For every college graduate, there is a high school dropout. For every yellow-skinned individual, there is a multitude of other physical appearances.

However, I am not just saying that whites can justifiably call themselves Asian American. I am only acknowledging that I have no more of a claim to the definition of Asian American than anyone else, even whites. There are some non-Asians who can speak Asian languages or who have studied Asian cultures better and more than I ever have. In a world filled with "half Asians," "quarter Asians," "eighth Asians," where is the line drawn for membership in this community I envision? Are whites any more outside the boundaries of Asian America than I am?

I dare not even wager an attempt at defining this community for anyone other than myself.

I was born Chinese, but I have been Asian American for most of my life. The first statement I did not choose; the second I eventually and proudly did. Yet, by speaking it aloud, I chose to enter a community (however imaginary and illusive) and to embrace its inevitable diversity.

Senior Year and Looking Ahead . . .

My thoughts return again to the instance when I felt momentary restitution in my student's encounter with reverse racism during my student-teaching. I thought I had encouraged my classes to dig deeper into their studies, yet I discovered that we all sorely needed more practice in looking beyond the superficial. For most of my life, "race" has simply denoted a group with the same geographic history and similar physical characteristics. Yet race cannot just scrape the surface. Whatever it means, it must be accompanied by a way of thinking, a sense of responsibility, an awareness of community.

I devoted most of my senior year to earning my teaching certification. One of the most important lessons I learned in my education classes involved a simple fraction. Ask any child to draw you a visual representation of "one-half," and more likely than not, she will draw you a circle with half of it shaded in. This image of a semicircle has been ingrained in so many of us as the archetypal symbol for "one-half." But I could easily draw any other polygon with half of the area shaded in, a black-and-white checkerboard, or even a yin-yang, and all of these would accurately represent "one-half." The lack of choice I felt I had during my identity crisis is much like the often singular concept of "one-half." There seemed to be only one option, and that was the choice that was made for me. I was an Asian American because I looked like one. Although I was thrust into Asian America, in my development as an adult, I definitely *chose* to remain there.

We only stand to gain by opening up the definitions of "race," "Asian American," "one-half." Every day as a teacher, I have the opportunity to help kids define these terms for themselves. Ironically, as I assist them, I assist myself. I have come a long way in my views on race, but even as a recent college graduate, how much do I really know? It is humbling to realize that at twenty-three years old, I know little more than I did at thirteen.

Yet such knowledge has never really been my goal. I do not seek definitions. After all, knowing the meaning of the term "Asian American," if that is even possible, would only be the first step in making that term *meaningful* to me or any other inquisitive young person of color.

I now mentor a girl who recently emigrated from China. When we talk, we do not discuss our race, our culture, or our neighborhood. Instead, she wants to know about clothes, magazines, movies, boys—"regular teenage stuff." I often wonder about her feelings about racial identity; does she even question it, and if so, does she have the same questions I did when I was growing up? She is an Asian person in America, so some would say she is Asian American. But she is a non-English-speaking immigrant, so others would say she is not. Yet the distinction is often comical in the face of more pressing concerns.

To my mentee, knowing the definition of "Asian American" is a useless tool. This definition will not help her learn English; it will not get her parents better jobs; and it will not help her graduate from high school. She is Chinese, that she knows. One day, perhaps, she will choose to be Asian American.

That is not a choice that I can or will make for her by defining an "Asian America" in which she is a citizen before she has chosen to be.

Definitions are often as advantageous as they are limiting. Sometimes they are desperately sought; other times, they are barely given a second thought. They will push, pull, and stop you all at once. In the end, do not just define "Asian American." *Define yourself* and you will have succeeded.

Priscilla Chan is from New York City, New York, and graduated from Harvard University with a degree in environmental science and public policy. She is currently teaching math and science in New York and studying environmental and occupational health sciences at Hunter College.

18 Lost and Found in Asian America

Jessica Kawamura

I can still remember that day . . . It must have been during the first week of my freshman year in high school. I was sitting in the auditorium, when this kid behind me taps me on the shoulder and slowly says in a surprised voice, "You're Japanese?"

I respond, "Yeah."

But he continues, "Japanese and what?"

And I say, "Japanese and Japanese."

Apparently this is not a satisfactory answer, as he repeats his inquiry and I respond, trying to find the right answer. "Japanese and Japanese? Japanese and American? Japanese and what?" Finally he seems to figure it out. I explain to him that both of my parents are of Japanese heritage. This seems plain and simple to me, but it seems to leave him in some state of shock. It turns out that his mom is from Japan, and his dad is from Thailand but is of Chinese descent. Apparently, he had never met any peers who were quite like me. Later on, not surprisingly, he was astonished to find out that I did not speak Japanese. I was amazed that he connected so much of his identity to speaking his native tongue.

Soon I figured out that I was really the exception at my school. My American history teacher, an African American man, and another student, who was born in Vietnam, were surprised to find out that I was a fourth-generation American and that my great-grandparents had immigrated to the United States in the early 1900s. In Asia Club, I found myself somewhat disoriented, as I was one of two Japanese American students, and discussions focused on Asian culture and not on Asian American issues. I was immersed in a group of students who loved Asian pop culture and truly identified as Asian. Yet, being a *yonsei,* or fourth-generation Japanese American, I do not identify as much with Japan as I do with America, and honestly, despite the friendliness of the members and their desire to include me, I just didn't fit in. Yet at the same time, I enjoyed being around other Asian American students and soon found myself eating Chinese food, buying *boba* tea drinks, and writing on Korean stationery.

Participating in Asia Club activities helped me learn about my own heritage through others' views of the world. I learned that first- and second-generation Asian American youth often identify with their parents' country, and that I do not identify with being Japanese but with being Japanese American. Being around first- and second-generation Asian American youth gave me a sense of what my great-grandparents' and grandparents' worldview must have been like. In a discussion in American history class, my Vietnamese classmate stayed away from argumentative discussion and preferred just to go with the flow and to not cause conflict. Even when another student made a racist joke, he just brushed it off. At first, I couldn't understand how he could not react, because in the same situation, my first reaction would have been to fight. But then I realized that what he had done was similar to what my great-grandparents' generation did at the time of internment. Rather than fight their government, they just packed their bags and went along peacefully.

Having grown up in a tightly knit community, I identify strongly with being Japanese American. Throughout my childhood, I participated in activities with other *yonsei* youth. I played basketball in the local community league, attended a Japanese Christian church, and went to Japanese American cultural enrichment summer school. After seven years of "Japanese school," I still cannot put together a sentence in Japanese. Instead, I have learned about immigration, about backbreaking work in the fields of California, and about internment. It was these stories that touched my heart more than any project in flower arrangement or calligraphy. Perhaps this is because I am *yonsei,* because I am so displaced from my Japanese ancestors, because I hardly know their names. Instead, I seek the stories of my grandparents' generation, those of internment in the deserts of Utah, of fighting World War II in the forests of France, and of liberating prisoners at Dachau.

I have realized that "Asian American" can mean many things to many people and that each person is molded by his or her own experiences. This is why there is such a gap between first- and second-generation Asian Americans and fourth- and fifth-generation ones. Our experiences vary so much that it is often hard to relate to each other. But it is this diversity which makes our community so interesting, because there is so much to learn. In the future, Asian Americans as a group will only become more and more diverse and there will be more need for coalition building. It is important to recognize our differences and share our experiences so we can better understand each other and form a cohesive Asian American community.

Jessica Kawamura is from Berkeley, California, and attends Head Royce High School.

19 Brown in
Faded Blue Genes

Janet Miñano

My search for an Asian identity in America has been a long process. I have searched through books. I've read prehistory chapters on the inhabitants of the islands before they were known as the Philippines. I've bought tapes on how to speak Tagalog, the national language. I know how to carry a basic conversation. I have watched movies in Tagalog in order to observe the customs, formal wear, and people so that I could identify with people of my likeness. I search because I feel a need to fill a void. The need to find out more about who I am began in college.

I enrolled in a speech class and was given a sheet of paper with a special assignment: to explain who and what you are, and how your background has affected you. My professor went on to say that he saw all kinds of people in class and that we were all different. He would be looking for an interesting speech from each of us for our first grade that semester. "You!" he said, pointing at me. "What is your background?" I told him I was Filipino. "Well, then, that will be a fascinating speech," he said. "I don't know too much about the Filipino Americans. What a great lesson we shall have!" I stared at my paper. I didn't know too much either. Suddenly, I felt as tall as the twelve-point font. I did not really know what it meant to be Filipino.

When I was born I lived in the heart of a multicultural Chicago neighborhood. The adults and kids were all kinds of colors and ethnic backgrounds. The neighbors on the left of our house were black, and the neighbors to our right side were Filipino. I had three best friends: One was an Indian, another Puerto Rican, and another Chinese. It seemed as if you could find any culture from any continent on or around my block. Color did not matter until I moved forty-five minutes away from the city to an all-white neighborhood called Schaumburg.

I leaned against my grade school's brick wall during recess. I didn't like some of my peers because of the comments they made toward me on the bus. A boy in my class called me an Indian. "But that can't be right because she doesn't smell like curry." Another kid said that I had chinky eyes. I resented my classmates and my Asian features. I never looked at myself as being different from other children because of my upbringing and surroundings. The people who lived around my family accepted and respected all kinds of people. Fortunately, I moved again in high school.

At Jacobs High, I was known as the Hawaiian Beauty and Caramel Princess. My peers were mostly Caucasians with very few minorities: one international kid and me. I became popular because I was different. My long black hair and tan skin caught attention. I would tell my friends that I'm not Hawaiian. I am a Filipino. "Same difference, Orientals are Oriental," someone would say. I just shrugged it off. There was no use in pulling out a history text and geography map to explain the distinct differences between Koreans, Chinese, Malaysians, Filipinos, and so on. If it was not taught in American history class, it was of no significance. "Who the hell cares?" was the overall attitude. Most Asians seem to deal with that. I just ignored the comments. After all, Asian is Asian. That was my thinking at the time. I had a temporary feeling of being part of the crowd, or a crowd. Finally, acceptance, I thought . . .

Then, we moved to Georgia.

I dated a Southern Caucasian. He seemed open-minded. His family wasn't, particularly his mom. He told me that his mother hated people of other races, such as blacks and Hispanics. It was "okay" though, because I didn't fit into either category. I cocked my head at that comment. "They'll like you, the way I do," he said. I'm great with parents—I thought. But his earlier statements made me feel anxious before I met them. When I finally arrived at his house, his mother looked me up and down twice. I began to feel insecure. She was glaring at me with pursed lips. I stood in the hallway and looked down at cherry-wood tiles. I felt as if I could count every single splinter in one tile. Then, she finally invited me to sit down in their living room. I tried to talk to her, but she would cut me off, talk to her husband, or ignore me.

A couple days later, I found out that his mother despised me because I was "black" and not white.

She told her son that he shouldn't consider dating or hanging out with a person like me because I was trying to escape my race, and to be with a white person is to move up the social status ladder. She also said that I was overly tanned for an Asian. "She also called you a nigger," he told me. Well, great.

Welcome to the Deep South, in the late 1990s, where progress could mean taking three steps backward. I pondered my skin color after that comment. I didn't think that color could and should matter that much. I grew up not favoring or judging one group or another because of their lightness or darkness. I am what I am. I could do nothing about my skin tone. But somehow her comment made me feel ashamed. And a host of other feelings flew inside my head.

I was shocked that someone would say something that derogatory nearing the year 2000. Afterward, I was angry that ignorance continues to live on while people make hateful, hurtful comments. I was also sad because I already felt self-conscious and unaccepted because of my Eastern features. Being brown is difficult, but one learns to tolerate and ignore ignorance. These statements only fueled my search for a place where I could reconcile my two different cultures. My parents tried to help my search by taking my siblings and me to the Philippines.

We could touch our roots. We went during the year of the Filipino Centennial, celebrating our freedom from Spain. When the plane landed in Manila, Filipinos were clapping their hands and standing beside their seats. Others looked as if they were crying because they were happy to finally be home. "Mabuhay ang Pilipinas!" some people cheered proudly. Yes, I agreed, long live the Philippines. During that single moment, I felt proud and looked forward to meeting my family.

My cousins weren't as tan or brown as I am. They were more yellow than me; it seemed like they had either Japanese or Chinese ancestry in their blood. When I met my cousins, they commented that I was *maganda*, beautiful. Then they said, "Maganda kahit siya medio itim." I could not speak the language well, but I could translate everything. She's beautiful even though she is dark. It all went back to flesh tones, in America and in the Philippines. It's inescapable. I began to think about where such a comment would derive from. When the Spanish colonized the Philippines, the paragon of beauty was based on their own kind of women, who had white skin and dark features. They took whole groups of Filipino people and made them into domestic servants, slaves, and slaughtered others in the name of imperialism and religion. In dividing the people, the Spanish held clout. Then another invader colonized the Philippines, but this time it was the American. I could get a massive headache just by thinking of everything. My cousins broke into my thoughts. They asked me if I could speak Tagalog. "Not well," I told them. They shook their heads from side to side and clucked in disbelief. Their reaction bothered me. It's not as if I did not want to learn the native language.

At home, my parents rarely spoke phrases in Tagalog to me. They spoke it to their friends and each other. I seldom saw them because they were busy working. They came to America to give my siblings and me opportunities that they never had growing up, a better life and better education. My parents were sold on attaining the American Dream. So the chance to learn was not an option. I later asked them why they never taught us Tagalog; they said that they didn't want Tagalog to be confused with the English language. I wanted a different viewpoint so I asked my uncle why he didn't have his children learn Tagalog, and he told me that it wasn't a useful language to know. Still, I made a fervent effort to learn about my culture.

Books and tapes in Tagalog were of no help. I know how to ask where the nearest post office is, but that won't get me anywhere. Knowing choice profanities will not win me any popular attention. My sources made me stop, think, and look around. They led me to think about the different types of Asians in America. I felt a slight pang of jealousy.

I was a tiny bit jealous of the Chinese and Japanese. I have noticed that these two particular groups, along with the Koreans, have language schools for their young. The parents speak to their youth in their native tongues, and their children comprehend and do not respond in English but in Chinese, Japanese, or Korean. I think it's wonderful that these people have maintained their cultures in America. As for myself, I have felt cultureless.

Filipinos seldom have language, history, or culture classes across the United States. But I should be used to feeling out of place. I had physical commonalities with people in the Philippines. Yet I still struggled with being Filipino American. To find a peace and place in America was not any better.

In America, I am said to be "whitewashed," like faded blue jeans. My friends have called me a "Twinkie." I am Asian, and most Asians are affiliated with the color yellow, yellow on the outside and white on the inside.

(It is really exciting to be reduced to a piece of clothing or food with discriminatory connotations by the peers of your own ethnicity!) I'm told that I sound funny when I speak. They say that I sound like a reporter on TV. "You sound white for a Filipino." Remind me again of how the sound of white goes?

I look at my countrymen and wonder how it is possible for them to judge me when they have embodied traits from other cultures and made those traits into their own. I read our history and I ask what it truly means to be Filipino. My Filipino peers take a different approach to answering the same question. They look to other oppressed races for answers on how to fit in. They do this because other minority cultures and their traits are readily available. This is apparent when I go to a Filipino function where I see boys dressed like P. Diddy or girls mimicking the New York accent of J.Lo. It's easy to want to grab immediate answers to identity questions, but it's not easy to carefully peruse textbooks and literature books on Filipino identity when it appears that many of them contradict one another. I get frustrated to the point where I want to pull my hair out!

A Filipino friend said to me, "Don't be drivin' youself crazy, aight?"

All right. For me the answers to fitting in are not that easily found or personally accepted, but I need someone to listen to my ordeal. I then turn to my other culture and speak to my American friends. "You're in America, not Asia, so what's the problem?" they have said. The problem is that when I look in the mirror I do not see brunette hair, white skin, and green eyes. I don't have Barbie-like features. Just because I was born an American does not mean that I have felt comfortable in my own skin and blended in with my white peers. I sigh. I can't blame them for not understanding because they have no frame of reference. Whites can easily blend in with one other. A person can be German, Polish, Scottish—or whatever ethnic European background—and they still mesh with each other. Asians don't intermingle the way that whites can. Asians stick to their own kind. Koreans hang around Koreans, Vietnamese gather among themselves, and so on. I see all these ethnic groups clique to only their kind when I look around. Americans, on the other hand, view their ethnicity as an ornament.

"I'm part German, part Irish," I overhear a person say. That can possibly mean three things: He can do something different at his funeral or eat pickled meats on occasion, or maybe he can just claim Irish roots because of the pale skin, red hair, and freckles. Overall, he is still white. But what your typical

American does not see, or experience, is that being a minority in the U.S. can affect who you are on many different personal levels. It can affect the way you're spoken to and treated. "Can you un-der-stand my En-glish?" Sure, I was only born in A-MER-I-CA. Being a colored minority can also affect your employment, your salary, or even the neighborhood you're trying to move into. It doesn't seem difficult to be part of the majority. They can blend easily enough. Where can I blend in? A Thai friend of mine said that I would like the West Coast and that I would feel like I was at home there. While visiting California, I discovered that a very Western internalization had taken place within me: I had gotten used to being the minority.

I went to San Diego and saw all kinds of Asians. I felt weird that there was so much brown and yellow. I asked my cousin Sharon, who lives there, where all the whites and blacks were when we visited Plaza Bonita. She laughed. "Are you serious?" I was. I also found something wrong with my question: Instead of embracing the fact that I was surrounded by people that I could relate to, I felt uncomfortable. I looked the same as everyone else. I had no distinct features among a crowd of Asians. All Asians are the same. My mind had innately adopted that Western concept. I felt that nothing made me different in a crowd of other Filipinos. I had gotten way too used to the South.

I had gotten used to living in the margins. Nearly all my life had been lived in all-white suburban neighborhoods, and most of my school classes had consisted of only white peers. I've realized that my identity construction was based around my homogenous environments, and now I have a better understanding of myself. However, my journey to bridge my identities continues on in "my" very broken, divorced America.

Janet Miñano is from Chicago, Illinois, and graduated from Georgia State University with a degree in English literature. She currently is a teacher.

20 Out and About: Coming of Age in a Straight White World

Michael Kim

Author's note: I have changed the names of places and people—including my own—in this narrative, in a sense to protect the innocent, or those critical people in my life to whom the sensitive details contained within it are not yet known. I struggled somewhat endlessly with this decision, as it alternatively seemed to me a renunciation of that which I had worked so hard to achieve. I now understand and embrace the reasons I still feel that anonymity is necessary at this stage in my life, but I have also come to understand the elegant way in which changing names universalizes identities and not only helps me objectify my own experience more productively, but, I hope, helps to better depict the resonances that my story can have with that of Everyman.

If I found a genie in a bottle, after my Upper East Side Manhattan townhouse and BMW 760, I would wish upon everyone in the world a coming-out experience. Forget sexuality, I am talking about the kind of critical existential moment that provokes unsettling questions about faith, religion, truth, society, and norms. I am talking about the kind of terrifying moment in which one perceives the limits of provincial sensibilities and questions the intellectual and moral constructions of one's upbringing. This moment might come in meditation on the logic of Christian belief and on the reasons for being a Christian apart from parental admonition. It might arrive in the exploration of the personal and social complexities of being a second-generation Asian American. Often, it comes in dealing with being gay. In this essay, I will ask—you and myself—what it means to come out at the intersection of all three, to consider the complex but underexplored world of a gay Korean American Christian man.

I spent every Sunday morning from the time I can remember until the time I graduated high school at Grace Baptist Church, a 3,000-member Southern Baptist congregation that practiced compassionate conservatism well before George W. Bush gave it a label. The congregation enjoyed Sunday-morning fellowships, Bible study, a 150-member choir, a thirty-piece orchestra, and a transcendently charming preacher. My family thrived within this warm and inviting community, without any feelings of exclusion despite the fact that we were one of three Asian families in the entire congregation.

As a child, I demonstrated a special aptitude for playing piano and as a result came to be celebrated and embraced widely within the church community. I became the church pianist and organist and made myself blissfully indispensable to the music ministry of the church. I played so happily for choir rehearsals and with the orchestra that this welcoming bunch of white Christian adults took me in collectively as their adopted son. It was of no consequence to them that I was Korean American; perhaps more important, it was of no consequence to *me* that I was Korean American.

In addition to my musical success within the church, I managed somehow to be a theological success as well. Given my particular propensity for memorization, I was a star student in knowing Bible verses by heart, committing to memory all the Bible stories and even their accompanying moral lessons. These were lessons designed for small children like me who were not yet involved in abstract and complex thought. God is good, Satan is bad; marriage is good, divorce is bad; pro-life is good, pro-choice is bad; straight is good, gay is bad. I swallowed these doctrines whole and washed them down with a swath of Bible verses to back up all the dogma, because, as Jerry Falwell has amply demonstrated, you can find a Bible verse to prove just about anything.

The danger here, in the church of my childhood, was not that these doctrines were oppressive but, on the contrary, that they were comfortable. If one does happen to be heterosexual, married with children, and lacking a personal relationship with anyone who has aborted a fetus or who is gay or who has been in an unhappy marriage resulting in a divorce, the sparse environs of dogma are a very comfortable place to be. Before I was perceptive of even the most rudimentary inklings of my sexuality, Christian fundamentalism was an easy place to live intellectually and to make friends and to be loved.

The societal calling of my life had been laid out for me from the start—I was meant to marry a woman and have children, an ideal set out not only in cultural terms but also in moral and ethical terms. This was the prevailing model of successful Christian living; the sociocultural iconography was eminently white and heterosexual. It was a fantasy to which I legitimately had access—not only could I be a straight man, with all the behavioral baggage that entailed, but it was what I was meant to be. Outside of my own family, I constantly fed on images from white suburban America: fathers who looked like Tommy Hilfiger models, mothers who looked like Ann Taylor models, children who looked like Gerber babies. I wonder if straight white men realize the extent to which they are idolized and societally normalized; so much in my culture made me yearn to be a straight white man. Even when I did experience ethnic diversity in my social circles—at school, or indeed within my own family—the model was still fundamentally nuclear, familial, and heterosexual. This, then, became normative, both culturally and ethically speaking, and success was framed similarly. The norm—white and straight—became a model of success that I would never achieve no matter how diligently I tried.

This is a profundity of white America that continues to confound me. It would be enough, one would think, for the institution of whiteness that springs from colonial settlement to explain the thoughtless ways white Americans often inhabit a sense of entitlement and egocentric normality. But when that entitlement becomes married to an acute perception of moral authority and clarity borne of a patriarchal and Anglocentric notion of rectitude and religion, the outcome, I venture, is acidic and threatening to nuanced or complex thought. A white man, I would suggest, has to think less about the implications of his racial heritage for his social station. Similarly, a straight man is rarely forced to confront his sexuality in such acute ways as a gay man must. Diversion (or, as it is phrased in the convention, deviance) from the norm is not simply unacceptable but often an unreal scenario, as within the Southern Baptist Convention particularly, the vast majority of families do exist within traditional categories of American familial structures. The tendency toward homogeneity of thought and lifestyle makes the entrenchment of doctrine a natural outgrowth of the lack of complexity among congregation members.

The institutionalization of this doctrine, and the ways in which it was ingrained in my moral consciousness, made the coming-out process even harder than it might ordinarily have been. Every thought I had about being gay was construed in my mind as a moment of deviance. In high school, I was more drawn to washboard abdominals than to voluptuous breasts; my sexual fantasies were about men, not about women; and whereas I experienced physiological reactions to attractive men, I could only aesthetically appreciate even the hottest female. But because I had been so carefully conditioned to think that homosexual thoughts and desires were never acceptable, simply deviant, I had to bring myself to the point of repentance every time I went down that road in my mind or in my actions, rather than considering the legitimacy of these thoughts. More inwardly, I would feel that I had failed twice—once by not being white, and again by not being straight. Despite all my other successes as a student, a pianist, a son, a friend, I carried the weight of these perceived flaws with me well into my early college years.

It was not until I reached college that I began to think outside my narrow Midwestern suburban provinciality and to explore my other internal spheres. I began to write, under the auspices of *Yisei Magazine,* about Korean American immigration, about American identity politics, even about Asian American male sexuality. In intellectualizing the Asian American experience, I affirmed the Asian American components of my own existence and thereby began to feel comfortable with myself, to take an active role in fostering my own self-esteem by growing to not merely live with myself but to embrace and accept myself.

In fact, as I would later realize, I had begun the business of becoming less narrow; this process was, in many ways, my first coming out. I started listening more, and accepting the idea that I might be wrong, or that absolute truth might be more elegant than my specific cultural lenses could perceive. As I studied ethics, I came face-to-face with gray areas, nuances, and ambiguities, and I became receptive to the idea that homosexuality is not an abhorrence. Dogma is easy to espouse in the abstract, but when the controversial issues are personified, dogma crumbles easily. Indeed, I was generally fine with my repressed "straight" self and the complex theology that I had to twist to support it. Then I met Patrick.

Patrick was, quite simply, my first love. He lived in my house, across the hall from me. We would eat together, go to concerts together, email constantly—

we even appeared in a documentary photo shoot together. And as we spent more time together, we noticed striking similarities in our personalities, our behavior, the way we talked about things, the way we looked at people. We had even been born on exactly the same day. I had found my soulmate, I thought, and I never thought I would be able or want to make such a sappy admission. There were many valuable levels on which Patrick and I connected in a platonic sense. We were very great friends, and Patrick was gay. This was how we framed it in the beginning—he was gay, I was straight, and how great it was that a gay guy and a straight guy could be such close friends. I even thought of it in terms of Patrick helping me accept homosexuality— that I as a straight guy was so cool with my sexuality that I could be really good friends with a gay man.

But underneath the guise, there was another level on which I was attracted to Patrick. He was tall, dark, and handsome, had beautiful eyes, a warm and endearing smile, and he always smelled great. The line between romance and platonic friendship became blurred for me (after all, what really is that line?), particularly when we began to sleep together. Though never in any overtly sexual way, we would cuddle—he caressed my hair when I slept, he held me, I would snuggle up against his chin.

All of this before I "came out." In addition, I had never dated anyone before—never kissed anyone, never held hands romantically with anyone, and obviously never slept with anyone in that way. During all of this, I never thought explicitly about the morality of what I was doing, nor did I chide myself for being a corrupt and base sinner. On the contrary, it was the first time that I had been able to express my bourgeoning sexuality in such a fulfilled and nurtured way. I was so in love with him that it took me a long time to realize the extent to which that was true.

It took months, in fact. It would become one event in the larger continuum of my coming-out process, but I was incapable of discussing it until I had arrived at a point of at least marginally accepting my homosexuality. That point is particularly difficult to arrive at with a traditional Asian family looming large and eighteen formative years of fundamentalist dogma weighing on the mind. Throughout the process of my coming out, Patrick would gently prompt me, asking me indirect and sometimes direct questions about my sexuality, and how much I had thought about it, and how sure I was of it. I would always gently deflect his questions, tossing them aside or coming up with stock answers to them.

There came a point, though, when I had to be honest with myself and recognize that I did not simply love Patrick but that I was in love with Patrick, and even more than that, that I was gay. I had nurtured a fantasy in which I would come out to Patrick and we would start dating and live happily ever after; it was only the impetus of this hope, in fact, that prompted me to "come out" to my closest friends before even telling Patrick. All were unflinchingly supportive and understanding of the confusion that I was feeling—a conflict between what I knew to be my true desires and inclinations and what I had been taught was right and good. It was in these formative conversations that my best friends became my family, not in a substitutive sense but in the sense that there seemed to be no way I could share something so deeply personal and controversial with my parents.

With a modicum of self-assurance thus in my back pocket, I found the nerve to approach Patrick and to tell him something that I thought would delight him, namely that I am gay. I thought I was reading all the signals correctly—we hung out all the time, called and emailed each other constantly, and furthermore, who spoons someone unless he's attracted to him? We had the conversation late one night after coming back from a Britney Spears concert (of all places), and after a series of evasions, Patrick made it quite clear that he was not attracted to me, that I had been misreading the signals, and that he was not interested in pursuing a further romantic relationship, though he hoped he and I would still be friends.

Thus began my tailspin into the bowels of unrequited love, a feeling that has no parallel in human experience, I feel. It surpasses, in my mind, vomiting, painful diarrhea, even acute hunger. Actually, it seems rather a combination of those three things, intensified to the nth degree. Above all, it was an intense hurt. I felt that in one fell swoop, my coming out had thwarted one of my best friendships, my first love, and my first potential boyfriend all at the same time. The fallout was crushing.

The painful vicissitudes of unrequited love have been well described by such popular artists as Céline Dion and Mariah Carey, forever known for their prophetic wisdom, so I'll not elaborate on how much it hurt. But for the purposes of this essay, it behooves me to remind myself of where I was at this point. I loved someone who did not love me back. I would never be friends again with Patrick. It took me a year to have any sort of objective perspective on the situation, and even to this day, though a recent conversation has brought closure, I still have residual hurt and anger. I had just come out, which meant I was on shaky ground with my own internal barometer of what was right and good. Because my best friends had become my family, I had become more sensitive to my inability to share an enormous part of who I am with my biological family; the distance between my family and me seemed as if it had just suddenly widened even more dramatically.

Indeed, the Patrick fallout forced me to deal with being gay not for the purposes of being in a relationship but simply to accept who I am. I had to confront, for the first time, the realities of being gay not as a deviance but as an orientation and life that I was only now beginning to comprehend. The most difficult part of this process, I think, entailed dealing with the familial strictures that made being gay so difficult and so undesirable.

Growing up in a Korean American household as the firstborn—and in my case the only-born—son requires a good measure of emotional fortitude. It is a surpassingly nurturing and loving environment, but even those words fail to describe the extent to which Korean American first-generation parents invest themselves in the lives of their *yisei* children.[1] I was my parents' life; they never went out on weekends, they never hired babysitters for me so that they could go socialize. Their entire existence was devoted to making my life beautiful. This is not some selfish proclamation; it is an overwhelmed statement of fact, and the debt of gratitude I owe them is insurmountable. Everything I have wanted has been mine, whether an opportunity or a shirt or a particular food—they live to make my life better.

My life is theirs—and insofar as this is a wonder, it can also be an oppression. Their gifts—least of all material, but more personal, emotional, and spiritual—cannot possibly be reciprocated, and yet I cannot but try to reciprocate by living to their standards. I owe it to them, in a sense, to get good grades in school, to go to a good college and medical school, to get married and have kids. This is what they want for me; this is their dream and, sometimes, mine too. But as I confront the upcoming life passages that await me, particularly marriage, I cannot help but feel uneasy and in fact terrified.

When I was a child, I would construct a fantasy of my ideal wedding. I had all the music picked (since I had played at hundreds of weddings); I had the church, the pastor, the groomsmen, the tuxes; and I even had the bridesmaids' dresses and bride's gown picked out, as well as the flowers (this should have been clue number one to me that I wasn't batting for the hetero team). My parents would reinforce these imaginations, affirming the importance of finding a good wife and having good Korean children (it continues to be particularly important that my wife be Korean for the sake of the children and for better mutual cultural understanding).

Now, as my high school friends start to marry off, I face a daunting reality. Unless laws change in the United States, I will never have a wedding. My parents will never get to see me kiss the bride on my wedding day. I will never pick out an engagement ring at Tiffany's (not that I could necessarily have managed that anyway). And my parents will never get to come to the hospital to see my wife deliver our first, second, or even third child. That will never happen for me.

Objectively, I can deal with this because it is an outgrowth of the new life I have come to embrace. But it seems to mean trading the happiness of my parents for my own personal happiness, and that is a trade-off that no one should ever have to make. I witness it in so many families of friends—my Jewish girlfriend who wants to date a Christian guy, a white buddy who is in love with a black girl. Familial constructions of domestic happiness are unexpectedly pressing and weighty, and the desire to stray from them results in a torturous balancing game.

This dilemma acquires particularly painful valences when the success of one's family is so tied to one's general success, as I perceive it is in the Korean American (and Asian American) community. It is a single-elimination game—I could go to Harvard, Harvard Medical, do a surgical residency at Massachusetts General Hospital, and if in the end, I am still gay, I end up with a big fat zero. The resulting dialogue within the Korean community will go something like, "Well, my son didn't go to Harvard, but at least he's not gay." The fact that gay men cannot have children in the same way that heterosexual couples can further compounds this effect, for success is also measured in these communities by the success of one's grandchildren. It is a highly artificial and constructed view of success, based on brand names and appearances, and it is tormentingly oppressive. I cannot make choices based on what I understand to be true and right; I must factor in the happiness and standards of family and the entire Korean community.

These structures are reinforced by the ties of the Korean community to the Korean church. As a religious institution, it is naturally a locus of community-building and socialization, but as a human institution and moreover a center for expression of ethnic solidarity and community, it often becomes highly politicized in community terms and frequently devolves into hierarchical posturing and gossiping. My parents are respected for their success because of my achievements.

When cultural success is thus attached to religious and moral accomplishment, the stakes in my case become even higher. My mother tells me that she prays for a good wife for me every morning and every night. This is perhaps the best illustration I can offer of the powerful nexus of social forces that make being gay in a Korean American Christian community so impossible. For me to come out to my parents and to the Korean community would be, quite literally, the ultimate failure—moral, social, and personal all at once. It would nullify everything good that I have done and would stand as the single mark upon me. It would be the ultimate shame upon my parents, and shame is the worst offense in my family. They have spent so long being proud of me that I don't think they would know how to cope with the shame of it all. Consequently, every time I go back home to visit with my immediate and extended family, I go back into the closet, a process that feels like anathema to all that I have come out of in the past few years.

There are simply no models for understanding homosexuality within my Korean community. My parents and aunt and uncle are painfully elementary in their ability to discuss or even understand homosexuality. We once watched an episode of *Will and Grace*, and it never occurred to any of them that any of the characters are gay. It is simply not something they think about, much less accept. There is no explaining why the constructions of success are so artificial and inflexible. That is the way things are in the Korean community, and I have no choice but to accept it. But of course, I cannot. It is not who I am, in all senses of that phrase.

I do not consider myself singularly or even especially burdened. Every person has his load to bear, every person has her bridges to cross. It can be painfully trying to be something you know you are when your background, your family, and much that surrounds you (and much that is within your head) tell you that it is wrong or deviant. There was, and still remains, an existential nag about how maybe it is still not right to be gay—perhaps I truly am an unrepentant deviant. Escaping that anxiety is something I still struggle with, particularly because it's compounded by staunch familial and religious expectations.

Through the trenches of these existential ponderings, I can only cling to the divine joy of knowing myself, and to the new comfort of being able to ask difficult questions and grapple with answers that are more than one word long. This is a satisfaction that springs from realizing that coming to terms with my homosexuality is a process not so much of coming out to the world but of more fully coming into myself. It is like finally fitting into that blazer that Mom and Dad bought for me three years ago; it was always too big, and only now do I possess the equipment to fill out the form much more completely.

"Coming out" has been a much broader development, personally and spiritually; it has meant, quite simply, understanding who I am. It has taken me twenty-one years to arrive at a point where I have just begun to be able to say with genuine honesty that I know who I am, that everything I took in but didn't process makes sense now.

It is an unfinished process that will likely outlive me. But it is a process I wish on absolutely everyone—searching within to understand who you are, why you believe, and what it is that is truth for you. Coming out is not fundamentally about being gay but about more fully and truly living, about maximizing potential. I cannot imagine a more rewarding and socially productive endeavor.

Note

1. *Yisei* means "second generation."

Michael Kim is from Dayton, Ohio, and graduated from Harvard University with a degree in history and science. He is currently studying at Oxford University.

21 Understanding Life, Ma, and Me

Joyee Goswami

"Your priorities have changed. You're exceeding the limits and values of this house and family."

"What is that supposed to mean, Ma?"

"You know exactly what it means. You cannot keep pretending that something is not going on between you and that boy. We did not grow up like this; we did everything our parents told us, and we did not question them. How could you have changed so much in such a short amount of time?"

"Ma, why do you always think my being different means being wrong? Why is change necessarily a bad thing?"

The first memory I have is of slapping my mother in front of dozens of shocked adults at a party . . . Granted I was only three at the time, yet still I have never forgotten (or perhaps more appropriately, my mother has never *let* me forget) the pinnacle incident that marked my rebellious entry into society. There are many memories from my childhood that are my memories only because they are my mother's.

My mother was married to my father at the ripe age of twenty-four. Finishing her master's in political science in India, she had planned on continuing her studies to become a professor or a lawyer. But then she met my father. Or rather, her father met my father . . . My parents were married to each other in 1975, without ever having seen each other until their wedding day. On a hot summer day in Calcutta, my parents' eyes met for the first time, in front of hundreds of excitedly noisy people. "What did you think of him when you first saw him?" I ask her excitedly every once in a while. She just blushes and says, "We don't talk about things like that, dear."

A few months after meeting my father during her wedding, my mother suddenly found herself moving to America, where my father had just been offered a job. My mother moved to a foreign country with a man she had just met, far away from her parents and siblings. I consider the adjustments she had to make as a young Bengali bride in New York: wearing pants for the first time in her life, learning to cook edible dishes, teaching herself how to drive . . . accepting the snow, a one-room apartment, and a new lifestyle as a path in her journey toward fulfilling the American Dream . . . Perhaps it was her youth that allowed her to accept her new life with open arms, without complaint or disappointment. Or perhaps it was her hope to let her children live the American Dream—full of opportunities galore—that gave her strength and guidance.

Beginning with the birth of my brother, my memories about life at home become much clearer. I remember the day I brought flowers to my mom in the hospital, dressed in terribly mismatched clothes that my father had somehow managed to assemble. I remember peering jealously at my mother as she sang a lullaby, *my* lullaby, to my brother to get him to sleep. And I remember the huge amount of love that was always present in my house.

My parents were undoubtedly the best parents a child could ever dream of having. Their priority was always their children, above anyone else, especially themselves. I remember after a long week of school being chauffeured around to singing lessons, softball games, dance practices, math tournaments, piano lessons, science competitions, volleyball tournaments, and more. My extracurricular activities became my mom's extracurricular activities; my being a "well-rounded child" meant my mother became well-rounded as well.

The arguments between my mother and me began when I entered high school. Finally free from the plaid-skirt school uniform, which my mother had always caringly made sure was down to my ankles, I decided to experiment with different styles of clothes.

"I know you're not wearing THAT.*"*

"But Ma, the skirt goes below my knees."

"It's too short and your shirt is too tight. Go change."

It was tough to reason with her. Shorts were out of the question. Even for gym class. I remember wearing sweatpants in the middle of April while playing basketball with my classmates. Is it any wonder so many kids made fun of me in school?

Then came the dilemma with high school dances.

"What would you do at a dance, anyway?"

"Dance, Ma."

"With everyone else watching? And with whom? You know we won't allow you to go with any boys."

"I know, Ma."

I remember going with a group of friends to my first dance during my sophomore year in high school and thinking it was strange and uncomfortable. I also remember coming home and telling my mother what a wonderful time I had had, simply to keep her from getting the satisfaction of knowing she had been right about me all along.

My outlook on life changed most notably during the four years that I spent away from home during college. I recall my first few lonely weeks in the dorm: not understanding the obsession with partying all night, being homesick and wanting to see my parents, coming to terms with reality. As the months went by, many of the things I had grown up accepting started to make less sense to me. Why is drinking alcohol so unacceptable? Is it really that difficult to balance having a relationship with a boy with still being in school? Am I disrespecting my family by having these thoughts? *Who am I?*

The arguments about clothes and dances were now replaced with much more serious questions regarding my religion, values, lifestyle, culture. Ideas that had taken twenty-one years for me to understand I now wondered about each day. And I hated myself for it . . . I hated the fact that I was questioning my values, the values my mother had painstakingly instilled in me. The ideas she had given up her career for, the morals that meant she had never left me at home with a babysitter, the goals she had imagined me achieving to validate her sacrifices and love for me. *But how could I fully accept anything without questioning it and then deciding on the best path for me? Was it wrong to be different, to change?*

Relationships and dating were the biggest topics about which my mother and I disagreed. She continued to envision me having an arranged marriage to a bright Bengali boy, while I tried to reason with her about the impracticality of such a situation.

"What is so wrong with arranged marriages? Your father and I got married that way and look how happy we are."

"Ma, everybody cannot have a fairy-tale marriage like yours. I think what both of you have is special and unique, but realistically I just don't think it will work for me."

"What is wrong with finding a boy from a good family with similar values?"

"Nothing is wrong with it, but the same can be said about dating. I think it's a just as good, if not better, way to eventually find the right person for you."

My mother and I gradually talked less about our varied opinions on relationships, love, and marriage. This change was mainly due to our mutual acceptance of each other's differences. I finally accepted the fact that I could not change my mother's entire worldview and should not try; her opinions and ideas were just as valid as mine. Likewise, my mother began to accept me for who I am. We soon began to discuss issues that were neutral or those upon which we agreed. Surprisingly, there were quite a few things we had in common.

I realized my interests in Indian music, the Hindu religion, and the Bengali language all stemmed from my mother's efforts to pass on our heritage to me. More profoundly, my passion for knowledge, my dedication to family and friends, and my ability to love people completely with my heart had come from her as well. We were both idealists, sensitive, and stubborn. We both remained silently strong.

Thinking back to the days when I attempted to define myself, I wonder why I struggled so much to create an identity distinctly separate from my mother, and why she fought so hard to remind me of the futility of my efforts. Perhaps it was because in me she saw the person she wanted to be. And possibly I saw in her the person I once was.

These days, I think of getting through medical school and wonder what the future holds for me. *How will I balance a career and a family? How will I know when I meet the person with whom I am destined to spend the rest of my life?*

I do not worry right now about such thoughts, however. There is time. And there is Ma . . .

Joyee Goswami is from New Orleans, Louisiana, and graduated from Rice University with degrees in biology and Asian studies. She is currently studying at the Louisiana State University Medical School.

22 Another American Mutt

Cavan Reagan

It's odd and sweetly ironic to think that the one time in my education when learning about colors seemed such a large part of the curriculum was the small chunk of my life when I did not think to consider my own color. We learned the spectrum in grade school: red, blue, yellow, green, black, white. We learned to mix two shades to get another. We learned that mixing too many would create a brownish mess. We were taught to identity the color of everything we saw, except, of course, one another.

The board could be black. My shoes could be black. But no one, to my recollection, ever looked at Chuck or Shaunee and said, "Mrs. Clausen! They're black too!" People were not colors.

But that was grade school, and my ignorance did not last long, though I think I enjoyed the bliss of it longer than most biracial children. I remember learning of my own ethnicity mainly through the taunts of other children.

When I lived in England, one of my best friends was transferred to another class, and I rarely saw her afterward. I sat across from her at lunch several weeks later and was trying to talk to her when a bigger girl next to her grabbed her arm and whispered, "Don't talk to him. He's a Chinese motherfucker."

My friend laughed and left with the other girl. Her explanation for it later was, "It was funny." Cursing was funny to us at that age, but I think the humor in the comment was the addition of "Chinese." We had learned to identify normal motherfuckers. I must have been the first Chinese motherfucker the school had seen.

Years later, after moving back to the States, my older brother was playing basketball in the driveway with some other neighborhood kids. I had never taken to sports, and sat in the lawn playing by myself. After a little rough play, one of the kids from the losing team broke away from the group, pointed at my brother and then me, and proclaimed us Japanese motherfuckers.

Odd. I was clearly still thought a motherfucker, but I am neither Chinese nor Japanese.

My mother is Taiwanese. My father is white, from a family hailing from Ireland. Any child must look upon his or her own family as the most normal of situations until they learn otherwise, and this was the case for me. My vocabulary did not include the terms "biracial," "mixed," or "interracial marriage" until recent years, and even now I do not use them to refer to myself or my family. My classmates, apparently, knew before I did that we were not the typical white American family.

As I said, my mother is Taiwanese. She is from Taiwan originally. She is not from Thailand and she is not Thai. She is from an island in the Pacific Ocean, and yes, that does mean I check the "Asian/Pacific Islander" box on forms, if I check a box at all.

Living among two cultures is difficult. The remarks about biracial children not being white enough for the white kids and not being Asian enough for the Asian kids are clichéd but true. If I walk into a group of people and tell them I am Asian, I am told either that nobody could "tell" I was Asian or that I am not "really an Asian, just part." If I say nothing about my ethnicity, it's ultimately questioned, and people are quick to remark they knew I was not white, because of my "slanted eyes," but they couldn't tell what I was.

I am not a what. I am a person. I am a left-handed, vegetarian, biracial college student studying English and journalism who was raised in Los Angeles, England, and the Midwest and is now attending a public university literally in the middle of Iowa. I am unique. I have a weird name. I am a mutt.

But I am not a what.

I don't mind the questions about my background at all. To be offended by such questions would be overly sensitive and touchy, and would make people feel even more uncomfortable about a subject they are already too scared to broach. But I've learned to detect judgment and prejudice, even in their smallest forms.

Sometimes prejudice is easy to spot. One of my good friends told me he did not like going to a friend's house because she had a "weird Asian mom." "I just don't want to have to deal with that," he said. Deal with what? Others? Of course the woman strikes a young Midwestern kid as weird. She was raised in an entirely different culture on the other side of the world, and she, too, can tell when people look at her and immediately think her accent, clothes, hairstyle, mannerisms, or culture mean she is a spectacle at the zoo.

I have been under the microscope, placed on a slide as a prime example of a "half-breed," for years. I like fried rice and spring rolls. I like martial arts movies, too. Yes, I own *Crouching Tiger, Hidden Dragon*. But many non-Asian people can say the same thing.

I do not know karate or Mr. Miyagi. I don't have "one of those big hats like Rayden from Mortal Kombat," and I cannot do complicated calculus equations without the aid of a calculator. And nowhere in my dorm room can you find a gong or kimono or any other icon Americans have come to identify with Asian culture.

People assume that because only one of my parents is Asian I will be okay with the remarks that led to the above comments. "You're not really Asian," a friend said. "Just half." Does that nullify half of me? Why not omit the white part of my heritage? Some see my being half-white as being "still half-normal." I do not. To refer to me as half of something is to ignore the other half of what I am. I do not look at my friends and say, "Well, you're only half-fat. Let's make fun of really fat people," or, "I'm confused about this part of who you are. Let's pretend it does not exist, except perhaps when you are drunk and more jovial."

It's humiliating to have someone I'm dating tell me how intrigued their friends and family are about their "new Asian boyfriend." After meeting the parents, there are comments about me not being nearly as Asian as expected (a sigh of relief from the grandmother, a sigh of disappointment from the younger brother, who expected Jackie Chan). I am, instead, demoted to only part Asian, and therefore only part interesting. I am the exhibit at the zoo only the stupid children will stop at.

"This colorful breed of human is the result of an experiment conducted on an air force base in California. He's not good at math, but he loves to read and enjoys odd foods that you do not." This is as far as anybody would read on my plaque before realizing a full-blown Asian was in the next cage over and running off. And there I would sit, half on a straw mat meditating, half on a La-Z-Boy recliner watching television. This is how I live to many people—there is no in-between, no medium between the two bizarre cultures. East met West and Cavan appeared. Then both parties rushed back to their own hemisphere and never spoke again, leaving the boy to straddle the globe in a constant state of confusion.

I'm not denying the confusion I went through trying to figure out who I am as an Asian American. I wish I knew more about my mother and her life before she met my father and moved to America. I wish I knew more about Taiwan and its people. But Mom made every effort to raise her two sons in America—despite the military dropping our family in random European locations. Mom's a Buddhist, Dad's an Irish Catholic. My brother Aaron and I were, as a result, raised without a household religion. We celebrated Christmas and grew up in the mainstream of American culture for the most part.

Confusing as it was to handle my ethnicity as a teenager, I wonder who I would be now if my parents had raised us in a household with strong Taiwanese and American influences. I say that with a grain of salt, of course, because my parents' very presence provided strong influences—they just did not create an environment in which I thought of myself as different from any other kid. That job was taken over, as I mentioned, by kids on the playground.

One of the first things I did when getting to college was join the Asian/Pacific American Awareness Coalition. Ashamed as I am to admit it, I spent my first meeting feeling horribly out of place. I had been in groups of Asians before, but never in such a social context. I am shy in the first place, and jumping into a group of people who were already friends made me incredibly self-conscious about being "Asian enough" for them to accept me. The people never did anything to make me feel uncomfortable about being of mixed ethnicities, though for several weeks my imagination played tricks on me: "Why does he come to the meetings? Is he even Asian? Isn't he white?"

All of my white friends eventually joked that they would come with me to meetings, too, if they weren't white. "You don't have to be white," I tried to explain, joking that they only had to be aware of Asian Americans to be a part of the group. None of them came with me to a meeting, and I see now my joke was slightly too accurate for many of them. They weren't aware of any Asian presence on campus, despite hundreds of Asian American and international students.

The coalition fought to change the ease with which most people overlooked Asian students, sometimes called the "silent minority" or even the "model minority."

"Don't take this the wrong way," my first roommate told me, "but I always notice a lot of Asian students studying in the library and doing well in class." Needless to say, I was not offended by a stereotype that grouped me among such scholars. But even these positive stereotypes have to be broken down in order to truly understand who we all are—and I don't just mean Asians. Stereotypes cross race, gender, sexuality, age, profession, geographic location, and much more. The coalition just wants to eliminate stereotypes of one sort, but the task is too daunting for the group to ever imagine accomplishing it.

Another stereotype that has plagued me as a student who excelled in high school and continues to do so in college is the stigma attached to minority-based scholarships. I do not pay to attend Iowa State. My tuition, books, and a large chunk of my room and board are covered through more than half a dozen scholarships awarded to me through either the university or outside agencies. One of these many scholarships can be described as a minority scholarship. And although it had academic requirements that I still must meet, I have been told to my face that the only reason I could get a full ride to this or any other university is because I am not white.

Make the argument, if you wish, that scholarships should not be given out solely on the basis of race. But do not belittle those who received awards for their academic achievements simply because they are not white, especially if you are not deserving of such an award yourself. If you're not, what harm did it do you anyway? You would not have received the money. And if you are, what are you doing complaining that you are "too white" for a scholarship? There are millions of dollars in financial assistance available; go look for a scholarship tailored for you.

Being told I am not really a minority and not deserving of any minority scholarship upsets me, generally because it makes it sound as if my achievements and my background are somehow linked. They are not. My Asian background has given me a solid sense of self, because I have taken the time to learn about who I am and to ignore comments about my being a half-breed or having weird-shaped eyes.

But I am a person, not a culture clash, zoo exhibit, or science experiment.

And I'm taking what I've learned about being both Asian and white and using it to help me reach my goals. I'm using what I've learned about both of my cultures and making sure I am somebody who can be a part of two worlds and still be one complete person.

Being biracial affected my childhood in a way of which I was not even aware. Growing older, I began to learn about being both white and Asian, and about being an Asian American. That learning process continues every day, not only as I try to learn more about my heritage but as I begin to recognize the influence my cultural background has on my decisions and views. Confusing as it may be, I would never wish for my mixed background to be otherwise.

I am comfortable with being unique. I am comfortable being a mix of yellow and white paints. I am comfortable with eyes that curve slightly upward and the color of my skin and even the expectation that I am the resident expert on all things Asian, though that's an accolade I cannot truly claim.

I wish it weren't stretching the truth to say that everybody else is as comfortable with my cultural identity as I now am. But that's an idyllic world still in the making. Till that day comes, I'm just fine chowing down on fried rice and apple pie.

Cavan Reagan is from Omaha, Nebraska, and studies journalism and mass communications at Iowa State University.

23 Shen ai shi ren

Wendy Hu

神爱世人

The pigtails on my seven-year-old head swung like mini-jumpropes as I scurried into the breakfast nook. In between gasps for air, I excitedly announced, "Ma Ma? Ba Ba? Wo jue ding le! Wo bu yao jiang guo yu le. Oops. I mean, Mom? Dad? I've decided! I'm not going to speak Chinese anymore. I'm going to speak English only. Well . . . starting now."

All four of the Chinese adults turned and stared at me in dumbfounded wonder, startled from their casual conversation as they sat around the dining table. My dad, mom, uncle, and aunt, whom I respectively called Ba, Ma, Yi-Diong, and Ah-Yi, had been sitting together, peacefully snacking on dried watermelon seeds, when I made my unexpected and unwelcome announcement. I do not remember what they said next, if they said anything at all. I was much too excited to care about their response. This was to be the greatest moment of my life, the decision to affect all decisions. I was about to correct all of my faults in a single move and make myself anew. I had assumed that my family would be equally ecstatic.

I explained to them in a high-pitched, euphoric voice that I had been inspired by Ru-Ru. Only eleven years of age herself, Ru-Ru had become my new role model because she could speak English relatively well. If she could be Chinese and speak English at the same time, then I could too. I did not stop to wonder about what would happen to my Chinese if I spoke only English. Chinese was not something of value to me. It was a skill that I had always possessed, but had never desired.

Shen ai shi ren (Chinese saying). Direct translation: *God so loved the people of the world*. Found in the Book of John, chapter 3, verse 16.

Although I was born in Santa Barbara, California, my parents, recent immigrants from Taiwan, raised me to speak Mandarin Chinese. People tell me that my Chinese-speaking capabilities were impressive. By age two, I was forming complete and articulate sentences, all in impeccable Chinese. My parents took me to a Chinese church and surrounded me with Mandarin-speaking relatives, so I never felt out of place primarily speaking Chinese until my first day of school.

Kellogg Elementary may have seemed like an ordinary, harmless elementary school. Set in the suburbs of Santa Barbara, it had everything an elementary school was supposed to have: a playground, blacktop, classrooms, a small cafeteria, and a nice grass lawn where students could sit and eat. To me, at age five, it was a terrifying place. I had entered a completely new world. Every child spoke perfect, unaccented English and dressed fashionably. I immediately felt out of place with my broken English and my well-patched pants. I felt so estranged that I would always eat lunch by myself or with Xiao-Shen, whose name in Chinese sounds like "Little Noise." Usually, I chose to eat quietly by myself. I eventually began to dread lunch and recess because those would be my loneliest periods during the day.

I remember when Ma Ma approached my first-grade teacher about my social problems. "Hi, Mrs. Strickly?" She spoke slowly and carefully. "I'm Wendy's mom. Is Wendy okay at school? I think she doesn't have many friends."

Oh no! I cringed internally at every word that fell from my mother's mouth. I felt like I was trapped under a waterfall. I could see my mother's words falling like rushing water, but I had no way of stopping them and no way to escape. I held my breath, hoping against all hope that Mrs. Strickly would not tell my mother the painful truth, that I really did not have any friends at all. I would never be able to bear the shame. Not only would I be a loser at school, but I would also be one in my mother's eyes.

"Well, Mrs. Hu, she doesn't seem to talk to many of the other children. She will only play with one other girl. They seem to exclude the other children because they only play with each other."

Who was she talking about? What girl?

"Oh," uttered Ma Ma as she paused to think. She stood there, thinking, while I grew increasingly embarrassed with each passing moment. She finally ended the silence with a simple question. "What can we do?"

"Well," Mrs. Strickly shrugged, tired of the conversation, "maybe

Wendy should try playing with other kids."

I would not have minded becoming like the Wicked Witch of the West and melting into the floor right then.

It's not that easy, I cried silently. *I'm scared of the other kids. I don't know what I can say to them to make them want to be my friends. What if they laugh in my face?* Watching the others play tag from afar was lonely, but at least it kept me safe.

Whenever school became too lonely to bear, I would seek out Xiao-Shen, or Little Noise. She would not reject me. Like me, she was an outcast. We had both been stuck in the English as a second language class, which had distanced us from the regular student body but brought us closer to each other. As I got to know her better, I realized how little I enjoyed our time together. Our ethnic backgrounds had thrown us together, but all I wanted to do was run away from her.

Little Noise reminded me of everything I did not like. She had a terrible fascination with worms, while I thought worms should stay underground— deep underground. Worst of all, she reminded me of myself. The other day, a boy had made fun of the yellow and green shirt I was wearing. It had the name of my parents' Taiwanese elementary school written in large, bold Chinese characters across it. I couldn't find any words to respond to my cruel classmate, so all I could manage to do was stand there while he laughed at my expense. Little Noise also wore hand-me-down shirts with Chinese lettering on them. Like me, she could not speak English as well as she could speak Chinese. Every time I saw her, I saw my own weaknesses reflected in her. She was a constant reminder that I could not escape my out-of-place clothing, or my Chinese accent. Little Noise forced me to see things that I could not bear to see.

"Wendy! Ni kan!" Little Noise giggled as she held up a long dangly earth creature close to her nose.

"What? Look at what?" When I turned to face her, I almost lost the contents of my stomach.

Is this how the other kids see me? This must be why they do not invite me to their birthday parties, why they laugh when I pick my nose in class. They must think I am so gross, so weird, that they could never be my friends. Hey! Didn't Mrs. Strickly say that the kids don't play with me because I play with one girl too much? Maybe she was talking about Little Noise. Maybe everyone thinks I'm just like Little Noise, a weirdo. Maybe if I made myself as different from Little Noise as possible, I could be normal. I can't change the way my mom dresses me, but I can change the way I speak. After all, Ru-Ru taught herself to speak good English. I can, too!

For the rest of the day, I skipped instead of walked, and dreamed of the possibilities before me. I had a chance to leave the muddy puddles that I played in with Little Noise, and to join in the blacktop games with all the other children. I simply needed to improve my English. Then they would not see me as different. I could be just like them. I would come to school speaking perfect English. The other children would hear me simply speak a word or two, and realize what a grave mistake they had made. *I'm not weird. I'm just like you,* I would say. Then I would leave the lonely corner of the blacktop; I would abandon Little Noise, and play tag with all of the other normal first-graders. This had to be a win-win situation.

The day I announced my decision to speak only English was also the day I began running away from the Chinese culture. Because being different was wrong, and Chinese was different from the norm, I saw anything Chinese as a hindrance. My English improved rapidly. By the time I moved to San Jose with my family in the third grade, I was all that I had hoped to become. I spoke English well and had been able to make five or six friends. I had even found myself a best friend. My master plan had worked; I would continue fitting in until I had enough friends.

Little did I know or care that there would be a price to pay for the abandonment of my native language. When I was about six years old, I had begged my parents to enroll me in Chinese school classes. Now these classes were meaningless to me. I rebelled in Chinese school. San Jose Chinese School continued promoting me even though I received Ds and Fs on all my exams. That is how I got through eight years of Chinese school and still did not know how to write a sentence without using Bo Po Mo Fo, the Chinese alphabet system.

I stopped feeling close to my dad and mom. I detached myself from my parents in order to run further away from my native culture. In addition to losing the language connection to my parents, grandparents, and many other relatives, I had begun to look down on the culture that my parents had grown up with. The more I found out about their culture, the more I pitied them.

Oh, how sad, I thought, *that my parents couldn't have been raised in America. Maybe then they would have more confidence; maybe then they would have better manners.* This arrogant dismissal of their culture became the foundation of the wall that grew steadily higher and higher between my parents and me. We could discuss the necessities of everyday life, but never the small, personal details of one's day that are supposed to be a joy and a treasure to share with loved ones.

After I entered college, I found freedom from my parents and all their many Chinese organizations, including the Chinese church in which they had raised me. I finally could choose my own religious organizations. At Berkeley, I sifted through the Christian groups, which are also known as "fellowships." I immediately shied away from the Chinese and other Asian fellowship groups. I chose to join Intervarsity Christian Fellowship (IV) because it was supposed to be ethnically diverse. I told my friends that I had grown up in Chinese churches and was sick of seeing so many Asians. Ironically, it was in that fellowship, the one that I had joined to avoid my Chinese culture, that I was forced to confront the fact that I was, and always will be, Chinese American.

Following a peculiar line of events, Intervarsity at UC Berkeley had become mainly Chinese. No other Intervarsity chapter in the U.S.A. had such a large percentage of Asians. Since I did not want to be in an Asian fellowship to begin with, I immediately identified this characteristic as a drawback. I decided that our fellowship needed more Caucasians, more African Americans, and more Latinos. In short, IV needed more of anything but Asians. Only then could we become more diverse.

When the IV staffworkers started speaking about how important it was to appreciate different ethnicities, I promptly agreed. They spoke about how God had created different races for a reason. They pointed to the book of Revelation, the last book of the Bible, for their evidence: "This book, which is believed to be a revelation of the future, describes many tongues in heaven praising God."

After reading the passage myself, I understood that even in heaven there would be different languages and different ethnic cultures. Then I thought, *Oh, how grievous our fellowship must be! There are too many Asians! And among the Asians, there are too many Chinese. We are too massive, too intimidating to the underrepresented ethnicities.*

Being at a campus that seemed overpopulated with Chinese, I had grown comfortable with apologizing for my race. *I'm sorry our number increased when they banned affirmative action. I'm sorry that my presence means Berkeley and my fellowship are that much less diverse.* After awhile of beating myself up for being Chinese, I began realizing that I had been on a journey of self-hate. No matter what situation I was in, I found a reason not to like Chinese people, which, in a way, meant not liking myself. When I was the only Chinese person in a group, I disliked my race for making me different. When I was among many Chinese people, I disliked my race for making me a part of an overdominant majority. This journey had begun on the day years ago when I made my simple declaration to my parents, and had developed into a winding, destructive road where I was in danger of losing who I was.

In order to regain a bit of what had been lost, I looked to God. I had spent so much time and energy into remaking myself that I had forgotten who I really was. I did not know where the exit to my misery lay, had no idea how to depart from this twisting road of self-hatred. I needed and asked for help.

On a whim, and perhaps out of a bit of laziness, I signed up for Chinese 5, Beginning Chinese for Native Speakers. UC Berkeley had created this class for students who used to be able to speak the language but did not realize the value of their skill until too late. It felt satisfying to speak Chinese again. I felt like I was opening my thirsty mouth and letting raindrops slide down my dry and parched tongue. Little did I know that this was the beginning of the journey of healing that God had prepared for me.

In the winter of my sophomore year, I went to a conference in Urbana, Illinois, appropriately titled "Urbana." At this conference, the organizers made a point of embracing cultures from many different nations. We sang songs in Tswana (a South African language), Spanish, Haitian Creole, and many other languages. I wouldn't have made the slightest noise of protest if we had gone through the entire conference without playing a single Chinese song. I could be perfectly happy singing songs from other cultures. *They don't need to make Chinese people feel affirmed,* I figured. *There are too many of us anyway.*

On the second night, the worship team's talented violinist made a surprising announcement. What was surprising was not what she said, but what language she said it in. "Da jia hao! Hi, everyone!" My ears perked up as I heard her communicate in impeccable Mandarin. I was surprised and a little pleased to know that they cared enough about my fellow Chinese to have the violinist lead a song in Chinese. My heart beat with excitement as I prepared to sing in Chinese. I could not wait to show off my rediscovered Chinese skills.

The Chinese violinist explained the pronunciations for the song, standard Urbana procedure for teaching a new song in a new language. The audience fumbled with the words, but I didn't mind at all. As the whole group of people, all nineteen thousand of them, began singing a worship song in my native tongue, I felt tears roll down my face. My heart softened. I saw that this beautiful song, this song that was pleasing to God, was symbolic of my people, who were also pleasing to God. I felt in my heart God saying that He loved my people just the way they were.

Really? Since when?

"Since always, Wendy." God reminded me that He loved the Chinese people enough to send the word of Jesus to them. Then my parents were able to meet Jesus and introduce me to Him.

Okay. So You loved us. How about now, though? Don't you wish there were less of us and more of other types of people?

"There are not too many Chinese people," I heard Him say. "You are not worth any less because you are Chinese. You are just as valuable as a person of any other ethnicity."

All night I listened to God affirm His love for me. "I love your people, just as you are; you don't have to change or become like any other culture for me to love you."

That night I cried, but I had never felt better about my ethnicity in my life. I cried out all the self-hatred I had, all the disdain for my culture that I had been holding inside. God loved my culture, He loved my family, and He loved me. Knowing this encouraged me to begin doing the same.

In one night, God had brought me over the hump, healed me by showing me how much He loved who I was. I did not have to become non-Chinese for Him to value me. He made no mistake in making me Chinese American, and *Ta ai wo,* He loves me. Now I could embark on my journey to find God in other cultures, learning to love all people, just as they are.

Wendy Hu is from Santa Barbara, California, and studies mass communications at the University of California, Berkeley.

24 Brown Skin

May Ling Halim

Freedom. The closing prayer had just released my classmates and me from the clenches of Sunday school, lessons of Daniel and the lions' den fleeing far from our minds as we stampeded to the foursquare court in the back church parking lot. Boys untucked their collared shirts, stuffed their clip-on ties in their pockets, and all threw their punch-stained Bibles to bake on the asphalt. The first task: picking teams.

"Let's play girls against boys!" shouted one of the boys.

"No!" my two girlfriends and I yelled back. Though we could hold our own individually, being just as big and just as strong, if not bigger and stronger, the herd of boys outnumbered us four to one.

"Chinese against Laotians! Chinese against Laotians!" bullied Jeremiah, a fourth-grader who was rumored to only eat meat.

I attended a Chinese Christian church, but church volunteers vanned in Laotian kids every Sunday for our children's program since their church didn't have one. It had been that way since our church started, never questioned, never wondered about. That was just the way things were. Although we grew up with the same Laotian kids year after year, suffering through memory-verse recitations, Bible-reading checkups, and hour-long sermons alongside each other, there was always a divide. They spoke accented English and got in trouble for speaking Laotian in class. The girls used hair spray and wore gold jewelry. Jeremiah shouted this divide, as salient as sex, without even a second thought.

Eager to get on with the game before parents, siblings, or church volunteers came to collect us, Chinese and Laotian kids scrambled to different sides of the court, lining up to get a turn.

"But I'm half-Chinese and half-Thai!" I distressed aloud.

"We'll take your Chinese half! They can have the other!" Jeremiah guffawed, delighted by his cleverness.

Growing up with a Chinese dad and a Thai mom in America made for some interesting identity searching. I didn't qualify as *hapa*, didn't quite pass for a Chinese American, or even a Thai American. You could call me Chinese Thai American, Thai Chinese American, or my favorite, à la Tiger Woods, Chai American, like that yummy Indian tea. I didn't know any other Chai Americans besides my two older sisters, but I wasn't about to ask them about "finding their ethnic identity." At the time, I didn't even know what I was looking for. There was, however, an abundance of Chinese Americans around me constantly—at church Sunday mornings and Friday nights, at orchestra rehearsals Wednesday nights, and at family gatherings about once every two months. It's not surprising that I started to itch about not being fully Chinese American at the beginning of high school. Who was I? How come I wasn't like everyone else? Why weren't there more people I could relate to besides my two sisters? The differences between my Chinese American friends and me, between my Chinese American cousins and me, started to really matter.

The biggest difference was how I looked. One time in fourth grade, I went to a local supermarket with my blond best friend from school and her mother. After picking up some Hawaiian sweet rolls, chocolate cereal puffs, cream-filled sugar-laden cupcakes, and other delicious treats that I never got to eat at home, we stood in the checkout line to pay for the groceries. As we waited, my friend's mom pointed to an Asian girl on the cover of a magazine and said good-naturedly, "Look, that looks just like May Ling." I looked toward where she was pointing, smiled shyly, then looked away. Granted she had long black hair and bangs that cut straight across her forehead, but the similarities stopped there. The girl on the cover of the magazine had pale skin and small eyes. She looked like my cousins, my orchestra friends, and my church friends. She didn't look like me. I had brown skin and bigger eyes.

And no, my brown skin was not just a tan like some Asians get after tennis season. I had brown skin all year long, a fact that I repeatedly had to convince my Chinese American friends of. Braiding my hair for me, one Taiwanese American friend suggested, at the sight of my pale scalp, "Maybe if you stayed out of the sun for a very, very long time, you would go back to the color of your scalp."

"Maybe." I thought about it for a while. "But I think I was born brown. Yeah, in all my baby pictures I already have brown skin."

"Really?"

"Yeah."

My dark forearms also had this magnetic force that attracted the forearms of my paler Chinese American friends. It was like a ritual that took place every few weeks. Go on vacation, get a tan, come back, attach forearm to May Ling's, and exclaim, "You're so dark!" or "You're so tan!" In return I would give them a small smile or reply, "Yep." They didn't know how much their skin-color comparisons affected me.

Skin color may seem like a superficial difference, but it mattered a lot to me because it made me different from my Chinese American peers and made me stand out in what I thought was a negative way. My bigger eyes and double eyelids didn't bother me so much because these physical attributes were sought after by East Asians as a mark of beauty. My brown skin, however, according to East Asian standards at least, made me ugly.

"I'm too dark!" my Taiwanese American friend would complain to me every Wednesday night in the backseat of my mom's Camry while we carpooled to orchestra rehearsal. "I don't like it." I would always keep silent. Dark is bad? Dark is ugly? I had darker skin than she had.

"He called me Tugly," my Vietnamese American friend told me one day, lips moving slightly up, eyes relaxing, referring to a lost love.

"Tugly?" I asked, eyebrows screwy.

"I never told you?"

I shook my head, watching her.

"Tan, ugly," she replied.

"Ugly?" Ugly? That was an endearment?

"No! I told him that I always thought I looked ugly when I was tan. After I told him that, he started calling me 'Tugly.'"

"But I'm tan."

"No! You look good tan. I look ugly."

I couldn't help but wonder about the truth of that.

"You're so tan now!" one girl said to the other, touching the other girl's forearm, smiling.

"I know," the other girl, in the shade of a tree, said, pressing her lips together, frowning. "I have to stay out of the sun."

"Why?"

"My mom got mad at me when I came home like this during spring break."

"She did?"

"Yeah. You know how Taiwanese moms always think dark skin is ugly and fair skin is beautiful."

"She stayed out of the sun for two whole months before her wedding!" my friend informed me, referring to her new sister-in-law as we looked at wallet-sized wedding pictures, fresh from Taiwan.

In high school I started to find myself with more and more Chinese American friends. My high school had a bigger population of Asians in general than my middle school did. Also, students started to separate into groups according to race. I drifted apart from my white friends from elementary and middle school soon after orientation week. For some reason, it suddenly seemed like I could relate so much better to my Chinese American friends. We could talk about similar conflicts with parents over clashes between Asian and American culture. We could commiserate over pressures to succeed academically. We could laugh at impressions of our parents' accents without offending anyone. It just felt more comfortable and easy. Forming most of my close friendships with Chinese Americans, along with learning about what clothes were okay to wear (only name-brand) and what music was okay to listen to (hip-hop, techno, or Korean pop), I also learned who was okay to date (only Chinese Americans, Korean Americans, or Japanese Americans). Any aberration from these preferences—for example, wearing clothes from a discount store, listening to alternative music, or dating white guys—quickly met with disdain and disapproval. So I started to wear only name-brand clothes, much to the dismay of my money-conscious mother. I started to listen to hip-hop music on the radio, forsaking my longtime favorite golden oldies station. And I started to have crushes only on Asian boys.

Freshman year of high school, I got to know a Chinese American boy at church who was three years older than me. He drove an immaculately clean SUV, always had a supply of fruit gum to share, wore a uniform of ironed khakis and polo shirts, and perpetually smelled of Calvin Klein's Eternity cologne. He befriended me and we talked easily. He always asked if anything was wrong and I always said nothing was wrong. He confided in me things that he claimed he told hardly anyone else. I felt special, and I fell for him. He went away to college to pursue his big business career, his phone calls stopped, and I was crushed. My explanation? Comments I heard about the ugliness of dark skin, skin-whitening-cream advertisements I saw in Asian magazines, pale beautiful heroines I watched in Chinese movies and TV dramas, white-skinned girls on the posters and desktop wallpaper I spotted that Asian guys put up, all came back to me. I wasn't pretty enough. My skin was too dark to be beautiful. I didn't fit into that mold of his ideal girl. I could imagine her in my mind. She had paler skin.

Junior year of high school, I met another Chinese American boy at a weekend orchestra camp. Handsome, over six feet tall, played the cello, destined for Harvard. Girls followed him around, but he didn't seem to notice. When I saw him I thought I had no chance. Then he sat across from me at an In-N-Out burger place. Our knees touched, his legs were so long, we flirted. On the last day, after our concert, he introduced me to his mom, had his mom take a picture of us together, asked for my email address. The courting began. Months later, after lies and heartbreak, it ended. Why? I must not be pretty enough. I must not be pale enough.

I started to hate the color of my skin, hate the Thai part of me. Maybe Chinese American boys would like me more if I didn't have that half-Thai part. Maybe their parents would like me more.

Attempting to control my fate, or at least how I looked, I started to try to make my skin paler. I bought SPF-45 sunblock at the drugstore and avoided going to the beach like I did going to the dentist, only my mom didn't make me go to the beach. One summer I flew to Maui with my high school volleyball team. While all my teammates slathered on tanning oil and sunbathed in their string bikinis on the many beaches we visited, I would sit alone underneath some trees away from the ocean, wearing a hat, sunglasses, a shirt, and pants.

Needless to say, slathering on sunblock and hiding from the sun proved futile. It didn't make me more Chinese American. It didn't make me more attractive to Chinese American boys. First of all, I couldn't really make myself look paler. Wasn't I the one who told others that I was born brown? I could make myself look a little more sickly, but not as pale as those girls in the skin-whitening-cream advertisements in Asian magazines, as those heroines in Chinese movies and TV dramas, or as those sex symbols on the posters and desktop wallpaper that Asian guys put up. Plus, once I went to Disneyland for a day or to some other fun outdoor frolic, the color would come back.

Second of all, even if I had achieved the palest of all skins it wouldn't have made me more Chinese. It wouldn't have made me fit in any more with my

Chinese American friends. My Chinese American friends had accepted me all along. Maybe my friends who liked to compare their forearms to mine were always so startled because they just thought of me as one of them. Maybe they thought I could return back to the color of my scalp because I should look the same as them, since they considered me the same as them. In fact, a Chinese American friend of mine had come up to me once at church and said, "I always forget that you're half-Thai." I just smiled in return, but what she said stuck with me. Maybe I had created this division between my Chinese American peers and me in my mind. Maybe I blamed my Thai half when I felt rejected to protect my ego.

One day at the beginning of summer vacation, a friend told me his friend's girlfriend was also half-Chinese and half-Thai, and I might meet her Wednesday night, since his friends were arranging an outing to see a movie. I had never met anybody half-Chinese and half-Thai before besides my sisters. Would she look like me? I envisioned getting a chance to talk to her and casually bringing up our shared mixed ethnicity. We would instantly bond, chatting and laughing about our shared experiences of being an ethnically mixed Asian. I hoped for a rare connection to a rare individual who shared my heritage. Friday night came and our friends arrived in clumps, driving separately. We stood outside a movie theater waiting and discussing what movie to see. "Look, that's her," my friend whispered, nudging my side with his elbow. My head whipped around to take a look. I probably stared longer than I should have. Alongside an old friend, she walked up to our group and smiled politely. Highlighted shoulder-length hair, a nice smile, fresh makeup, and brown skin. "She doesn't look like me," I thought, eyebrows raised, a slight frown on my face, although she did have brown skin.

We made eye contact, and I gave her a smile. "Hi," I ventured, "I'm May Ling." I wasn't sure whether or not I should put my hand out there to shake hers. I kept my hand at my side, deciding to see what she would do first.

"Hi," she responded with a smile, much cooler than I. "I'm Elena." No handshake.

We fidgeted, shifting our feet, looking to our friends for something to talk about.

I racked my brains for something to ask. "What movie do you guys want to see?" I asked her and her boyfriend.

Elena looked up at her boyfriend. Her boyfriend answered that he wanted to see the new inane teenage gross-out movie. I tried not to raise my eyebrows or scrunch up my nose. I always wondered who actually went to see those kinds of movies. I looked at Elena to see if she had any opinion, but she quickly looked away, like she didn't want me to know that she was looking at me.

"Is there anything else you guys want to see?" I tried to think of an excuse to watch another movie. "I think it's opening night for that movie, so it might be sold out or we might have to sit all the way in the front." In my peripheral vision I spied Elena looking at me again, not out of curiosity but rather out of something like checking-out-who's-prettier competitive girl cattiness. We were supposed to be talking and laughing right now about "Oh, Thai culture is so this, and oh, Chinese culture is so that," not seeing who was prettier. I looked at my watch. It was getting late. I had to get up early the next day for work. I didn't want to see the teenage gross-out movie. We ended up not seeing a movie together.

Eve Ensler, the author of *The Vagina Monologues,* spoke on my campus once. She ended her amazing talk with the charge, "Be the one you're waiting for." For her it meant getting rid of the notion that there was someone out there who could save her from the pain of childhood sexual abuse, that there was someone out there who would make the world safer for her. It meant taking up that responsibility herself, healing herself and others through her writing and activism. For me, meeting Elena made me realize I was waiting for a mythical person or group of people exactly like me, who shared my experiences and would accept me and understand me wholly. I needed to be the one to accept myself.

During college my outlook began to change. Out of interest, I took Introduction to Asian American Culture sophomore year. We read books by Japanese Americans, Korean Americans, Vietnamese Americans, and Chinese Americans. I never knew that these groups had such different histories in their immigrations to the U.S. Reading these autobiographies and novels made me appreciate more the differences among Asian Americans. It made me value more my mother's experience as a Thai immigrant. I also began to take cultural psychology classes with open-ended research papers. I used these opportunities to explore Thai culture and skin "colorism." Turns out African Americans and South Asians deal with skin-hue issues too, people valuing paler brown to darker brown. I started becoming more active in the Asian American community, interning for a film about Asian-women stereotypes and leading a sexual- and intimate-partner violence-prevention program for Asian women. All these experiences combined made me more open to the complexity of my ethnic identity.

I am growing to appreciate being both Chinese and Thai. I have always loved my Thai mother with brown skin like my own. She is beautiful. I want to look like her when I am her age. She brings wonderful warmth to our family, no doubt through her generous spirit but also through her Thai culture that encourages expressing and sharing emotions. I appreciate that our family can hug and kiss each other to express affection. Even though sometimes I shy away, it's nice when my sisters and my mom try to hold my hand and link arms with me when we're walking in the parking lot from our car to the mall or along the pier. My Thai heritage doesn't take away anything from my Chinese American identity. It only adds to my ethnic identity.

May Ling Halim is from Fountain Valley, California, and studies psychology at Stanford University.

25 The Confession: Part Two

Shiv Desai

Please, God, forgive me for my sins. Forgive me for lying for all of these years about who I am.

You see, I have always looked a little different ever since I can remember. The comment I hear most often is, "You're Indian? You can't be." Even Desis would ask me this trite question.[1] After I tell people that I am Indian, they still don't believe me. For the longest time I thought it was a curse from Bhagavan.[2]

As a young child, I was really lucky to grow up in an area where most people were tolerant of new immigrants. I was lucky to have friends from all different backgrounds and religions. Perhaps it was my innocence, but it seemed like ethnicity and religion did not matter then. We all enjoyed playing games and creating childish mischief.

As I entered middle school, my family moved. Even after moving, my pride in being Indian persisted. When I was in the sixth grade, I remember my teacher lecturing us every day about the evil realities of racism, discrimination, and prejudice. To me, it was all hot air. In my short life, I could not relate to her words or understand her stories. I could not foresee that in another two years her words would ring true, producing a lingering echo that would reverberate with the harsh sounds of discrimination and prejudice.

As is true for so many adolescents, eighth grade proved to be a major turning point. My family had moved yet again. Up to this point, I had never felt ashamed or embarrassed about being Indian. This was all to change one afternoon in a public library where I was doing a research project. While standing at the card catalog, I noticed a girl looking intensely at me. *Did she like me?* She finally approached me and asked if I was Puerto Rican. I replied no, and continued with my search. She asked if I was Arabic. Again I said no. "Well," she said, seemingly irritated. "What are you?" Without hesitation I enthusiastically replied, "I am Indian." A look of befuddlement appeared on her face. I continued, "You know . . . India . . . the land of the Taj Mahal and the Himalayas."

In an instant, her mood switched. Suddenly, she was shooting away insults about being a Hindu and being an Indian. I did not know what to do. I was stunned—paralyzed. She continued to follow me—unrelenting with her insults. Boy, do I wish I had hit her, had shut her up and had flung insults so hurtful they would have turned her mute. Instead I ignored her and managed to get rid of her momentarily. *Why are Indians so damn passive?* I was frazzled and did not know what to do. I quickly got my stuff and proceeded to leave. Outside the library, I saw the same girl standing with a group of boys. The small crew approached me with hate in their eyes. They yelled, "Get that red dot! We gonna teach him a lesson!" In my panic, I ran without looking back. This would be the first of many times my legs rescued me from a beating.

I retreated to my bedroom shocked, afraid, and angry, without saying a word to my family. For the first time in my life, being an Indian felt shameful. I wondered what she had against Indians, and why her crew had wanted to hurt me. *Sticks and stones may break my bones but words will never . . . Can words hurt this much?* It was at this moment that I first understood the incredible strength of words. After a few days of reflection, I was able to brush off the incident; however, my pride was wounded.

In the next couple of weeks a few other incidents happened. They happened on the basketball court and in my school. It seemed like everywhere I went I was being picked on for being Indian. Throughout history, every new immigrant group has felt the wrath and the hatred of all previous groups. We were the new group in the community, the outsiders. No one knew anything about us. They could not understand our language or our customs. What they did know about us came from *Indiana Jones and the Temple of Doom*, *Gandhi*, and *The Simpsons*. They saw women wearing strange clothes and putting red dots on their foreheads. Thus, I became an easy target.

It was not uncommon for groups of boys to vandalize deli stores owned by Indians. The attacks would all follow the same pattern. One or two boys would enter the store and ridicule the Desi in that annoying fake Indian accent. Next the rest of the crew would bum-rush his store by stealing merchandise. *Why didn't the owners do anything? Why did they take this crap from these punks?* Sad to say, I did not do anything either.

Later that year, the final incident came when I went to Little India. I had to get some food for *mari* mummy as well as some Bollywood movies and tapes for her.[3] As I left Little India trying to juggle the bags, a local gang called the "dot busters" approached me. They said, "What's inside the bags?" I tried ignoring them and tried to walk a little faster. One of them said, "What? We are not good enough to talk to?" I knew whatever I said I would get heat for it. I decided it would be better to keep quiet and keep walking. By now, the dot busters had decided they were going to find out what was inside the bags one way or another. I was like a hockey puck. One member after another took turns pushing me. They ripped the bags from me, spilling the vegetables and fruits, the spices, the Amitah Bachan films, and the Kishore and Lata tapes.[4] They accomplished their mission of finding out what was inside the bags and got the added pleasure of giving me cuts and bruises.

I was steamed as I picked up the groceries. *Why didn't I say anything? Why didn't anyone help me, especially my Desis?* I should have defended myself. I should shown more courage and been a warrior. Other thoughts sprang to my mind, but the most important one was how I would explain to my parents what had happened. As I came home, I knew I could not fabricate a story. I had to tell the truth. Surprisingly, my parents were not mad and told me to keep my head up. My dad prophetically said, "See what happens when you are not educated. *Beta,* this is why we tell you to study so hard.[5] You can live in a nicer area and have a nice life with a good education."

All I thought was: "This is the second time I got jumped for being Indian." It felt like being Indian was nothing but trouble. We were picked on for being nerdy, ridiculed for the way we talked, derided for our religion, and scorned because we smelled.

I thought I had to protect myself. I was tired of getting harassed both physically and verbally for being a Desi. I especially hated to hear people make fun of my religion and my culture. Moreover, being an Indian felt like it was a disadvantage in this new area.

The solution: I would no longer tell people I was completely Desi. I would only be half-Desi. For the first time, the way I looked wouldn't be a curse. Since I had never looked Indian to begin with, it would not be difficult to lie about my background. At the time, I thought I was protecting myself. But today I regret the decision. I sacrificed my identity to protect my vanity.

I entered high school with this plan. I would simply be whatever people wanted me to be. I spent the first weeks of school blending in smoothly until the first day of soccer practice. We were taking shots on the senior goalie of the team. No one could score against him, except me. The keeper asked me what my name was. I told him, and he asked if it was an Arabic name. *My first experiment with this new plan: Would it work?* I told him yes. From that day on, I became half-Egyptian and half-Indian.

Yeah, being half-Egyptian would not be so bad. They built the pyramids and had a marvelous civilization. It turned out it was a bad time to be an Arab. Saddam Hussein had invaded Kuwait, and the U.S. was involved in Desert Storm. Furthermore, Arabs got picked on as much as Indians. I was constantly being bombarded with cracks. Every day I was called a camel jockey, a sand nigger, a towel wearer, a terrorist, and given a stupid nickname: "Aknad." I thought to myself, "At least I am not being made fun of for being Indian anymore." The year progressed and the insults continued to mount; it seemed like everyone had something negative to say about Arabs at the time. It became unbearable. Even though I was not Egyptian, I felt the pain. The words were piercing to my heart. I started to defend Muslims and Arabs. I had to—I was one. I realized that being Egyptian was not going to cut it. I had to find a new identity.

I was kicked out of my high school for constantly getting into fights and was sent to a Jesuit school. Alas, this would be my opportunity to pick another new identity. I entered the school trying to figure out what I should be next. This proved to be a difficult task. The first identity I chose was being Guyanese. I had learned from a friend that a lot of Guyanese people look Indian. This would be an easy switch, and it would not be a complete lie. Pretending to be Guyanese proved to be difficult, however. I had no clue about Guyanese or Caribbean culture.

I then said that I was part Tanzanian. *Mari* mummy grew up in Tanzania. Apparently, there were a lot of Indians in Tanzania and many other parts of Africa who had been brought over by the British to work as servants and in the fields. This quickly diminished because no one believed that there were Indians in Africa. They all thought you had to be black to be African. Finally, the answer came to me one day from a girl.

I was riding on the bus to go home. I saw a pretty girl sitting by herself. I quickly made my move and started flirting with her. Somehow, I fascinated her, and we engaged in conversation. Toward the end of our chat, she asked me what I was. I said, "Guess." She replied, "Puerto Rican?" I delightedly said, "Yeah!" The girl had given me her digits as well as a new identity.

I would try out being *half–Puerto Rican* and *half-Indian*. It turned out I would spend the rest of my high school years with this new identity. Puerto Ricans were in, just like blacks. Hip-hop was starting to dominate urban culture and everyone wanted to be a part of it. My dates with girls quickly shot up. As soon as girls found out I was Puerto Rican, they would throw themselves at me. Platano fever was in full effect. The girls even thought it was so cool that a Puerto Rican had gotten together with an Indian. The only thing that mattered was hitting skinz. *But was having sex more important than my culture? Was it so important that I should deny my identity?* At the time, the answer was a resounding yes. Today, I realize that my priorities were screwed up. I realize that the most important thing is to know who you are.

The guys did not pick on me as much either. They would just make the same rice and beans jokes. It seemed they respected me more now. As a matter of fact, I did not get jumped at all after I became Puerto Rican. I was cruising now.

Wrong!

In school, my teachers held lower expectations for me now that I was Puerto Rican. Unexpectedly, I was getting more detention for the littlest things. Suddenly, my work was poor. I could not go into a store without being followed. And cops could not keep their hands off of me.

On several occasions, I faced police brutality and racial profiling. Police would call me a spick and tell me that I was just trash ruining their community. Being Puerto Rican was not all that great either.

So I decided I would leave my state and go to a college that was out of state. There I could be Indian again. I had learned that no matter what ethnicity I was, I would still face the same problems of racism, discrimination, prejudice, and hate. My sixth-grade teacher's words were loud and clear now. These ills were and are inescapable. I would never deny my heritage again. I would never be ashamed of who I was and pretend to be someone I was not.

Sadly, I did not go out of state; however, I was still determined to show my Indian pride again. I went to college with the hopes of finding out who I am and who I could be. I thought it would be cool to try to find some Indian friends and tried joining the Asian Indian Association. I quickly found out it would not be that easy.

Desis are weird. I learned this during my first semester of college. If you did not look a certain way, talk a certain way, or already belong to the Desi clique, you weren't allowed in. The first problem was I still did not look Desi enough. I was constantly confused with being Latino. So when I arrived at Indian events, I was considered an outsider. On several occasions, I had to pull out my driver's license to prove my Desiness. Every Raksha Bhanden, I would wear my *rakri* for months just to prove my Indian-ness.[6] *Why weren't my own people accepting me? Why were they treating me like an alien?*

I found myself feeling frustrated. Perhaps it was my fault. I had pretended to be someone else for so long that I did not know how to be an Indian. *Maybe I did not belong in the Desi community?* I made friends with Filipinos, Latinos, and blacks. It was so easy to hang out with them because we had so much in common. The greatest thing was that they wanted to learn about the Indian culture, and I, in turn, wanted to learn about theirs.

I tried to take classes on Indian culture, hoping that I could finally hit it off with some Indians. I took a class on Hinduism and actively participated. I found the subject exhilarating. In all of my years of schooling, this was the first time I was learning about my culture, my heritage, and my religion. No matter how hard I tried to make friends with the other Indians, however, I just was not being accepted. I was looked upon as an outsider.

Again, I cursed Bhagavan for these looks. *Why did I have to look so different? Why couldn't I look more Indian?* I found my savior my junior year in college. I took a class on spoken word and read many poems about people who struggled with their own identities as well. I was not the only one who faced this problem. There were so many other people who shared my pain. I picked up a pen and paper one day, started writing about my struggles to find myself, about being an ABCDEFG, and about being a chameleon.[7] I started going to open mics and reciting my poetry—opening my heart for the whole world to see. I felt as if I was confessing my sins and cleansing my soul. I felt like a huge burden had been lifted. I was like a flower blooming for the first time.

Finally, I had awakened. I had found my Atman, and I had destroyed my Jiva.[8] I had begun my path toward self-realization. I had finally asked Bhagavan to forgive me; and He did.

Notes

1. "Desis" are Indian people.
2. "Bhagavan" is God.
3. The word "*mari*" means "mine." "Bollywood" refers to Hindi films.
4. Amitah Bachan is a famous Bollywood actor, and Kishore and Lata are famous singers.
5. The word "*beta*" means "son."
6. Raksha Bhanden is a religious holiday. A "*rakri*" is a bracelet worn on that holiday.
7. "ABCDEFG" stands for "American-Born Confused Desi Especially from Gujrat."
8. "Atman" is the Hindu term for the true self. "Jiva" is the Hindu term for the material self.

Shiv Desai is from Fort Worth, Texas, and graduated from Rutgers College with degrees in psychology and urban planning. He currently studies at Teachers College for Educational Leadership.

26 The Jazzian Singer

Francine Di

Donned in a sleek, pinstriped suit, the jazz singer assumes her place at the microphone. She faces a waving sea of swing dancers; they rise and fall in perfect synchronization with the music's smooth beat. Behind her, a thirty-piece band blares out a brass-inflected introduction. The throng turns to her, hesitantly yet expectantly. And she starts to sing.

Whispers waft easily through the crowd. "I *love* that song." "Do you know how to lindy?" "Wow, she's really good." All are happy. All resume dancing.

The jazz singer is Asian. I am the jazz singer.

What race was the jazz singer you pictured in your mind? Black? Latino? Maybe even white. But not Asian, and certainly not this Houston-born, mostly Chinese-blooded chick. The thought stretches even my imagination—some jazz singer. I can't even envision myself at that microphone, because I grew up with society telling me that Asians can't sing. Idols of American music littered my childhood through the eighties and nineties, but not one was Asian. I saw no singers who looked like me, had no role models to look up to. So I ask myself every day: *How did I ever get here?*

One of my earliest memories is of climbing up a tree to sit amid its smooth, gray branches and sing. At the time, Ariel, the little mermaid, was my heroine, and I'd often sing songs from the Disney film. My neighbors' father, in the midst of watching his kids play baseball, once heard me singing and came to sit under the tree. I felt the odd sensation of being tickled—I had an audience! Granted it was one person, but never before had "gadgets and gizmos" taken on such life! I decided to spice up the performance with some interpretive gestures. I almost fell out of the tree. But it was worth it. He thoroughly enjoyed my performance. He said that he thought I had a "beautiful" voice. And an addictive thrill took root in my brain that day. I was seven years old.

For the next few years of my life, I remained a closet singer. My tastes matured into mainstream pop as I approached adolescence, and when Mariah Carey debuted in the early 1990s, I was hooked. The first cassette I ever bought myself was *Music Box*. I'd crank up her songs on the radio and listen, awestruck at her seven-octave range. In the safe, contained haven of my room, I'd emulate her voice's every trill and turn. She doesn't know it, but she was my first voice teacher. In addition, music videos began comprising a huge chunk of my decidedly American culture. Michael Jackson, Paula Abdul, Madonna . . . these iconic "American" singers flooded my childhood television screen. I watched MTV daily, addicted. Not one Asian ever graced the screen.

The exposure of Asian singers in this country is practically nonexistent, the culture certainly not supportive of them. I never consciously digested that fact, but the images took their toll on my own definition of "singer," effectively discouraging me from singing for years. The public's tacit yet blatant prejudice had me fully convinced throughout my childhood that I could never be a successful vocal artist. So I kept my voice to myself, like a terrible secret. And like a secret, it refused to stay hidden, slipping out on numerous occasions. Like an insuppressible urge to sneeze or cough, it would force its way out of my throat. I tried to ignore it each time, hoping this anti-Asian *thing* would pass by unnoticed. But people did notice it. And people told me it was good. Those who heard me sing advised me to pursue it more seriously. But I blew them all off. In the youthful illusion of my own omniscience, I thought—foolishly—that they failed to realize how simply looking Asian incapacitated me. All the while, I should have noticed how *they* had been able to see past my race to hear my voice as something special. More important, I should have wondered why I couldn't see this for myself. Instead, I sulked in self-pity and let the thrill of vocal performance drain slowly out of my life.

Then in middle school, eighty exhausted girls and I were on a school bus at 1:00 A.M., returning home from a regional drill-team competition. Unlike most of the young passengers, I was wide-awake and heard a friend across the aisle complain of being unable to sleep. Someone suggested she be sung to, so in true team spirit, I chirped up with Céline Dion's "The Power of Love."

Three girls sitting in front of us swiveled around in their seats to watch me. Across the aisle from them, our coach had turned around to look at me as well. I thought that she was about to tell me to keep quiet. Instead she became ecstatic. She poked her boyfriend beside her and made him listen. She called to her brother at the front of the bus and made him listen. After our arrival back in Houston, she dragged me off the bus to her mom and made *her* listen. Everyone looked at me with these huge eyes and told me I had a great voice. The secret was out again. And that mysterious thrill from years ago rushed back into me like a flash flood of emotion.

I would never have spoken a word about my own voice unprompted. I had learned the Chinese law of silent, submissive humility well. But for once, I didn't just smile shyly and say, "No, no, my voice is terrible." Instead, I laughed to myself when their eyes grew round and said, proudly and unabashed, "Thank you." They saw a skinny little Asian girl; they heard a voice come out of her mouth that countered their expectations. But once they forgot I looked Asian and began really listening, they liked it. So I belted it out for them. That old tickled feeling grew until it pounded in my brain. It flooded my veins and completely conquered me. For me to sing to people and have them enjoy listening felt so awesome. You'd think, then, that the next logical step in my life would have been to pursue singing. I didn't.

In March, I was accepted into the High School for the Performing and Visual Arts (HSPVA) . . . but not for vocal performance. I had passed an audition for the classical piano program. Coach responded to the news in an absolutely perturbed fashion. "PIANO?! What about her voice? She can really sing!" Unfortunately, I had already made up my mind that playing the piano was an acceptable path to follow while singing was not. I was "mature." I could be responsible and practical and pursue a more realistic goal. Hadn't my (Asian) piano teacher informed me of my natural talent and musicality? Surely she knew what she was talking about. After all, Asians play the piano. They don't sing.

The truth, of course, was that somewhere in the core of my mind, I still didn't trust my voice as anything more than just that. It's not as if I could have escaped it—I heard it every day, chanting the mantras of most Chinese children, reciting the bilingual vocabulary of my daily life. I could not, however, accept it as a musical medium, as an instrument. It would then have become something that conflicted with the rest of my Asian package. And it's a strange use of the word, but I was still too ignorant to overlook my own ethnicity. I let it stay in the back of my mind, undermining my confidence, barricading me from singing.

I practiced the piano instead—a decidedly "acceptable" pastime for an Asian girl. My life became filled with Bach and Mozart and Chopin. Not that classical music isn't unquestionably beautiful in its own right, but I didn't want to sing Mozart or Schubert. The songs most tempting to me would seduce me each time I turned on a car radio. Unable to suppress my clandestine urge to sing, I tried to cram it in on the side, but due to the number of class conflicts, I couldn't join the choir at HSPVA. Besides, I had no business doing so when the choir was comprised only of vocal majors. I got another chance to sing my junior year when I came upon the girls' audition piece for *Sweet Charity*, that year's schoolwide musical. For once, the song lay perfectly in my unusually low range. I sang it secretly to myself, on and off for a few weeks. I toyed with the terrifying prospect of actually auditioning—for about two seconds. Me, an Asian girl, in a 1960s American musical? Yeah, right. And that was that. The already fragile relationship I had with my voice seemed to die.

Then, two weeks before Christmas my senior year, I passed my friend Charles improvising on the choir room's piano. Having no destination in particular at the moment, I went in to say hi. He was having a blast. As he churned out a gospel-sounding version of "Oh, Holy Night," this *thing* started fighting and raking its way up my throat. I couldn't stop it. Before I knew what was happening, I was just singing along, slipping a taste of Mariah Carey into the holiday standard. It was a high I'd forgotten all too well. It was electric. It was amazing. Charles stopped playing. I stopped singing. We looked at each other.

"Girl, I never *heard* an Asian sing like *that*." He paused. "No offense or anything . . ."

And that was the day I finally snapped.

Offended? Was he kidding? I was floored. I was flabbergasted. I felt flattered to no end. I knew Charles meant no animosity toward Asians—his words reflected only the reality that he saw. It was the same reality I had seen all my life. I had swallowed it daily like a necessary pill, accepted it matter-of-factly as a worldly given. And as I began looking around through new eyes, I grasped the full weight of the reality I had so submissively complied with. Our modestly populated arts high school boasted a grand total of (drumroll, please) one Asian vocal major, a Vietnamese girl from the northwest side of town. Houston, I thought, is an extremely diverse city with one of the few large concentrated Asian populations in the nation. Surely this was not a representative year for Asians in our prestigious music institution's vocal department. I flipped through old yearbooks that night, expecting to dig up buried treasure, but with little luck. There had only been one other Asian vocalist in the past four years, a Chinese guy who, incidentally, had also been class president (surprise, surprise). The bulk of the Asian student body was—where else?—occupying the classical instrumental sector. I suddenly felt very sorry to be a piano major. There I was, there we all were, dutifully solidifying the cliché of the Asian prodigy with impeccable technique and insanely diligent practicing habits. Besides being string players and pianists, a handful of Asians were visual arts majors. Hardly any were in theater or dance, and practically none were vocalists. I saw all the music videos of my childhood flash before my eyes. I saw myself caught in a miniaturized version of the world I had grown up in—a world without Asian singers.

Meanwhile, Charles's words looped endlessly through my head. For the first time in my life, I seriously contemplated what someone had said about my singing. I wonder whether his being black made me assume his opinion and experience in musical matters meant more than mine. It hit me how heavily African American artists tend to dominate our country's popular music, and how, whether or not I realized it, I had let this tendency dominate my own musical development. Since fifth grade, I had idolized Mariah Carey. I had emulated Céline Dion because "she sounds black." Even now, in college, Ella Fitzgerald is my personal vocal goddess, the symbol of my plunge into the sophisticated world of jazz. From Aretha Franklin to Bob Marley, Whitney Houston to Stevie Wonder, the voice of the American soul seems forever shaded in black.[1] Even country music boasts its own Charlie Pride. (Could you even imagine an Asian country singer??) These artists have managed to cross racial barriers, put forth their music in its innate, unfettered form, and become highly successful in gaining American listeners. Audiences see past these singers' race to discover the soul and honesty of their music. Black musicians, particularly singers, have become household names that represent a cultural facet of American music, regardless of the listener's race or age. But how many non–Asian Americans have heard of Lee Hom Wang? Coco Lee? One Voice? Mike Shinoda, or Joe Hahn?

On the other hand, how many Americans recognize the name Yo-Yo Ma?

DUH, right? It's as if Asian Americans are trapped in this sheltered world where it's kosher to perform only classical music or on classical instruments. Having watched numerous American pop singers on television, I have yet to see even one use Asian backup singers. I notice, however, that they don't hesitate to put an Asian string player on the stage next to them. The band Smashing Pumpkins includes a male Japanese American lead and rhythm guitarist: James Iha was born in Chicago. Both Shania Twain and Céline Dion have even used the same violinist, Roddy Chiong, on their respective tours. Why do Asian vocalists seem specifically singled out for artistic oppression? I think it's because the general public in America can't get over this assumption that Asians, or Asian-looking people, can't sing.

I've noticed that it's not unusual for American movies to promote their soundtracks. Such movies span almost all genres and age groups. Think about any Disney cartoon, *Dirty Dancing*, *Titanic*, or *Moulin Rouge*. Often, if the performers of the songs are not already established vocalists, the soundtrack can boost their popularity. Think back to Céline Dion, singing the famous *Beauty and the Beast* theme song with Peabo Bryson; it was the decisive jump start to Dion's American career. Let's consider, then, the Oscar-winning movie *Crouching Tiger, Hidden Dragon*. Its soundtrack was not only written by a Chinese composer, but the song "A Love Before Time" was performed by Coco Lee, the first female Chinese singer ever to perform at the Academy Awards show. The movie was a hit, and Coco's performance was well received. It seemed America was ready to embrace the Chinese singer into its musical world.

Coco's attempts to cross over in 1999 with an all-English album, however, proved unsuccessful. On the other hand, Latino crossovers like Ricky Martin and Shakira have become immensely popular here in recent years. Cuban singer Gloria Estefan broke into the American mainstream years ago. Céline Dion, a French Canadian import, has found huge success in America. Our audiences obviously enjoy their music and view them as talented singers. And while these audiences could easily argue that they don't like Coco Lee's music, why would the song she performs win an Academy Award? I think the greatest distinction between Coco and other crossovers is the fact that she's Asian. As far as many Americans are concerned, she doesn't even exist on the same playing field. People assume she's not talented based on her race, preventing her from finding popularity among American listeners.

This utter lack of opportunity is not limited to native Asians. Born in

Rochester, New York, and a graduate of Williams College, Lee Hom Wang sings, composes, plays various musical instruments, and remains one of Taiwan's most popular musical artists. Recently, he wrote and performed a song from the *Spiderman* soundtrack, "Like a Gunshot." The movie was a smash hit at America's box offices. Yet how many Americans even recognize Wang's name? Why has he uprooted himself and moved thousands of miles from his homeland to record albums, perform, and tour? Why couldn't he have just stayed here? Probably because no one in this country thought an Asian kid could sing. It's a tacit message from America: Go home.

This unspoken racism has plagued us for years, and it hasn't stopped yet. Through an online message board, which will remain unnamed for our purposes, the prominence of racial prejudice against the Asian American image becomes clear. Comments like "The Asians are at home because they can't sing" and "They [Asians] weren't good enough like the rest of these nationalities" proliferate on the Internet. One person suggests we "go to India" because "they have a million singers." Another asks, "[Based on] image alone, does my friend, a Chinese guy, look like an American pop star?" Well of course not, if the bulk of Americans still see seventh-generation Asian Americans as outsiders. The key words here are "image alone." In my personal experience, the moment someone fails to see past my Asian features, my voice assumes a race. Then the music I create isn't music anymore. Someone might as well stamp it as yellow noise. I can't perform if it doesn't give people enjoyment. For many, the fact that I look Asian prevents them from ever enjoying the music behind my physical appearance.

Even more disappointing, Asians themselves seem to embrace the prejudice against Asian pop singers, internalizing the public's stereotypes. My own ESL students said to me laughingly in Mandarin, "Chinese people can't sing!" While trying to promote an all-Asian girl group to sing at a local function, a producer met the Asian show coordinator, who asked him bluntly, "But can they *sing*?" After he had played a recording for her, she looked at him blankly. "These girls are ASIAN?" If even other Asian Americans don't support my calling, how can I convince myself that I can be a vocal artist?

I had let them—this—everything—tell me that I could never be a singer. All my life, the racial conflicts had pushed me down and prevented me from trying. They had kept me from building a relationship with my voice. They had convinced me of the hopelessness of my cause. I had trapped myself within my own web of prejudice, applying a race to my voice instead of seeing it as a musical entity unrelated to color.

And by the time I finally figured out how much of my life was built on singing, it was running away from me. I was about to graduate from high school, ready to plunge into life, free to chase after the dream of a singing career. But I had no voice teacher, no voice training, no background whatsoever in singing. Since I had already auditioned for classical piano programs at five different universities and conservatories, it seemed useless to try turning back at this point. I finally settled on attending Rice University, right at home in Houston, where I would pursue a bachelor's degree in piano performance at the Shepherd School of Music. I promised myself, though, that I would not deny myself the joy of singing anymore—no matter what anyone said to me. And in my heart I had to believe that it was not too late to start.

The first thing I did was look for a voice teacher. I met a wonderful one who specializes in jazz. The first time I performed in one of her class recitals, she made me open the entire program (as if being Asian weren't enough of a stressor). I looked out at the dark little crowd of people. I could just imagine what they were thinking. "Look at that little Asian girl. Is she going to *sing?*" I wanted to die, right there on the stage. But in that moment I remembered singing in the little tree when I was seven years old. I remembered singing on the bus to all those people in middle school. I remembered most of all the awesome jam session with dear Charles. All these memories swirled around in my brain. I took a deep breath, opened my mouth, and just did the thing I wanted to do—sinking into every word, falling into every chord, and loving every second of it. And when I heard the applause and saw my teacher's beaming face, I knew I had done my job right. I had officially become a performing addict. I had found that unbelievable feeling again, and nothing would make me deprive myself of it anymore. I knew I had to perform more. So the very next day, I went to the registrar, where my friend persuaded me to sign myself up for the Rice Jazz Band with him. Unbelievably, we would be the first two vocalists to grace it in three years.

Although the director seemed genuinely excited about having singers again, I still felt nervous the first night I walked into the band hall. Oh, did I mention my friend is black? He had no problem blending into a jazz band— I did. I glanced around, and my insecurity couldn't help but make a quick count of races. I panicked when I didn't see any other Asians. If that weren't enough, the director had both of us singers sit up in the front, right next to the conductor's stand, so the entire band could stare at me. I sat there nervously, holding my breath, fidgeting with every and any earthly thing there was for me to fidget with, just waiting for someone to comment on my Asian-ness, to look at me sideways, to smirk and point and say something demeaning about me. No one did. In fact, everyone just said hey, greeted me as if I'd been part of the band for years. Later, a Vietnamese saxophonist walked in, so I didn't feel quite so much like a sore thumb. I stuck it out, and I'm so thankful that I did.

Here I am. I'm a senior, ready to enter the "real world." Scary prospect. But I'm still with my voice teacher. She has experience. She works me hard. Most important, she has faith in my ability. I see it every day when she pushes me to push my own limits. Her support has done great things for my own confidence. Also, I'm still singing in that jazz band. We recently performed an entire night's set for a swing party. I can't think of anything in the world more exhilarating than having an entire band backing me up on that stage. After so many years of muffling my voice, I can finally let it fly. It makes this whole Asian-and-singing thing seem like a breeze. I've almost started to believe that I made it all up. Almost.

At times I regret all the years of my life I wasted when I let the opportunities to develop my voice fly by me. Luckily, that only makes me more aggressive in my search for opportunities. I sing all the time now. I'd like to say I've figured out how to forget that people see me as an Asian, but that would be a lie. Every time I get up on stage to perform, that old feeling of inadequacy creeps up on me, if only for a second. I think, though, that those seconds are getting shorter every time.

In theory, we should view talent in terms of itself, not through the race of the performer. However, society has made this almost impossible. For years it warped my own view of my voice and belief in what I can do. I know now. I love to sing. But I don't want to have to run away from my homeland in order to do what I love. I don't want to be stuck with audiences that only question whether or not someone of my ethnicity can sing instead of enjoying the music I love making. I want people, in any country, of any race, to see me as a singer—not an Asian, not an American—just a singer. But before that happens, I have to achieve the same goal for myself. It's a difficult process, and a slow one, but I think I'm getting there. Like the song says, I just need to take it "nice and easy."

Notes

1. Marian Anderson (1897–1993) is often called "the voice of the American soul." Originally denied entrance to music school because of her race, she eventually rose to great operatic prominence, becoming the first black singer to perform with the Metropolitan Opera.

Francine Di is from Houston, Texas, and studies piano performance and English at Rice University.

27 Reminiscings

Shiuan Butler

Significant moments in my life that changed me forever and I will remember as long as I live, even with my shitty memory:

1. I have three memories of the time before I was six years old. One is of coming back home to our Taipei apartment and finding it ransacked by robbers. The other two memories are of being punished with my older brother. There isn't much more to say about the first memory except that my present fear of leaving the house and encountering strangers may very well come out of that incident. My other two memories are equally unpleasant.

My older brother and I would get punished on a regular basis by my birth dad. (I call him my birth dad because that's pretty much all he did—contribute to my birth. My second dad I call "Dad" because he legally adopted me, as well as raised me.) On recent questioning, my mom said that she would never punish us because he hit us enough for the both of them. Thanks, Mom.

So my brother and I are in the shower. Suddenly from nowhere my birth dad is beating my brother on his butt with a stick, for reasons I cannot remember and which are probably insignificant anyways. End of memory.

The setting for the second memory is also our tiny Taipei apartment. My brother and I are kneeling next to each other facing the wall next to the bathroom. We're being punished again for reasons I can't remember, and we can't get up until we apologize and feel truly sorry. Now, this is not as easy as it sounds or we would have simply jumped up and apologized. Oh, no. You had to stay there until you were truly sorry. That probably wasn't the best exercise for my three-year-old knees either. Thanks, Dad. So we're kneeling there and I turn my head in time to glimpse my mom being chased by my birth dad. He's holding a butcher's knife. (You know how we Chinese like to have our nice kitchen knives.) They rush by and disappear into the kitchen. End of memory.

2. My mom divorcing my dad changed my life. By leaving that marriage my mom gained back her life, and so did I. I respect my mom for doing what was best for her, even if it meant going against cultural tradition. I will always admire her for that.

3. Moving back to Taiwan during my middle school years helped me realized Chinese was more than just an annoying language that I had to learn on Sundays. I met my extended family for the first time in six years. I realized this was a huge part of who I was that was missing from my life. I returned to the U.S. looking to fill this gap. Starting at age fifteen, I began my involvement in Asian American organizations, clubs, camps, anything I could get my hands on. I haven't stopped since.

I'M NOT ASKING FOR MUCH
A Taiwanese brother sister someone who'll go with me to lunch
At a Chinese restaurant and won't ask for a fork
Someone I can eat with be with and won't feel like it's a chore
Someone who won't be grossed out by the fish tank
Someone who won't holler "why's this food stank?"
Someone who won't divide the bill equally to the last penny
And leave 10 percent tip. Hello! This is the twenty-first century!

I'm not asking for much
A common friend no diamond in the rough
A Chinese who can speak Mandarin
That'd be cool I'd be chillin'
An Asian who doesn't need to get high before they go out for the
    night
Someone who can use chopsticks without havin' their food fly
A Taiwanese brother sister they don't have to spend the night
Just someone to laugh with cook with and maybe share a cry
About how our parents came here and didn't understand a thing we
    were goin' through
And how they'd send us on Sundays to three hours of Chinese school
Where we didn't learn a thing about Chinese anything

The only Chinese I knew was ching
Chong that was from American school throngs
Where we learned national anthem songs
That sung about victory with guns
Killing my people that's how the war or quote peace was won

That's all I'm looking for
A Taiwanese brother sister to laugh with about all of this
I'm not looking for sex attachment or even a kiss
A Taiwanese brother sister someone who won't diss
Me for their boyfriend girlfriend whoever it is
That they always put first instead of their friends
A Taiwanese man who likes my boyfriend
A Taiwanese girl who claims the world hers
Who realizes the most important thing in life is to put herself first
Who knows she's the most beautiful thing next to me of course
I'm just playing with you
All this serious talk has given me a mental serial conditional mind
　　block

Anyways I think you've got my point
I just want a Taiwanese Chinese sister brother whatever aight?
Someone who can laugh at racism along with me
And not stare at me like I'm a freak
So if any of you out there know of someone applicable
Just give 'em my name and tell 'em to give me a call
Just tell 'em what I said about no shoes in the house
Stuffing yourself obscene amounts at your relatives' house
And if they're really Taiwanese then they'll know what I mean.

4. My first time having sex killed like hell. My high school girlfriend recently asked me if he had an extra big one or something. (If you're already grossed out I recommend you skip to #5.) I thought about it . . . not that I know of. It wasn't that small though. (See, last week she told me about her first time, which just happened a few months back in Germany, and so I told her mine. Now we're both nonvirgins together. Yay!) My doctor recently told me my vagina flips backward—like that. I wonder if that has anything to

do with . . . ? I don't think so. Who the hell knows. Anyways, it was the first time for both of us. He was very sweet.

So the first time was all pain from what I can remember. By the fifth time or so, the pain would only last during the first 20 percent of sex, then it was pure heaven after that. He would reassure me during the first few times, while I was cringing in pain, that it would soon go away and in his sweet, gentle voice tell me to just try and relax, okay? What do you think I'm doing? I thought, with my teeth clenched. Men . . .

5. When my dad walked in on my boyfriend and me having sex. Whoa, shocking, I know. It's okay. I walked out alive, barely. First, you need to know the kind of teenage girl I was so you can appreciate the true significance of the situation. (Although I *am* Chinese—what more is there to say?) It wasn't like I was a druggie *and* my parents walked in on my boyfriend and me having sex. No, it was more like, I was an A-B honor roll student *and* my parents walked in on my boyfriend and me having sex.

So, yes, my dad walked in on my boyfriend and me doing it, getting laid, getting it on, etc. Actually, he didn't literally walk in on us . . . um . . . he heard me first. Did I mention I'm not a quiet Chinese girl?

I was of course traumatized for days, weeks. When I told friends of the disastrous incident I'd start bawling. Now, years later, I can tell the story to horrified friends and reassure them and laugh. *C'est la vie, n'est-ce pas?*

6. Meeting my second boyfriend and present husband. At the time, he was a twenty-two-year-old, dark, Nepali man with long hair down his back and a tattoo on each arm. Needless to say, I, a quiet Chinese girl from the suburbs, was a bit scared of him at first. Now, to back it up a little . . .

Before then I had had all of two romantic relationships with men (none with women). Both were white. The first lasted one night or two weeks, however you want to look at it. (Okay, it was really a one-night stand that I stupidly tried to drag out into a long-distance relationship, which of course failed miserably.) The other lasted nine months—my first "true love" (the one where we were caught by my parents doing it).

At that time, I had never met any Asian boy that I liked in all of the white suburbs that I had lived in. The number of suburbs was many, the number of Asian boys was few. At age twelve, I told my mom, to her astonishment, I would never date an Asian man. (My mom herself had divorced a Chinese man and married a white American. I don't remember if I liked my Chinese dad or disliked him. But the two memories that I do have of that period are

not pleasant, to say the least. Let's see, both of them were memories of . . .
being punished, see #1.) Needless to say, I didn't grow up with wonderful
impressions of great Chinese male role models. So my mom should not have
been surprised when I declared that I would not date any Asian man, especially a Chinese one.

This promise was not especially hard to keep growing up in Belmont,
Massachusetts, the white middle-class suburb that it was, and still is. I remember one Chinese boy, Toby, told everyone he was not Chinese. He thought
his mixed features allowed him to pass as 100 percent white. Rather, his declaration made me conclude he was 100 percent stupid. The two other Asian
American girls in my class had white best girlfriends, as did I. The fobbish
ESL kids stuck together. It was only after high school that I found out there
were schools in which Asians actually hung out with other Asians. I was
shocked. When there was a large percentage of Asian American students,
they naturally flocked together. Naturally . . . does that mean they *wanted* to
hang out with each other? Interesting. So anyways, there's the backdrop. I
had vowed to never date an Asian man when, boom, I met Gagan.

Gagan was a twenty-two-year-old, dark, Nepali man with long hair down
his back and a tattoo on each arm. We worked together at Au Bon Pain. We
started taking breaks together. Mostly, he would talk and I would listen. I had
a hard time understanding his English at first, but I was too shy to ever ask
him to explain so I would just nod and listen attentively.

On August 6, my birthday, I sent my first boyfriend to the airport. (He
was leaving for college and had decided it was too hard to try and stay
together over such a long distance and unfair to ask the other person not to
date somebody else. Okay then. See ya later.) After saying goodbye to my ex
and crying leaving the airport, I went to work. That night, Gagan and I took
a break together as usual. During the break he asked our boss, his friend, if he
could take me out for my birthday. Of course he said yes, and we went out to
eat. It turned out to be a date because by the end of the night we had kissed.
That was five years ago. We've been married for four months.

7. Meeting my older brother again after fifteen years. That was definitely
a very moving experience for me.

GE GE
Fifteen years we hadn't seen each other

Reuniting with my own true brother
Didn't know what to expect
How would I react
Would there still be a *bond* between us though we had more than a
    decade of no contact

We drive from the airport / sweet smoky smell of Taipei in the air
We drive up to the front door / the anticipation's more than I can
    bear
I get out of the car / run my hands anxiously through my hair
We stand there staring at each other / all my emotions covering up
    the tears

He's all grown-up now / too big for Dad to beat now
When I tried to reach out and hug him / he just leaned over with a lit-
    tle bow
His four-month girlfriend knows him better than *I do* now
What the hell
Our parents got divorced / but that don't mean me and you can't con-
    verse
My friends call him slow / I remind them hey that's my brother
    you're talking about you know
But unlike me he didn't get to leave my dad when he was six years old

A man I considered for a long time a real asshole
Which I know now to not be true
He was simply very confused / growing up in a controlling house
    always getting told what to do
Let me tell you / he and his brothers are a fucked-up crew

Now this is a big deal for me a Chinese to be airing my dirty laundry
I just think it's important for us to share our stories and realize our
    problems are not extraordinary
My nuclear family is not uniquely out of the ordinary
There are Asian couples unhappily married / and brothers and sisters
    long forgotten and buried in their families' memories

So was my brother in ours
Now he had come back alive to me as if from the dead
I just wanted to hold him and hold him caress his sweet head
Awkwardly we exchanged questions and answers instead
Not feeling any closer to each other than when we first met
There was a feeling of disappointment sadness confusion
We were blood brothers and sisters / found similar things
    amusing
But there was something missing / I kept watching and listening
And finally realized it was he himself that was drifting
Away from the conversation / his body / his life
When I realized I was torn I just wanted to do right
By him for himself I wanted him to fight
When I realized
There's only a certain amount I can do / he needs to right his own
    plight
So at present I'm praying someday he'll wake up in the middle of the
    night
And realize
There's nothing more important than taking charge of his own life

8. My wedding four months ago. Mmm . . .

I DO
When I first met you I was scared of you
Your colorful tattoos
You told me your drinking days were through
Your easy laughter the graceful way you moved
Were what made me first fall in love with you
And now four years and nine months later I'm marrying you
You barely asked me and at first I wasn't sure I wanted to
Marry you now I'm just twenty-two and a half
Then I thought about you me us and your laugh-
Ter that'll help us get through most anything
And I thought about our love your life and my dreams
And I figured hey nothing's impossible
You're the sweetest and I'm glad I can help you become legal

I love you baby that's all I wanted to say
I'll never forget what we have for the rest of my days.

9. Two weeks later, telling my mom over the phone that I had gotten married. Mmmmmmm . . . I'll just say that she took it better than I thought she would. She's a strong, smart Chinese woman.

10. Slowly gaining my self-confidence through my friends and a process called Re-evaluation Cocounseling. By looking at the patterns or the misinformation that I was led to believe growing up, I am slowly gaining back my self-confidence and sense of self-worth. As for my friends, they are irreplaceable.

DON'T LET ANYBODY TELL YOU. SIMPLY REPLY, "SAYS WHO, YOUR MAMA?"

1. *That for something to be considered Asian American literature it has to have the word "Asian" in it. At least twenty times.*
2. *That they don't see color. That they're like a dog, color-blind. Really.* (Maybe you want to have your eyes checked then?)
3. *That they love Asians. All their exes were Asian. That proves it.*
4. *That you got accepted (to the company, school, etc.) because you are Asian.* (Says your mama.)
5. *"You're short" (if you're a girl) or "You're too skinny" (if you're a guy).* (Whoever's seen muscly six-and-a-half-foot-tall Asian men or women walking around Asia? Exactly.)
6. *That you're loud for an Asian.*
7. *That you speak English really well.* (So does your mama!)
8. *That they love Asian nights at clubs too!* (Yeah, okay. They're called "Asian nights" for a reason, honey.)
9. *That our culture is sexist.* (Well, it's a good thing American culture isn't! Whew!)
10. *That you must have permed your hair. "Oh my God! It's so beautiful and . . . curly!"* (Oh, thanks . . . I have curly hair in other parts too.)

Concluding Words of Wisdom

For those Asian Americans who live in white isolated worlds, the next best thing is to know that there are other Asians out there experiencing the same thing. You are not a freak, there is nothing wrong with you, only the outside oppression. That just because you don't see Asian American role models out there does not mean they are not out there. That in the rest of the world you are the norm. There is no norm. And that to be happy you must first accept and like yourself.

And if you like to write, jot down some notes. Any notes. On just about anything will do. Share your notes. Your voice and thoughts need to be heard by the rest of the world. The world needs to hear from young Asian American voices like yours and not Hollywood's or those of Asian stars like Jackie Chan (even though he is hot).

I have slowly come to realize who I am from the experiences I have been through. I am slowly realizing I want to be a swimmer, spoken-word poet, negotiator, good friend, and to be damn good at all of them. If you have a dream, I beg you to pursue it. If you don't have one, pursue finding one. Eminem put it well: "Do not miss your chance and blow . . . this opportunity comes once in a lifetime." Major opportunities may only come once in a long while, but at any time you can make your own opportunities. What are you waiting for? What are you scared of? Screw your fears. If you knew your dream would come true in the end, would you go for it now?

Shiuan Butler is from Taipei, Taiwan, and graduated from the University of Massachusetts at Boston with a degree in Asian American studies. She currently teaches English as a second language.

28 There's No Place like Home

Phillina Sun

A few nights ago, I placed my John Hancock on a rent check. It was my first rent check in years.

Squatting in an attic throughout life as a college student, you forget the reasons why you are so mobile in terms of lifestyle. My administrative assistant's paycheck financed lavish dinners, bar nights, late-night movies, flea-market finds, groceries from the farmer's market, a trip abroad.

Now . . . it's all *so* last year, so different now that I am broke and wondering how to make rent each month during an economy that is witnessing the abrupt tightening of white-collar and blue-collar belts everywhere, as well as the corporate exploitation of a temporary, underpaid, and uninsured workforce. I can't even imagine the dinner parties I used to throw. Friends comment, eyebrows cocked, *Get a job, cut your hair.*

Some (like my anarchist roommate) would say that rent is theft, the logic of which I don't fully grasp yet. All I know is that paying rent means that you should have a monthly income, and that rent should be no more than one-third of your income in order for you to live comfortably. (This was what the facilitator told us attic denizens when he tried to negotiate a settlement with what he called our "idiot" slumlord.) Having to pay rent every month, year after year, means that you have to be relentlessly employed, with little freedom to explore or to disengage when you become restless. You have to work. You have to worry about your bills. You have to get paid every two weeks, or the shit will hit the fan. You start to long for stability, to be able to put your money into something other than rent, because paying rent often feels like it goes to nothing. I mean, you could get evicted any day because your landlady decides to rent your place out for more money—despite whatever time and expense have been invested in making your apartment into a home—and where are you then? Back to square one, with nothing to show for all the money you paid in rent.

So you start longing for more income, enough money to pay for a house. Think about it. A place of your own! Seductive, huh? And, voilà! Assimilation into middle-class America, abetted by the (hegemonic) reality of having to pay rent. You have thoroughly invested in the system. Oy veh.

To live comfortably: That was all my parents wanted and would find beyond reach as marginalized nonwhite refugee speakers of wobbly (improper, bad) English. They worked hard in factories and one donut shop, toward an uncertain present of sore joints and brows creased with worry over the sense of never having enough. Was this the year we would have to sell our house? Every year of my adolescence, this question resurfaced.

This difficulty was what had made me balk, from early adolescence till now, at their dreams of a (recklessly) book-smart daughter living in a big house in the countryside, German-made car in the driveway, thousands of frequent-flyer miles in her back pocket. As someone growing up uncomfortably working-class among the wealthy in a predominantly white, upper-middle-class neighborhood, I was wary of these dreams; obviously certain people couldn't obtain them, as there was only a limited amount of wealth and resources to be distributed. I mean, who got tracked into the college prep classes? Looking around in my college prep classes, I saw mostly white and (non-Southeast) Asian faces. On the other hand, in my regular (i.e., non–college prep) classes, I was surrounded by mostly brown faces, by kids who were often bussed in from poorer neighborhoods. So much for the idea that segregation was a relic of the past.

The future my parents had mapped out for me just didn't fit with the future the education system was mapping for kids like me. My parents thought that I could be anything I wanted to be in America. Now I know it's the stuff of noontime soap operas and rags-to-riches stories, impossible goals toward which a straight and narrow path leads, a thoroughway that only a certain class and indomitable others will tread.

Not for me, I thought when the fallacy of this dream became apparent. Not for me the dream that my mother clung to, as she diligently fried hundreds of donuts each night. Instead I was gonna pursue a spectacular death: if not young and violent, then preferably after many lovers and globe-trotting adventures like childhood icon and dashing American imperialist archaeologist Indiana Jones . . . and then someone, preferably a grieving daughter, would open a suitcase out of curiosity and discover a dozen manuscripts by her dead and adorable mother. Once she had them published, I would be an acclaimed master of the twenty-first-century American English diasporic novel. Bigger than Amy Tan. Almost as big as white-tressed Maxine Hong Kingston. Required comparative lit reading.

And in order to accomplish my destiny, I did what I thought any self-respecting ne'er-do-well daughter of refugee/Cambodian/American parents would do:

1. Never get a driver's license, a big no-no in southern Californian suburban sprawl. This will allow you to be very unemployable, because since you've missed your bus again, the chocolate shop will have to fire you. (Oh big deal. As if I would miss my $5.15/hour wage.) Unemployability is key to being a no-good, useless, shifty, untaxable American citizen.

2. Avoid sensible majors, like engineering and computer science. Diaspora studies, what's that? *What can you do with that, A-Na?* my dad asked me, before launching into yet another anecdote, the one he never fails to tell me when we debate the profitability of my major, the one about the Asian policeman he knows. *Do you know what he take in college, girl? Creative writing. Now he regret it.*

3. Don't graduate. (Yet. That happens when you can no longer endure phone call after phone call from your parents, telling you, sighing, *Uncle ask about you the other day.* [Dramatic Pause.] *Did Na graduate? he ask. I tell Uncle, I don't know.* [Dramatic Pause.] *I don't know what to tell the family anymore, A-Na. Make money, Na. You're twenty-four.*

But you can only eat so much ramen and work so many hours and worry so much about your (untreated) dental cavities and aging parents. Living uncomfortably in the American capitalist machine and trailed by the hopes of my family, I start to think that the hyperbolic destiny I imagined for myself so many years ago is unattainable. Even foolish. Merely a fantasy concocted by a stubborn, untalented, lazy mind. And so I ponder all that is within reach for a former university student with a shockingly decent GPA and (this is key) excellent academic references.

All that is within reach . . . should I choose to repeat the lines prospective corporate employers want to hear, so that I could get a proper publishing job, for example, writing proper American English copy about proper American things, sellable things, you know, products. Then I would earn a reasonable salary that would pay for health insurance, rent, trips abroad . . . All that seems tantalizingly within reach, should I choose to participate in all the right, civilized, proper American ways of being.

If I became a good American citizen who abided by the rules of the State and of civil society, I could occupy (national) space legitimately. Safely, without fear of the acts that can happen to the people who do not act as good American citizens should. To be unsafe is to risk being blacklisted, or isolated in detention camps, deported because you look like a terrorist, beaten to a bloody pulp with baseball bats because you look like you're one of them, one of those people who are taking away jobs from good American citizens. Even tried and executed—as the Rosenbergs, and Sacco and Venzetti were tried and executed—because, since you are of the wrong political persuasion, you must also harbor inclinations toward dissent and should be eliminated before you become a real threat.

What terrifies and attracts me is exactly this: the bliss of being comfortable as a person who is normal, who believes that the State is looking out for them, who believes that it is so easy, so right, to have a place in American society as you do an apartment, accomplished through legitimate means, through simply following preestablished rules like paying rent, an ideal third of one's ideal income needed in order to live comfortably, ideally.

But it's not that easy, is it? It's only in reach of the few whose material circumstances are quite unlike the material circumstances of the many.

Sometimes I just want to feel like Dorothy, the girl in *The Wizard of Oz*, a teenaged daughter of good law-abiding white Middle American farmers. Be in her ruby heels, as she, tho' stuck in a kooky place called Oz, only had to utter a chant in order to reappear in a place so far away and now, ideally, home. *Yes,* I am tempted to think, *I should learn how to drive a car.* Then I could go places. I could get a real job. Yes, I want to chant, as if it were that easy, all you need is ruby heels and a wish: *There's no place like home. There's no place like home. There's no place like home.*

Because there is no place like home. Because for Dorothy, it would be safe. There would always be a roof over your head and a dog named Toto and parents who loved you despite every bad habit you had and would eventually outgrow . . . and maybe, just maybe, something bigger and better than what you had at that moment. The years you will never have to ask, *Is this the year we will sell our house?* A dream. A Big Dream. The Great American Dream.

When my imagination has reached this frightening conclusion, I switch. Gears, roles, sentiments, whatever—I just want to be Dorothy's black-tressed nemesis. I want to be like the woman I most (and secretly) identify with . . . and not be at all ashamed of her. The Outsider. That mean lady who shouldered a history of what must have been a really awful childhood and who glorified in her power, her anger, her desire to make history explosively. She wanted to ignite a new Big Bang, courtesy of magic and a broom wielded just right, out to undo a universe that had displeased her. Yes, it's true, I wanted and still want to be the ballsy green bitch who, as the Wicked Witch of the West, cackled, *I'm gonna get you, Dorothy! And your little dog, too!*

Who knows? Perhaps I'm already there right now, writing the first missive of an illustrious career as an Outsider. That's right. Making a history that counters the claims of civil society and the State, even as I write, regardless of whether or not I'll make rent this month.

Phillina Sun is from San Diego, California, and graduated from the University of California, Berkeley, with a degree in diaspora studies. She is currently an editor.

29 Thin Enough to Be Asian

Uyen-Khanh Quang-Dang

—2 hot dogs
—1 wheat bread w/peanut butter & jelly
—tuna w/salad, lots of olive oil
—Clif energy bar
—3 chocolate chip cookies
—corn bran cereal w/soy milk
—2 Cadbury Crème Eggs (regular kind)

Writing down a list of food that I had put into my body for that certain day would calm me down a little bit. It was as if writing each item down on paper allowed me to be in control of what I had eaten. In control of the chyme already churning inside my stomach, already being digested in my intestines, already absorbed into my body. Of course, I had no control at all but needed to pretend that I did. I'd stare at this list for fifteen minutes, reading each item over and over, then I would decide whether I should eat anything else for the rest of that day. Usually, I would vow not to touch another morsel: "Okay, don't eat anything else until tomorrow. No more. Very easy. Just don't eat." But inevitably, I would scarf something down a few hours later, something sinful . . . like a double-decker peanut butter and jelly sandwich on white bread. It was the part of me that desperately wanted to be normal (eating whatever I wanted to eat) teaming up with the part of me that finds ecstasy in eating, and annihilating the part of me that despised my "thick" thighs and "flabby" arms. After gulping down the last moist, sticky piece of bread, I'd go put on a loose T-shirt and oversized sweats, so that I wouldn't have to feel the disgusting feeling of my bulging body against tight, stretched cotton.

There are people who view food as sustenance—eating happens to them, but they don't go out of their way to make eating happen. Then there is the big group of people who are enthusiastic about food—those who take much pleasure in eating and get excited about going out for dinner. And then there are those like me, whose lives are dictated by food. We daydream about our favorite junk foods, our clocks tick in constant anticipation of the next meal, the quality of our days depends upon what we had to eat. My obsession with food has always been a significant part of me, but it didn't become a problem until I also became obsessed with my body image. These insecurities are rooted back when I was in eighth grade, when my world consisted of my three best friends and the wild adventures we shared. It was a time when I felt I truly belonged in a group; like most teenagers, I felt that there was nothing more important than belonging to a group. It was a time when boundaries of what I was supposed to look, act, and think like were built according to standards set by this group of friends I belonged to.

The Friday-night ritual of getting dolled up for a night out with my three best friends was unforgettable. Donna and Phung were both Vietnamese, and Sherilyn was Filipino, but we all passed for either ethnicity since the California sun tanned our skin the same bronze hue. Sherilyn was our designated hairdresser; she would style all of our waist-length, dark hair (curled, pulled up, straight), while the rest of us tried on different outfits and sang along with the blasting radio. By 9:00 P.M., preparation for hours of dancing in the clubs of San Francisco would be in full force. Slinky tube tops, sparkly miniskirts, brightly colored bras (backless, strapless, strappy—depending on how much skin the outfit revealed), and platform shoes (which added at least four inches to our five feet) littered the floor and bed, forlorn rejects of our ruthless auditioning. Then our faces would be cautiously painted, for we certainly did not want to look like "one of them hella gross, slutty girls." By 10:00 P.M., our scrawny legs would prance out the front door, and all four tiny Asian bodies would comfortably squish together in the backseat of our friend's Honda Civic, with plenty of legroom to spare. We were ready for a night of dancing on the stages of San Francisco's most popular club, with our borrowed IDs (courtesy of our friends' older sisters) safely tucked in a bra, boot, or the space between our underwear and tight pants. Half an hour later, as we drove by the mile-long line in front of the club, we'd strain our necks to check out the bouncers. At least one of them would be white, and Donna would always remind us: "Just remember to show your ID to the *white* bouncer." Then we'd all laugh smugly. "White bouncers think all Asians look the same and can't tell the difference!"

By the age of fourteen, I had learned how I was supposed to look. I had learned what was cool to wear, how to pluck my eyebrows, that Revlon's "Toast of New York" was the perfect lipstick shade. In the accumulated hours in front of the mirror, my body juxtaposed with those of my three best friends made it evident to me that I was the biggest of the bunch. My arms were a little bigger than those of all three of my best friends, my thighs a little chunkier. My tummy was all right, but everything else was just a little bigger. Bigger enough to be noticeable. Bigger enough to make me stick out, to make me different from the rest. Though I was not even close to being overweight, simply being a little bigger than all my best friends was just as devastating to me. You see, our friendship was characterized by the fact that we shared everything, from money to makeup to clothes. Thus, it was essential for us to be as similar as possible in appearance. We all fit into each other's size-0, Wet Seal clothing, and—though the silliness of this is much clearer in hindsight—the fact that we swapped baby Ts and flared corduroys was something we prided ourselves on. It was evidence of how tightly bonded we were, for we could care less what actually belonged to whom (though I, being the most anal about shrinkage and fading, was always the one in charge of washing our prettiest pieces).

Being in this Asian clique cultivated stereotypes of white people that I still find difficult to ignore today, though they've been undermined plenty of times since they were formed in my yet unwrinkled mind: that white people were too stingy and cautious about material things, and therefore would not be able to share with the carefree abandon that we did. In our high school, where Asians were as prominent as whites, blacks, and Hispanics, we had many white friends but secretly poked fun at their penny-pinching ways. *"Don't forget, Robert, that you owe me a dollar and thirty-nine cents from that time I bought you ice cream,"* we'd mock our white classmates as we pooled our money to pay for lunch at our favorite McDonald's. Our willingness to share everything without recounting who gave what, as we discussed on many occasions, had very much to do with the Asian culture of the communal family. Each of us had grown up living under one roof with not only our nuclear family, but aunts, uncles, cousins, and grandparents as well. Privacy was unheard of in our homes, and with it went the concept of personal property. Visiting the homes of our Asian friends, I remember seeing gaggles of cousins and relatives and bedrooms inhabited by two or three siblings. The homes of my white friends would rarely have more than five people living in them, each child with his or her very own room.

My early teenage years were when I shaped "the Asian ideal" according to the sizes of my best friends' bodies and those of the large Asian population in my hometown community. Later in high school, I learned what the stereotype of this Asian ideal was in American society's psyche through learning about the infamous "Asian fetish." I remember hearing for the first time about what an "Asian fetish" was. *What? I don't get it. Okay, a man who has an Asian fetish is someone who gets turned on by an Asian woman because of the way she looks? Huh? What the hell does that mean? Isn't everybody attracted to others because of the way they look? Oh . . . He likes any Asian woman because he's attracted to the typical features of the Asian woman: long, flowing, dark hair, small bone structure, thin limbs, soft skin, diminutive personality, eager to please, subordinate in public but a tigress under the covers . . . Lots and lots of men, especially white men, have Asian fetishes. You better be careful not to date one of those. They'll just treat you like an object, a prize they'll show off to their friends but not have any respect for.*

Though it was made clear that men with these Asian fetishes were not to be looked upon approvingly, the idea that this mold of the exotic Asian woman drove white men half-crazy with desire was fascinating to me. I was shamefully intrigued by the beautiful Asian woman, whose gracefulness, contained in her fragile, slim physique, I could never achieve. I wanted to be thin enough to be *the* Asian woman that men fantasized about; I longed to be thin enough to be shown off as a prize to the world, despite my dreams of becoming an independent, successful, world-changing woman.

High school ended, and I left my best friends on the West Coast to attend college on the East Coast. College was simply an entirely different way of life. The gorgeous all-year-round weather of northern California was replaced by the excruciatingly freezing winters of Boston. My comforting clique of best friends with whom I only partied was suddenly supplanted by brand-new classmates with whom I shared every aspect of my life. I studied with them, ate with them, and hung out with them. Because of such unceasing exposure to these strangers-turned-acquaintances-turned-friends (in a matter of days!) who came from all over the country and world, I was forced to become keenly aware of different facets of my identity, facets that as a high schooler I would have found too awkward to discuss. My religion, my ethnicity, my political views, and my physical appearance were in constant comparison with those of my peers. Though I became grounded in my beliefs through intense talks about such delicate issues, it was often tough in the beginning, when freshmen aren't sure about what their opinions really are yet. Home-cooked Vietnamese dishes became distant memories as all-you-can-eat buffets, complete with rich pastas, french fries, and more forms of cheese than I thought possible, were introduced to me. Classes were extremely difficult. I could barely decipher the chemistry lectures and the seven hundred pages of weekly reading assignments. I was on the premed track, so doing poorly in my classes, my innocent freshman brain thought, was equivalent to premature death.

But what was it that finally pushed me to become bulimic? What drove me to have binging and purging as a way of life? Each person with an eating disorder has a different reason from the next person. What makes eating disorders so difficult to treat and cure is that they're the result of a culmination of reasons, all enmeshed together, intertwined and inseparable. What reasons can I point my finger at? Low self-esteem? Brainwashing by a multi-billion-dollar industry that puts the same twenty faces and bodies on every single magazine cover, television ad, and movie screen? Depression from missing my family and friends back home? Seeing that other Asian girls were thinner than I was, feeling the familiar embarrassment of not fitting into the "normal" Asian female body? At Harvard, the average Asian female was even thinner than what I was used to back home, which I attributed to the phenomenon of the type A personality (the overworking perfectionist) which had allowed most Harvard students to get where they were. At least at home, I had other parts of myself to feel proud of that did not involve my physical shortcomings—my academic and leadership success. But at college, what had made me special dissolved into everyone else's basic characteristics. Perhaps the anxiety and shame about not being smart enough to get into medical school were too overwhelming, and I needed to exert control over my body since I was failing in other aspects of my life?

Or perhaps the most embarrassing reason, the most shameful reason of all—that my eating disorder was just about vanity? Was I bulimic because I cared much more desperately than the average person about my physical appearance? Many girls who have eating disorders will do anything to pretend that they don't have one. They pretend—*we* pretend, as proud members of the Harvard community—that we couldn't care less about the size of our waist . . . *Oh, we're just naturally thin and don't need to worry about such petty, inane things like ounces and calories. After all, we're busy worrying about how to become the leaders of tomorrow.*

What I need to admit is that the biggest reason why I suffered from bulimia is that I *did* care too much about my physical appearance. It is the thing I am most ashamed of about myself. It was only when I was able to admit this to myself that I was able to figure out exactly how I was going to get better, to escape from bulimia and move closer to normalcy. I think what shocks most people when they learn of my past experience with an eating disorder is that I am not overweight, and was never even close to being overweight. Actually, most who suffer from bulimia are within the normal body-weight range. Not only am I not fat, but I have been told that I am beautiful since I entered college. My friends to whom I revealed my secret ask incredulously, "Don't you know that you're beautiful? Why are you so worried about your appearance when many others would do anything to look like you? Can't you see that you're destroying yourself over something that you already have—beauty?"

I felt so special when random strangers on the street would approach me to talk to me. I've been told by friends, family, and boyfriends, "You are the most beautiful woman I have ever seen." "You are the most beautiful woman in the world." "I've never seen anyone more beautiful than you." I felt that it was the sole reason why I was able to meet people so easily, the reason why many paid attention to me at all. As a result, I believed that my appearance was one of the most important things about me—often the most important. I believed, subconsciously, that my self-worth was dependent upon my physical appearance.

It seems ironic that one who knew she was beautiful would look in the mirror and be disgusted by what she saw. But that's the way it worked. I was scared to death by the prospect of losing my beauty, for it was what made me special, to the point where I was horrified if I gained even just a pound. My insecurities about my intelligence peaked my freshman year in college, when I felt that I was always the dumbest student in my class and my dreams of becoming a doctor were shattered. I knew that my classmates would go on to become leaders and innovators who would improve the world and mold history. I could barely handle my studies and so didn't have time to even participate in activities, much less lead them. I thought that what I had to help me succeed was not talent or intelligence, but my work ethic, friendly personality, and beauty. But for three and a half years, I did not fully accept that much more important than my looks were my cheerful, open personality and work ethic. For three and a half years, I struggled between my Buddhist philosophy, which prioritized compassion, disattachment, and awareness, and my desperate desire to look beautiful all the time. When I gained even just three pounds, I hated myself and literally felt that I had lost everything. I was afraid to walk outside and see people see someone who had lost what had made her special in their eyes.

What finally pulled me out of the hell I had created for myself was *not* realizing that I couldn't lose my beauty by gaining ten pounds. My friends tried to help me by telling me that my weight should not be something I worry about, that I was already so beautiful. But all that did was make me continue to deem beauty more important than any other part of me. It was my boyfriend and best friend who first said to me, two years after I became bulimic, "You are beautiful, but that's not the reason why you should not have an eating disorder. You shouldn't have one because beauty itself should not matter to you. Your obsession with your looks is what degrades the compassion that really does matter about you, and matters most of all."

I've been recovering for one and a half years since my boyfriend first told me that. It took me that long to finally have his words ingrained in my head and in my heart. I've hit dead ends too many times, turned myself inside out too many times, and fallen into the sick cycle of eating, throwing up, eating, throwing up, eating, throwing up, too many times. I've seen myself fade away. I no longer cared as much about my friends and family because so much time was devoted to myself. I spent hours hovering over a toilet or trash bag choking on my fingers instead of spending time with those I loved. I once saw a reflection of myself in the shininess of the silver toilet handle. I was so ugly. Not just my face, with tears streaming down my vomit-splattered cheeks, but my eyes, windows to my soul, were dead and exhausted.

It's been extremely difficult to try to make my physical appearance no longer matter to me. I would be lying through my teeth if I said that I don't weigh myself anymore. But I've learned that beauty is not what will make me succeed in life and it isn't why my friends are my friends, or why strangers say hello to me. It's my smile that tells strangers I'm a good person and am easy to talk to, and it's my cheerfulness that makes them want to be my friends.

I can only speak about my own experiences with suffering. Because for a thousand girls there may be a thousand different reasons why they have an eating disorder, my experience and road to recovery may not apply to everyone, or even anyone else. What I do hope is that those who read about my experience will see that it takes painful self-examination to be able to get healthy again. Not thinner, but much more importantly, healthier.

Uyen-Khanh Quang-Dang is from Santa Clara, California, and graduated from Harvard with a degree in history and science.

30 Language and Identity

Jeffrey Ryuta Willis

"Guard the *gaijin*," they yelled, as I broke for the open space in the dirt field to receive a pass from my elementary school teammate.

What?

I kept running, elbowing my way through my opponents, as that word stuck in my head—*gaijin*.

My opponents kept referring to me with that mysterious and uncomfortable word for the remainder of the game, but not to any of my teammates.

Gaijin, I thought again, as the whistle blew and echoed among the concrete buildings that surrounded the soccer field. The word would not leave my head even as I joined my teammates in the traditional Japanese game-ending ritual. Both teams lined up at the centerfield, bowed to each other first, and then bowed to the referees.

That night, sitting in our new apartment eating tempura and rice, I asked my Japanese mom, "What does '*gaijin*' mean?"

For a moment she looked startled, but immediately regained her composure. "It means 'foreigner,' Jeffrey."

"How am I a foreigner here in Kobe? I go to the same public school as everyone. I speak Japanese, I read and write Japanese. I even watch *Doraemon* and the other cartoon shows that everyone watches. How?" I asked.

"Jeffrey, you're not. You're Japanese and American," interceded my father, an American cultural anthropologist. "People call you *gaijin* here because they just are not used to interacting with people like you yet," he said simply, though I could tell that he wanted to say more.

I nodded while my little brother, Luke, who didn't seem to care at all about this conversation, stuffed his face as usual with a sweet potato tempura.

My parents continued eating, slowly now. Luke's smacking seemed noisier than usual. I didn't feel like finishing my dinner and going to bed.

"Jeff," Josh, the senior proctor in my dorm, said, looking rather exasperated, "in the U.S., kids and chicks only use the word 'sleepy.' You need to say 'I'm tired,' not 'I'm sleepy.' Got that?" It was seven years after the soccer game in Kobe, and I was now a new sophomore at Phillips Exeter Academy, a boarding school in New Hampshire. Josh was making his rounds to make sure that the freshmen and sophomores were preparing to go to bed.

"Okay Josh, got it. 'I'm tired so I'm going to bed now.'"

"Cool. See you tomorrow afternoon then."

"Yup, I'll see you at soccer practice. Good night."

"Just say 'night,' that's cooler. And also, tomorrow, when we're playing, if Matt, the senior dude with the brown hair, gives you any trash, just say 'You're a waste of sperm.'"

"Okay," I replied, then "night," as I watched him walk out of my single.

When he was out of sight, I looked into my mirror, into my face, my eyes, and repeated, "Matt, you're a waste of sperm." I looked at my mirror again, and found the reflection of *Cat's Cradle*, not *Dragon Ball* and the other Japanese comics books that I read in my room in Kobe.

As the school terms passed and as I learned to say more than "You're a waste of sperm," I became more comfortable thinking that many of my peers had accepted me as one of them, an American. This feeling reached its climax during my junior spring when I found myself elected by my peers to become not only a senior dormitory proctor, but also a track captain and a soccer captain.

The realization that I fit into one of the most prestigious high schools in the U.S. made me even more nervous about perfecting the social language that was used in all the groups I associated with. The summer before my senior year, this trepidation fully surfaced when Coach D., the soccer coach, asked me to write letters of encouragement to my fellow soccer players.

"Jeff, just write a couple of sentences. Show them that you care about the team, about them. Show them that you're a leader on this next team," said Coach D.

"No problem, Coach," I said, lowering my voice and speaking from the back of my mouth to sound more masculine. I then steadily exited his office, looked back to make sure that I was out of sight, and checked my watch: two o'clock in the afternoon, so two o'clock in the morning in Japan . . . too early.

As time rolled along that day the number of times I looked at my watch became more frequent. Five o'clock P.M. showed its face and I could not manage to keep my hands off the phone. I dialed o–1–1, followed by my house number.

"Moshi-moshi," groggily replied the other end of the phone in broken Japanese.

"Daddy?"

"Jeffrey, what's wrong?" he said, a bit startled.

"I have a problem."

"What is it?" He sounded worried.

I explained the situation to him. I thought at first he understood but then realized he thought my anxiety was over the grammar in the letter. I told him I didn't care about the "goddamn" grammar. I just wanted it to be "good," a letter that would fit into Exeter Jock Culture. He told me that he could help and make it sound American if I sent him a draft over email.

That night, I worked feverishly on every sentence, trying to make the letter capture high school slang while also encompassing an authoritative voice. Every sentence frustrated me. I kept working that night, crossing out sentences, rephrasing words, and guzzling Mountain Dew. I never even considered using the letter I had received from my captain in Japan as a model. It wouldn't have fit in for an American team. Finally, my roommate helped me put something together with a little help from my dad.

My understanding of the social language or slang kept bothering me in both countries for months after I had completed that letter. I even started to fear speaking in Japanese in front of my friends because of the possible consequence of feeling different.

At the same time, however, I started to gradually fear less and less that my friends would refuse to accept me if I didn't talk perfectly like them. What I started to realize is that the structure of friendships is built more upon the mutual understanding of each other's personal qualities and mutual experiences rather than on the external constructs of an individual. This realization became apparent to me during my summer in Kobe before my freshman year at Amherst College.

That summer, while I taught English to Japanese elementary school kids, I went out with friends to clubs and restaurants in downtown Kobe and Osaka. One night, right after "Typhoon 17-gou" had left the region, a few of my old elementary school friends and I gathered together to hang out at karaoke joints in Osaka. As we walked down the windy streets of Dotonbori, a part of Osaka famous for entertainment, we chatted and laughed about the old days when we fought over who got to eat the leftover pudding at the school cafeteria.

Moving through the waves of people, I noticed that none of my friends had really changed since I last saw them five years ago. We were all bigger in every sense and our eyes reflected the successes and failures that we had gone through during the past seven years. As I looked at everyone again, I was not sure if we still had the connection that we used to have. In particular, I didn't know where I fit into the picture, now that I had been away at boarding school for three years. Popular words that my friends used in their sentences baffled and amused me. I had no idea what they meant when they used "choberigu" or "choberibu," which, as I would learn later, respectively translate to Japanese-English hybrid words: "cho-very good" and "cho-very blue." Furthermore, I created awkward sentences and stumbled to find words when the conversation became more intellectual and technical. Yet this type of conversation would have been easy for me to join had it been in English.

As the winds died down around us as we entered Ultraman-Club, a karaoke club, Takashi said, "Jeffu, nihongo no tsukaikata mattaku shogakko no toki to itsho yana" (Jeff, you still use the Japanese language the same way you used it in elementary school).

"Souka?" (Really?) I said, a bit defensively yet complacently.

"Kwaiikute eeyan" (Yeah, you sound cute), he said as he let out a soft laugh and walked into the club.

Following Takashi, I didn't understand what his soft laugh implied. But before I could think about it deeply, the other guys caught my attention and dragged me into the soundproof karaoke room.

Crunched into the room, the five of us picked some songs, started humming some old tunes, and started busting the rhymes as the music flowed through the humid air. I was initially hesitant to sing because of my voice, one that had crippled many school music teachers, but the guys got me going with their biting yet soft jokes.

"Jeffu, onchi no chikara was dekai-koe yazo!!!" (The only strength of a tone-deaf person is their loud voice!!!)

I let out a grumbling laugh and gradually joined their voices to sing the songs that we grew up with. "Manatsu no . . ."

That night, letting our voices loose in the overheated room, jumping up and down with the beat, and making fun of each other, I didn't feel embarrassed or alienated because of my inadequate control of the current slang or technical language. I simply felt comfortable around people that I knew and had grown up with, and sensed that my friends felt the same way.

Even though I understood in my head that acceptance into a particular group does not always necessitate certain external constructs, I continued to act and talk in ways that befit the group of my interest. Yet I slowly started to feel uncomfortable with myself and almost felt as if I were a full-time "actor." My dislike for how I was behaving crept up on me when my mother visited me in Amherst my senior year.

"Jeffuri, you know, it seems like your personality changes depending on the language you're speaking," said my mom as we sat down at the Blacksheep, a coffee shop.

"Yeah, sure, don't you think that everyone changes their personality depending on the people they hang out with? You change the way you talk when you speak with your colleagues," I said, sipping the whipped cream from the top of my mochaccino.

"It's different. It's like you think differently when you talk in English. You speak so directly and individualistically, like your father."

"I guess. That's how you survive in the States. You need to be confident, strong, and independent. Mom, you lived here for a couple of years with Dad, you should know," I said, wiping off the bubbles of whipped cream inadvertently attached to the tip of my nose.

"I know. It's just strange seeing you change like this. When you were in Japan, before leaving for all your school stuff here, your English was never like this. Same with Luke. When I see you or Luke speaking English with your roommates, it seems as if you are repressing some of your Japanese values, the values I know you have. Or maybe attending all these hard schools the last few years in the States has changed your values," she said, taking the first sip from her green tea.

"Mom, you can't say that *ne*. It's like I'm all evil and corporate now," I said, dissolving the last of the whipped cream into the dark liquid.

"Jeffuri, don't worry. I'm just saying all that so that I won't lose you and Luke to America," she said with a slight laugh.

That night, as I walked away from the Lord Jeffery Inn after saying good night to my mom, I heavily tossed around the idea of my present identity in my head. Had I become too American? Or perhaps too Japanese? Had my pursuit to perfect the social language that my peers spoke taken away the values that I truly believed in? Had the social language that I studied molded my personality into something that was not truly me?

Depressed and confused, I kept walking through the biting New England night, tossing around more questions with inadequate answers. Suddenly, in the background, I heard a voice. "Jeff. Wait up, dude."

I looked back and saw one of my track buddies sloshing through the icy slush.

"How's it going? Cold, huh?" I muttered.

"Totally. Messed up how cold it is in this part of the country. Got to go back to Cali. Anyway, hey, did you hear about Etricia?"

"Nah."

"Apparently she got in a fight with the coach. She's not running track anymore."

"Well, I guess that's her decision. Sucks for the team, however," I replied without thinking. However, intuitively I felt that what I had said sounded rather ugly. I wanted to say what my Japanese soccer coach would have said: She should have consulted the team first and thought more about the team before quitting. My coach's words echoed in my head: "Rest only when you believe that other people around you are more comfortable than you."

"Yeah, that's her decision. Sucks for the team—the girls' team might not even score at NESCACs [New England Small College Athletic Conference] this year," my friend replied.

I didn't say anything back. I wrapped my scarf around my neck tighter and kept walking quietly, listening to the bare branches howl in the New England wind.

I continued to dislike myself for not orally expressing how I felt in certain situations just because I wanted to use the social language that was most acceptable to the people in that society. I wanted to find a solution, but a positive one did not present itself until I started my internship at USAID (United States Agency for International Development) the summer after I graduated from Amherst. At USAID I was exposed to people from various international backgrounds, and was shown that an external construct such as language does not have to be used in a particular rigid way, but rather can be manipulated. I learned that I could not only use language to fit into a culture, but could also use it as a tool to create my own unique character. This recognition gradually occurred during my time at USAID, but surfaced most on the day I met a Japanese representative from JICA (Japan International Cooperative Agency), the Japanese equivalent of USAID, who was stationed in Washington, D.C.

Walking down the corridor of the newly built Ronald Reagan Building, I showed my ID to the security guard to enter the "need-to-know basis" section of USAID. Walking beside me was Ken-san, the representative from JICA.

Swiping our cards again in front of a magnetic ID detector, the two of us entered the Bureau of Population, Nutrition, and Health. Only two weeks had passed, but I already felt comfortable in this building that housed countless languages.

"Jeff, let me introduce you to a couple of people. Some of them have a lot of experience working in Japan," Ken-san said.

As he introduced me to each one of them, I found a different style in each of their greetings, and they were comfortable with the difference.

As we sat down and talked more about the HIV/AIDS epidemic in Botswana, I heard different languages move back and forth in the conversation. It was as if the speakers had created a new language, but one that made perfect sense in that conference room.

Suddenly, Ken said in Japanese, "Jeff, would you want to learn more about the AIDS epidemic?"

About to answer the question in a humble and indirect Japanese manner, I caught myself. I decided that I would rather tell them more confidently and directly that I would like to take the initiative to learn more about it. "Yes, definitely. How can I learn more about it? Could I get some background material?"

Ken smiled back and told me to ask the secretaries to get me some articles.

As I walked toward a secretary's office I felt in control of who I am and what I wanted, and no longer a complete extension of what I thought others wanted me to be. Since that day I have attempted to manipulate my language depending on the situation. At times, I note the importance of using language that follows the social norm. Other times, when I sense the need to express my values, I deviate from the rigid social norm to create my own words in that particular language that best express my values. Thus, through language I have been able to not only reflect upon my identity as a bicultural person growing up in both Japan and the U.S. but also understand that my identity is in my own control and not that of others.

Jeffrey Ryuta Willis is from Kobe, Japan, and graduated from Amherst College with a degree in economics. He is currently studying at the Johns Hopkins School of Public Health.

31 Who Am I?

Gordon Wang

I am a neuroscience graduate student at UC Berkeley. My name is Gordon Wang. I am Chinese in origin and American in national affiliation. Do you know me now? Can you say, "Ah, Gordon. I know him well." Not likely. We all realize that the identity of a person is much more than anything that can be named, categorized, and abstracted. Yet we all have the intuition that one's ancestry, one's profession, and one's affiliations matter. Is this just a mere delusion, or is there any truth in it? The answer is yes, there is some truth to it, and if you think that is an ambiguous yes, you are right.

Secluded in the Asian conclave that is California, I cannot claim to have a proper perspective on race relations in the rest of the United States, where Asians might not be a common sight, and Asian minimalls do not dot the landscape like Starbucks. Here in California, in the Bay Area, at the University of California, I do not feel particularly out of place. My identity has no special connotations other than the quirks and talents of my Self. True, I might have lived an isolated and protected existence, or perhaps I am just blind, but the tales of prejudice have not occurred to me. That is not to say that I do not believe in these tales, but they are not personal; they are not immediate. They are, to me, make-believe warnings, boogie men, and poltergeists. They are laced with hyperbole, construed to manipulate behavior.

All that said, there are times when I feel culturally isolated. In all ways I am a chimera, a mix-and-match identity that is neither American nor Chinese, but this dualism or contradiction makes me a bystander, a person with no true convictions against or for any racial issues. I have my moral opinions, but I can never take sides, because I understand, and my understanding traps me. My empathy binds me. This does not mean I am neutral. I am not, but my knowledge makes me fairer and in the end less convincing. For instance, I am deeply disturbed by the pop-cultural chicness of Asian culture. Asian culture is not a fad or a fetish. Asian chic disturbs through its blatant characterization of difference, the coolness almost bordering on kitsch, the novelty of the exotic. Yet it does signal a sort of acceptance. Is it a start or a false start? And how am I to presume?

The irony of my predicament is that I find the Asian discourse that is spread among the youth and sprinkled into the media to be too Western. When we talk of an Asian America, we are dealing with an intrinsic dualism. Western dualism is dialectical, which means that there are two poles: good/bad, black/white. It lends itself wonderfully to poetry and rhetoric. It is passionate and beautiful, but it is horrible for trying to understand the reality of the human condition. Asian dualism is based on mutuality. Think yin and yang. The symbol swirls around itself. Yin is within the heart of yang, and vice versa. The key difference between the two philosophies is that in Western ideology a mixing of the two poles is a weakening of both. Thus, black and white form grays. In Eastern philosophy, mixing the two poles is the key to life, to understanding and knowledge. It is not seen as weakness that white should contain black, and just like the yin and yang sign, they do not have to mix. There are no grays, their constituents are still pure, but they are more complete because of each other.

Asian discourse focuses too much on them and us. It tries to split the Asian American apart into the Asian and the American, and for a person who embraces both they are seen as gray. Diluted. I am not a gray boy. I lived almost half of my life in China. I know what it is to be Chinese, but I am more than just that. I am also American. My American identity does not make me less Chinese. Truthfully my identity has made me sort of an outsider to both worlds, and this perspective has made me realize one thing: It is not about races or cultures. It is and has always been about individuals. Racism and bigotry are projected by both the majority and the minority, and they can be both positive and negative. In my experience, racism is mostly ignorance, and partly insecurity. I think some of the worse cases of racism have been of in-group racism: Cantonese versus Mandarin, Korean versus Vietnamese, etc.

In light of all this I have chosen to ignore the idea of race relations, because it is all too relativistic. I like things that are more absolute; call it my platonic streak if you will. I think in terms of human relations. How we get along with one another is a personal business. It should not be about nationalities or affiliations. I treat everyone with the same respect and compassion that is due to any human being. Gender, nationality, and race should not matter, and I feel they do not to most people. In California, or at least my immediate California, I think most people, raised in a world of heterogeneity, love and hate based on personal differences and not on race or nationality, and that is as it should be.

I think Asian culture, as I have experienced it myself, is at a mass and age in America at which a transition is happening. It is sometimes painful, and because of the nonhomogenous nature of Asian Americans, groups are feeling the pressures of a greater force that is formed by the total whole of Asians in America. We are visible now. Our culture is starting to have a force in the mass culture. We are transitioning from a particle in tow to a satellite that exerts its own gravity upon the whole. However, we do not dictate this visibility in many cases. Furthermore, this visibility has brought conflict. To many it seems that the mass culture has usurped our own heritage from us, and is twisting us in its own lens. How we are portrayed is said to be problematic. I do not disagree with this, but I think we should realize that this is a game of give and take. Evolution and survival are dependent upon adaptability and not stubbornness.

I have friends who fight for equality, but insist on keeping their "uniqueness." I love them, but I think they are wrong. In this case, many can learn something from Eastern philosophy. The ideas of balance, of incorporation, of mutualistic dualism (remember yin and yang) are essential. Self-love can be a beautiful thing and in many cases, in small measured doses, is necessary; but do not let our narcissism fragment us. We can be right without having someone being wrong. Yin and yang, the symbol and the actual concept, do not really matter; it is the philosophy behind them that matters. "Asian American"—the term only exists because of a binary existence. They do not destroy each other. One breathes depth and reason into the other, and vice versa. To understand one you must know the other; yet being a part of both does not make you any less pure, because neither loses its fidelity.

Thus, to understand another group of people, to validate another culture, does not mean you have diluted your passion about your own. Mutual dualism is the key to existing in zealous harmony. This is something that to my dismay is not a part of the Dionysian and Apollonian world of Western society. Our heroes are uncompromising, and the ones who do compromise are weak. This is why Asian Americans and other ethnic Americans caught in this Western society become radical, revolutionary. They embrace this idea of a hero, an uncompromising *Mr. Smith Goes to Washington* hero. I feel that the Asians who fight the just fight for our place in America hardly represent Asians really. They represent Asian Americans, and they have to realize that. They have been trained in the Eastern life of their family units, perhaps, but they do not know the philosophy of being Asian. It is actually quite different from the familial practices that we are all raised with. Asian Americans, the ones who lead the fight, should take some time and study Eastern thought. They have been raised and educated in a Western tradition where the fundamentals of Western philosophy are deeply entrenched.

I think Asian leaders know America all too well and do not know Asia. This is why many first-generation or recent immigrants feel out of touch with these Asian leaders. It is the same difference as that between immigrant parents and their American-grown children. It is a difference of states. One feels they understand Asia because they are Asian and were raised by Asians, but that is not true. The other lives in and is engulfed by America and they feel they understand it, but they really do not. As an Asian American leader, one must be able to shift perspectives at will and not believe that they understand when they really just have a vague notion. We must study to fill the holes in our education; it is then that we can bring all the Asians together, and Asian and American together.

You see, the fight of Asian Americans to me is really a greater battle for the humanity of our society. We are really looking for a breakthrough, a break away from the old ideas of struggling for Asians, or struggling for Americans. We should start by saying, "We are all equally capable human beings, so what should we do to benefit all?" I believe that instead of a call for increased rights or exposure, we should be calling for education. When the mass understands us just as they understand their own people and heritage, then the conflict will be where it should be, between human beings.

So, who am I? If you have come this far then you know me better now, but I am more. Yet I can be less, depending on how you would like to perceive me. I am Asian, but if I were not, then how would it have changed how you feel about what you have read? Should it matter? If it does matter, then why does it matter? Finally, think about your own ethnicity. How has that affected your reading? Did it matter? If it did matter, then why did it matter? I am no traitor to the cause, and I am no sheep. I am just a well-adjusted China-born citizen of the United States. I have my issues, just as anyone

32 Doppelgänger

Frederick Macapinlac

At the start of summer, I got an email from my friend. It was about making this book. "Dope, I got a lotta shit I wanna talk about," I told him. Now that I'm actually writing this essay, I don't know where I'm going with this. So I think I'm just gonna let my thoughts run freely, and see where they take me.

I guess I'll start off by introducing myself. My full name is Frederick Manansala Macapinlac, and as of July 8, 2003, I am seventeen. My ethnicity is Filipino, but I was born an American in Norfolk, Virginia. Like many Filipino Americans, my dad was in the U.S. military. Like many Asian Americans, my parents were drawn to this country in the hopes of a better life for their family. In the second year of my life, my family relocated to Honolulu, Hawaii; three years later we moved again, to San Diego, California, where I am right now, and hope to leave pretty soon (insert smiley face for all you Internet people).

I really don't know how to evaluate my childhood. I was raised pretty strictly; in today's overly political correct world, you might look at what my parents did as child abuse. But the way I look at it, without them I wouldn't be the person I am today, plus compared to serious cases of abuse, mine was a cakewalk. I'm very thankful for my childhood. Ha ha ha, you could say I had discipline, morals, and my study habits beat into me. Actually, there was this funny incident in kindergarten where my teacher thought my dad had given me a black eye, but it was from being hit by a kid on a swing. Well anyway . . .

In a few weeks, I'll be in my senior year of high school. I just filled out my college applications and I'm really hoping I get into a good school. How smart am I anyway? Compare me to everyone else, I'd say I'm above average; compare me to the above average people, I'm a dumbass. But that's life, there's always someone better than you. For as long as I can remember, my goal has been trying to get good enough to be accepted into every college I can. The reason: to get away from here.

So now we get into what I'm supposed to be talking about. What's so bad about where I live, you say? It's a really weird situation. I would probably place my family in the lower- to mid-middle socioeconomic area. If I confused you, don't worry, I confused myself. That's like the lower or middle end of the middle class. Poor to some, rich to many. In my area you can see about every economic class there is. About five years ago there was a boom in the upper class coming from the dot-com millionaires. Needless to say, they're mostly white, but there are a few upper-middle-class and upper-class Asians as well. Looking at the area from west to east, it's kind of like a sandwich effect: affluent, nonaffluent, affluent; or just rich, poor, rich (trying to stay away from the word "poor," because there are differences between not being wealthy and not having money).

Now, the affluent-nonaffluent area we call Mira Mesa; the just affluent area we call Scripps Ranch. Each of these two areas has its own high school named after the area. My situation is that I live in Mira Mesa but attend Scripps Ranch High. Being in this unique situation has enabled me to look at the bigger picture and see what's happening to today's Asian American youth in this country. At Scripps Ranch High there are very few minorities; it's not like I'm the only Asian, but there are few minorities. Mira Mesa High, on the other hand, is filled with minorities. Here's the odd thing though: In both places, you see a lack of concern about culture and heritage.

How is this possible? In my school the lack of minorities gives very few Asians other people to identify with. Because of this, you see the Asians assimilating into the majority. In the other school, you see the exact opposite happening. Because Asians are the majority, there is little need to bond and appreciate one's culture; it's basically a lack of concern.

What we can find in today's Asian youth is that they no longer identify themselves as being Asian. In many cases we can generalize this as assimilating into either white or black American culture. There is the so-called banana, who rejects their culture and wants nothing to do with it, in the worst cases even insulting it. Then there's the wigga (wannabe nigga, to fit everyone), who will probably have all that AzN PrIdE junk, yet call everyone "nigga" or "nikka" trying to be black. To those who act like that because it's "cool," I say go to South Central or Oakland and call a random black guy "nigga." Now, some of these people will speak their culture's language and take that as proof of how "Asian" they are, but just knowing how to speak isn't being cultured. What good is being able to speak Tagalog when you want to be black or white?

That is the problem, so how do we fix it? This is a large problem within the Asian American community, especially with the youth, and in all honesty, if you don't want to identify yourself with your culture, there is no way to change it. But I'm sure that isn't a problem with those reading this, so here's how we go about it. First off, learning your language is an important issue; you should go about doing this as soon as possible. History is the aspect of culture which is disregarded the most. How are you supposed to know who you are or where you're going if you don't know where you came from? I would recommend reading books that relate to all Asian and Asian American history in general, in addition to your ethnic background. This broadens your knowledge of not only yourself but also others you'll meet in life. The greatest reason for conflict and violence is ignorance of each other. Also, talk with your parents or elders. I have noticed that in most homes, there's usually little dialogue between child and parent. Talking about a subject of general interest will bridge the gap, and maybe there won't be so many fights.

The best thing for the Asian American community is supporting one another. There's so much disunity among all the ethnicities. Chinese hating Japanese, Vietnamese hating Koreans, Filipinos hating who knows what. Why do we hate one another when we all came from the East? In this country we're the minority, and the majority doesn't even recognize our diversity. Walking out of a Filipino store, I noticed a Caucasian scream to his friend: "Hey (whatever his name was), there's a half-mile line of gooks in there!" This isn't true for all of America, but if you're shorter than a white guy and you have black hair, you're automatically a "gook," "chink," "jap," "slanted eyes," or whatever stupid racial slur they can come up with. Instead of fighting among ourselves, we need to get together and appreciate all our cultures. Yellow is beautiful as well, and if we can't see that ourselves, then how will the rest of America see our strength?

Many people don't realize it, but racism is another problem we face. It is not gone today—in fact it was never gone in the first place; it's still here. It's in the form of smiles, jokes, and apologies. How many times have you watched TV and seen them crack a racial joke? How about all the small-

Asian-man jokes in the movie *Rush Hour*? I'm sure you remember the mas-sage-house scene where Tucker punches Jackie, saying: "All ya'll look alike." That we don't notice these things is another reason why they call us the "model minority." Most African Americans will get pissed hearing some-one of another color say the "n"-word or even call someone "black." Yet when the Chinese rapper Jin tha Emcee was battling on 106 and Park all of his opponents called him "chink" or whatever. Don't get me wrong: I greatly admire the African American community, and if anything, I wish our com-munity had as much unity and sense of identity as they have (we need our own Harlem Renaissance as well). But this is just an example of how racism is not limited; it is affecting everyone: blacks to Asians to Caucasians.

This will not end anytime soon; immigrants are the backbone of this nation, and what we need to do is get the whole country to see that. It's okay to borrow ideas from other places, but when we try to imitate completely, we lose ourselves. We need to show our numbers, strength, pride, and heritage. Yet this will never happen until we find our identity. We need to find out who we were, who we are, and who we will be.

Frederick Macapinlac is from San Diego, California, and attends Scripps Ranch High School.

33 Caught between Cultures: Identity, Choice, and the Hyphenated American

Margot Seeto

"You know, Margot, you're really into this Asian thing,"

Some people of non-Asian descent keep thinking that I was either born in China or am a second-generation Chinese American. A fellow hallmate was surprised when she found out that the only accent my parents have is my mom's Boston accent. Yes, my mother is 1.5-generation, but I was born here, as was my father. I am a 2.75-generation Chinese American.

When people I know tell me that racism toward Asian Americans does not exist anymore, I think, "Wow, I guess I really can't be friends with white or white-washed people." Or just racially ignorant people, not to say that white equals ignorant, but I am angry right now. Allow me to rant.

 a.   "It might be hard to find shoes to fit your small Asian feet."
 b.   "It has always been my dream to be in a room full of beautiful Asian women."

How ironic. We were at the Wellesley Asian Alliance retreat in Cape Cod.

I. Attack

I cannot understand why some people, especially other Asian Americans, do not see the same importance of Asian American issues as I do. Unfortunately, my egocentricity is a dead giveaway of my immaturity, for I lack the patience for people to have their epiphanies concerning their cultural identities—whether they be friends or strangers. These epiphanies, however, may not even occur until well into the future, or perhaps even never.

Some people think I have nothing to complain about—and it is true that I have suffered few physical, violent acts of racism, nor did my race hinder my getting into the college of my choice. Most of the time, I can walk around San Francisco without having to worry too much about my race. Sometimes I even feel like the girl who cried racism, because there are times when even I think I am delusional. I cannot fathom how my predecessors lived through the 1800s or the 1950s, or even how present-day Asian Americans deal with being in isolated parts of America where there might not be a sizable population of Asian Americans. This is why I believe that some see me as some overly sensitive, polemics-spewing hyper–Asian American.

Then I catch myself. I remember things such as rediscovering over and over again that perverted Asian fetishes still exist, and the fact that I have to think twice as much about having long hair because of its exotic connotations. Then there are the rising number of hate crimes against Asian Americans, the Wen Ho Lee case and racial profiling, the hate groups that are alive and well, even in parts of my California, and all the Vincent Chins. And lately I have seen with painful clarity the thing that hurts me the most—fellow Asian American brothers and sisters who hate themselves for simply having black hair and brown eyes, who internalize the racism that is meant to cut them down.

Something else potentially more dangerous than physical violence exists in the attempted slow and silent genocide occurring before my very eyes: the Amazing Disappearing Asian American. It is an attack on our minds—our gross underrepresentation in the institutional pillars of this great nation has some of us trying to erase ourselves. This cultural imperialism eventually tricks some of us into committing cultural suicide. So I guess I really am into this Asian "thing." Part of the reason why I am perceived to be active is because I feel the need to overcompensate for the people who have not had their epiphanies yet. I am trying to repair the damage that America has done. In all truth, I am scared—scared that if my Asian American sisters do not have their epiphanies, their potential cultural suicides will leave me to be alone. I wish I were not in the minority of Asian America.

Although I have consciously had a strong interest in Asian American issues since sixth grade, I started to become more visibly active my junior year in high school, after an unpredicted racial incident at my otherwise liberal high school, Lick-Wilmerding, occurred. In the handicapped stall of a girls' bathroom, the searing words "NIGGERS, SPICS, AND CHINKS DON'T BELONG" were scrawled across two walls. I suppose this is when one of my epiphanies occurred. I wrote a letter to the editor in a special edition of the school newspaper covering the incident. After discovering the cathartic value of speaking out and getting compliments on the content of the letter, I realized that my voice is important. My voice is valid. After that incident and its dramatic aftereffects on the community, I vowed to immerse myself in Asian American and multicultural affairs once in college. Keeping true to my junior-year promise, this past year I have served on the Asian Student Union Executive Board, and will continue to do so next year, in addition to being one of the co-coordinators of the Wellesley Asian Alliance. Ironically, my predominantly white high school probably sparked my activity more than if I had gone to my very Chinese American other school of choice, Lowell High School.

But since arriving at Wellesley, there have been times when I truly felt that being an Asian American separatist is the only way to go. The colony would be a think tank where word would get out by recording the ideas and plans of action for empowerment and mobilization, and then sending those out to the outside world—America. This system would facilitate production without impediments. I desire this colony only because I am frustrated with the backtracking that must occur in every new encounter, such as when people ask me where I am REALLY from or when people tell me racism does not exist anymore. Just when I feel as if I am on the brink of enlightenment, I am cruelly pulled back into the reality of others.

It is not so much the college itself that is the source of my frustration, but rather the act of living in a place other than San Francisco, California, which has spoiled me. Although the city is not perfect, it looks like heaven compared with most of the United States. I forget that relatively liberal San Francisco is not like the rest of America. San Francisco—the birthplace of so much Asian American activity and the hub of so many resources. I always forget that where I grew up is not typical of the United States. I did not have to grow up in blond-haired, blue-eyed Middle America without many others like myself, let alone support groups and open, active dialogue. I forget that the majority of people come from rather homogeneous places. Asian Americans, after all, do only make up 4 percent of the American population. So maybe I'm the odd one out.

I see that there are holes in my worldview, seeing as I am an all-knowing being at my ripe old age of eighteen and all. Since turning eighteen, I have noticed that my worldview has suddenly expanded, even to the point where I can see and understand things like my parents' perspective, much to my horror. But included in this slightly expanded worldview is the realization that we teenagers tend to think that we are the first ones to feel the emotions we feel, that our perspectives on the world are fresh and original. Well, unfortunately, most of the time they are not new to the rest of the world. I can be like a bitter troll sitting under the bridge, getting mad at everyone else for crossing my path. But I have to realize that someone out there thinks the same way about me. I can help educate instead of berate. Everyone is on her own timeline. I enjoy challenging and uncomfortable questions, even if I cannot answer them. However, my initial shock about the racism in today's society does not surprise me much anymore. Welcome to the real world, Margot.

I sound like I am full of hubris in my secret (or not so secret) admonishment of everyone who does not think like me—especially the Apathetic Asian. Sometimes my overconfident attitude, gained only after starting at Wellesley, worries me. Tory, in my writing class, tells me, "You focus a lot on the external, and not enough on the internal." This is when I realize that I have to calm myself down and not just write while my heart is racing and my blood is raging. Otherwise all I see is red.

II. Vindication

Sometimes I just have to throw out the PC crap to get to the real issues within myself. For me to say this is difficult, as I would consider myself to be anally PC; to let down my guard and admit this is one of the hardest things for me to do. So here I go. It is time for me to attack myself.

This year I have found it harder to be friends with white people. While other Asian Americans are irked by the fact that their circle of friends might be mostly Asian American, I am happy with it. In fact, I have come to prefer it, even though my roommate—one of my closest friends—is white. Though as I have had a chance to calm down in recent months, I am not so militant about my stance with white people at present.

In recent years, some people, strangely enough, have thought I was *hapa haole* (half-white). And, strangely enough, there were times when I was flattered by this mistaken identity, though I wish I had never felt that way, seeing as how I am all the while fighting against the white majority and am irritated by the high rate of out-marriage among Asian Americans. When people first mistakenly thought I was mixed, I was baffled and even offended, since I think I look 100 percent Chinese and most of the people making the mistake were also of Asian descent. I thought, "Don't you know your own people?!" But as such incidents reoccurred, I noticed that most of the people asked with fascination and meant to compliment me with their incorrect perception. As if looking whiter was better.

Professor James Kodera told our Asian American Experience class that JFK said it is easier to change one's mind than it is to change one's heart. And unfortunately, the hegemony formed an impression on my child's heart before I knew what was going on. It was not until recently that I realized I might have been more whitewashed than I previously thought. Most of the stories that I wrote as a child had white characters, because most of the books I read and TV shows I saw had all white characters. White was my standard. In sixth grade I wanted to be *hapa* because I thought it was cooler to be mixed, though I wanted to be part white, not black or Latino. But even at that young age, I wanted to be mixed in part to lessen my guilt about not knowing as much about Chinese culture as I could. The funny thing is that I wanted to be mixed and not fully white. Maybe it was my way of wanting to be able to participate in the mainstream culture completely while still retaining who I originally was. Was I exoticizing my own race, or was I exoticizing the white race because it was the grass on the other side? I still do not know.

I am still working on freeing myself of the damage the hegemony wreaked on my childhood, though I know I will never completely get rid of the scars. This is the first time I have said that I, too, suffer from the indoctrinated inferiority of nonwhite races. Though I am fighting it pretty well nowadays—the characters in the stories I write are Asian American now. My classmate Minnie, a fellow member of the Wellesley Asian Alliance (WAA), openly admits that she is a "recovering whitewashed Asian," and I admire her for being so open about that weakness. But the defensive part of me says that I never was fully whitewashed. I had no continuous period in which I wished I was white, but rather little spurts here and there. And I never altered my appearance to look whiter, such as by wearing light-colored contacts. I just hate to admit I was affected more than I would like to think. And I hate to admit that the desire to be whiter, intentional or unintentional, is a rather common experience among Asian Americans, with many suffering worse than I did.

So to counteract that suffering, I have evolved my thinking into this prepackaged, prejudged stockpile of verbal and mental counterattacks against racist thinking. Why? I want to perfect no-fault arguments on the existence and effects of racism. However, I have recently realized that I hang on so tightly to my almost militant pro–Asian American stance because, just like everyone else, I am trying to find myself. Even though I am comforted in knowing that I am more Chinese than I realize at times, I also cannot claim to be completely in touch with my roots when I still prefer hip-hop to Chinese opera, and speak Cantonese like a four-year-old. That is why I so strongly hold on to my self-proclaimed title of 2.75-generation Chinese American. It is a well-known fact that by the third generation, members will have completely assimilated into the mainstream culture. If I tell myself that I am 2.75, that I am not yet third-generation, there is still time for me to retain and regain what I once had. I am saved. I am hanging on so tightly because I want my identity. My activism reflects a movement toward not so much a cultural but rather a sociopolitical identity. This activism, however, still rings strongly with my cultural chase because I am around and fighting for "my" people. Though sometimes I wonder: If I were not a minority in America, what would I do? What would I be like? This Asian American fight is a huge part of who I am and who I want to be.

Lin, another fellow member of WAA, feels this tension between not wanting to claim the role of the victimized minority and still feeling this anger toward America. I actually see that there are a lot of angry Asian American girls out there, unknowingly brewing a disjointed revolution for quite some time. Though I am not just angry. Often I hear my peers complain that minorities band together mostly because of harmful experiences. I am saddened when I realize that most of the things I rant about are negative. Group identity is usually based on shared experience, whether positive or negative, and one has to embrace everything to understand the entirety of the experience.

But of course I have felt and feel the fierce pride and joy of being Asian American. My Asian Pride is apparent not only when I participate in a protest for Asian American causes, but also when I feel the heat of a spoken-word piece by the likes of I Was Born With Two Tongues or Yellow Rage. My

Asian Pride shows when I learn from the works of Asian American scholars, authors, and peers. My Asian Pride shows when a friend and I share the inside jokes and struggles that come with being Asian American. My Asian Pride is there when I eat dim sum with my family. I am celebrating and advocating in just a few ways.

At the 1999 National Association of Independent Schools People of Color Conference, one person commented that having tea with your grandfather is a way to show Asian Pride, and that one need not always be belligerently yelling and attacking. I did not realize the value and truth of his words until this year. While I continue to fight and still see an aggressive and assertive approach as necessary, I also know that I do not cease to advocate when I participate in the quieter aspects of being Asian American. Resisting and rejoicing can take many forms.

Margot Seeto is from San Francisco, California, and studies Asian American studies and psychology at Wellesley College.

34 The Paradox of Being Too Chinese and Not Chinese Enough

Bryant Yang

I grew up in Monterey Park, California, the first suburban Chinatown. During the influx of Asian immigration in the 1980s, Monterey Park went through a dramatic transformation as large numbers of Asian immigrants, mainly Chinese immigrants, settled in this small suburb of Los Angeles. Many of the white residents attempted to keep the Asian and Latino immigrants out through English-only legislation and other xenophobic and racist methods. When those attempts failed, they moved. Now, Monterey Park is composed of approximately 61.5 percent Asian and Pacific Islander Americans, 28.9 percent Hispanic/Latino Americans, and 9.6 percent other. Monterey Park has the most Chinese-owned businesses and entrepreneurships in the United States, which is evident from all the Chinese characters along downtown Monterey Park. We also have almost every aspect of Chinese culture and food accessible around the corner—whether it is dim sum, *boba nai cha* (pearl milk tea), Chinese pop music, temples, karaoke, etc. In fact, Monterey Park has become a Mecca for Chinese immigrants and Chinese Americans in southern California, who often travel many miles to enjoy their favorite meal or to shop for items they could not purchase anywhere else.

Growing up in the San Gabriel Valley, where Asians and Asian Americans constitute the majority, race was not an issue. I hardly faced any racism or discrimination. I also never had to completely hide my culture or lose it, trying to assimilate, because Monterey Park had an abundance of Chinese culture. In fact, the only non-Hispanic whites that I regularly came in contact with were on television or were "tourists" trying "ethnic" food and/or shopping for culture. The only racial tensions that arose were between Latinos/Latino Americans and Asians/Asian Americans. This occurred in the late 1980s, when Latino gangs and Asian gangs fought for turf. However, through increased police presence and the cooperation of Latino American and Asian American leaders, the tension subsided. By the time I entered junior high, racial tensions were down to almost the point of nonexistence.

Although the relatively homogenous demographics of Monterey Park prevent major racial discrimination, this does not mean that none exists. There were clear stereotypes and prejudices in Monterey Park while I was growing up, especially within the Asian and Asian American community. The prejudice that most blatantly stands out in my mind, because of personal experience, is that of Chinese and Chinese Americans against Southeast Asian Americans and Pacific Islander Americans, specifically Vietnamese and Filipinos, who make up a significant portion of the Asian/Asian American population in the suburban town. Whether this is because Southeast Asian and Pacific Islander immigrants tended to be poorer because they were refugees or because preimmigration nationalism carried over, I am not sure. Though the reasons are hard to pinpoint, the prejudice and stereotypes are clear—Vietnamese and Filipinos are violent gang members, who have little or no family and moral values.

I used to get really angry and frustrated when anyone would falsely assume that I was Vietnamese or Filipino. Being active in high school, I was involved in several sports, including tennis and cross-country. During the sports seasons, I got really dark because I was always out in the southern California sun, and so fellow high school students would assume that I was Vietnamese or Filipino because of my skin tone. Whenever I received comments like "Oh, I thought you were Vietnamese/Filipino," they would hurt and annoy me because of the negative connotations that the Vietnamese/Filipino identity or label has in the Asian/Asian American community of Monterey Park. I did not want to be identified as Vietnamese or Filipino; I wanted to be "seen" as Chinese, not because I really am ethnically Chinese but because being Chinese did not carry the same demeaning stereotypes.

For similar reasons, I also chose to not ever embrace my Burmese heritage and culture. Although I am ethnically full Chinese, I was born in Myanmar (formally Burma), along with my parents and siblings. My parents identify themselves as Burmese. Our family speaks Burmese, eats Burmese food, has family back in Myanmar, and so forth. We have maintained our Chinese culture and traditions, but our family—for the most part—is Burmese. Yet I never identified myself as Burmese when asked about my ethnicity. I always answered that I was Chinese, as I secretly hoped that the questioner would not ask me where I was born or what dialect I spoke. To this day, I am not sure if I was ashamed of my Burmese heritage or I just simply wanted to fit in with the Chinese/Chinese American majority.

In addition to the prejudice of Chinese against Southeast Asians and Pacific Islanders, there was prejudice from Asian Americans against recent Asian immigrants. Derogatory terms like "FOB" (fresh off the boat) and imitation of accents were routine weapons used to belittle Asian immigrants, especially in schools. Anyone who revealed that they were "too" knowledgeable and in touch with their Asian heritage was looked down upon. In fact, the social hierarchy of schools, especially high schools, tended to situate Asian Americans as the upper elite. Asian Americans were the leaders of student government and student clubs, the star athletes, and the kings and queens of dances.

Deep segregation among Asian Americans and recent Asian immigrants was also pervasive in elementary and secondary school. Many times, the level of your English class and your math class determined your entire schedule and curriculum. Rarely was any class proportionate in its composition of recent Asian immigrants and Asian Americans. The segregation in the classroom spilled over to the playgrounds and cafeterias, where it was made clear to which group—Asian American or Asian immigrant—you belonged. Thus, there was almost no interaction between Asian immigrants and Asian American students, which only fueled the stereotypes and prejudices.

Growing up as a 1.5-generation Asian American, I was able to experience both the rejection and the acceptance of other Asian Americans. It was extremely difficult for me to deal with the snickers, the jokes, and the constant pointing, along with having to learn a new language and having to adapt to an American lifestyle. Oftentimes, I hid my Buddhist wooden bracelet, hated my no-name-brand shoes, and tried not to speak in classes in fear of being ridiculed for my accent. The only time I allowed myself to open up to people was in ESL classes or when I was around recent Asian immigrants. However, as my English proficiency grew and my Asian American identity formed through the years, I became a part of and was accepted into the Asian American student community. With that acceptance, I took on the role. Sometimes, I instigated FOB jokes; and other times, I refused my heritage, like not admitting I knew how to speak another language.

Not until the summer of my senior year in high school did I fully accept my racial, ethnic, and minority identity. I was wait-listed for John Hopkins University, and I wanted to make myself a better candidate through an internship at the end of the school year. It was because of this superficial reason that I obtained an internship with the Organization of Chinese Americans (OCA) and the Asian Pacific American Legal Center (APALC) in Los Angeles. Despite the selfish intentions, the internship completely changed my life and my perspectives. Throughout the summer, I was able to work on Asian and Pacific Islander American issues such as hate crimes, redistricting, and voter empowerment. The experience opened my eyes to how under-served our community is and how many problems are plaguing our APIA community. Most of all, it made me realize that real or perceived race, eth-nicity, nationality, sexual orientation, gender, religious affiliation, and so forth, all matter and affect every aspect of American society.

One defining moment of my transformation and identity empowerment was a candlelight vigil for Joseph Ileto and the Jewish shooting victims in Little Tokyo, Los Angeles. Both helping to set up the whole event and just watching the speakers truly changed my views as an Asian American. You see so many violent crimes in the media and you shrug them off. At the can-dlelight vigil, I was face to face with Mr. Ileto's sister, brother, and little nephew, real people, not numbers or names. It was just extremely moving and very sad. The event made me realize that people in America are still being killed, tormented, violently abused, and looked down upon just because of the color of their skin and the religion they choose to practice. I realized that we don't live in a perfect society and that racism against Asian Americans DOES EXIST.

Since that summer, I have gone through a tremendous transformation. I have reclaimed my Chinese/Burmese heritage, and I now feel secure and proud of both my Chinese ethnicity and my Burmese culture. I now believe that when you lose aspects of your culture, you lose a part of yourself, of your identity. Recently, I started to teach myself how to read Chinese and Burmese. I have been researching Buddhism, listening to Korean, Chinese, and Japanese music, and learning about my family's various traditions, all in an attempt to recapture part of my identity that I might have lost growing up. In a way, I feel ashamed that I have lost so much of my culture and heritage. I am disappointed in myself for not being able to carry on a conversation in my native language, for not understanding the prayers our family chanted when my father recently passed away from lung cancer, and for so many other reasons. In a rush to assimilate and be Asian American—to be American—I gave up parts and pieces of myself. I did not realize, as I do now, that being American does not entail losing or hiding your culture, that true patriotism is the celebration of our rich diversity.

I have also come to terms with my very prejudiced and backward past. It was wrong of me to get angry over fellow students assuming that I was Vietnamese or Filipino; it was wrong of me to allow myself to associate those horrible stereotypes with the two ethnicities. Now I do not get upset when people mistake my ethnicity. Lately, the vast majority of people have assumed that I am of Korean descent. I correct them, but I only find humor in the situation. Furthermore, I have become vigilant in my perception of recent Asian immigrants, making sure that I always regard them with the respect that every human being deserves. I now understand that recent Asian immigrants resemble the ancestors of Asian Americans who came in the 1800s. They are like my parents. I am similar to them, and we are all connected in this cycle of immigration, of a search for a better life, of oppression, of headache and heartache, of American history.

However, my Asian American identity has been most influenced by the organizations I have participated in and the people that I have encountered. UC Berkeley and the surrounding Bay Area are extremely progressive, which has greatly influenced my views on who I am and the values I hold. I have become active in serving my communities—Asian and Pacific Islander, student, people of color, immigrant, etc.—through organizations like the Asian Pacific Council, the Asian Political Association, the Student Advocate Office, and the Berkeley Police Review Commission. The people I have encountered and the activities I have participated in have all made me actively question my values as an Asian American, what "Asian American" means, and who is Asian American. A prime example of this occurred when Abercrombie & Fitch marketed T-shirts that were insensitive and derogatory to Asian Americans. In helping lead the campaign against Abercrombie & Fitch at UC Berkeley, I had to seriously question and critique myself. I had been an avid A&F shopper before the incident. It made me extremely angry and frustrated that I had supported a company that is perpetuating racist stereotypes and that has refused to diversify its advertisements to reflect the multiple shades of America. Moreover, I was ashamed that I had bought into Abercrombie's savvy use of sex and the upper-middle-class white image to sell their sweatshop clothes. I have come to a point in my life where I can no longer shop at Abercrombie, Gap, J. Crew, and so forth, specifically because I am Asian American. The incident has made me associate being Asian American with being someone who is politically and socially active, not just someone who is an American of Asian descent.

Being active in serving various communities has also influenced my having a broader, more encompassing identity. Although I consider myself Chinese American, I identify myself as an Asian and Pacific Islander American. As such, I tend to identify with various issues from many ethnic groups within the API category, such as hate crimes against South Asians post–September 11 or the loss of thousands of jobs by Filipino airport workers after the Patriot Act. I do not even really like using "Asian American" because I have interacted with Pacific Islanders, who have taught me that they are often marginalized both by mainstream society and by other ethnicities in the API category. I also consider myself very much an immigrant and a minority. In addition, though I cannot identify with them personally, I am now able to acknowledge and strongly support women's rights, black and Latino/Chicano issues, LGBT issues, and so forth.

The process of my Asian and Pacific Islander identity formation has been a long process, full of twists and turns. Though it has solidified, I believe I am still forming my identity and finding myself. However, in the process, I have found one sure thing. I have found that I want to serve Monterey Park and the surrounding San Gabriel Valley. Wherever life takes me, I know I will eventually settle back in the SG Valley and serve my community. There are so many issues facing my community that I want to help confront and solve, such as failing public schools, lack of resources for newly arrived immigrants, underrepresentation in public office and media, underdeveloped elderly care, and racial tensions. True, there were a lot of personal identity issues I had to deal with growing up in Monterey Park. Oftentimes I felt trapped in a paradox of not being Chinese enough and yet being too Chinese at the same time. Whether or not growing up in the San Gabriel Valley was a good thing for me, I am not sure. However, in the end, it is my home and it is where I belong, where I want to serve, and where I think I am most needed.

Bryant Yang is from Monterey Park, California, and studies legal studies and ethnic studies at the University of California, Berkeley.

35 I Am Going Home

Duncan Zheng

It is windy. The sun hides behind a dark gray ceiling and lets people outside shiver. It will rain soon. From an invisible loudspeaker a voice penetrates my inner silence: "Last call for Lufthansa flight 443 from Berlin to Boston."

My parents help my eighty-four-year-old grandmother to stand up. They say, "Take care of yourself. Be careful with new people and call us as often as you can." They speak without looking in my eyes.

But I can see their eyes; they are red and wet. My grandmother's lips are shaking. She touches my face with her tender but cold hand and says, "Study hard, and if you can, come to China to see me!"

Outside, it starts to rain. I pick up my drawing portfolio and stand there motionless, voiceless. Then the word "good-bye" slips from my lips and, in what seems a second later, I am in the sky. I feel a hard object in my pocket and discover a platinum ring. It is my grandmother's ring. My nose becomes sour and I close my eyes.

Hitler's favorite architect, Albert Speer, designed the building of the Immigration Bureau of Berlin—sharp-edged concrete in cold gray, magnificent windows three times as tall as they are wide, and a marbled foyer so lofty and vast that inside it one feels like an ant in a Gothic church. An androgynous voice calls my name but only the echo is audible. From behind a wooden door whose nameplate reads "Frau Herzog," a middle-aged blond woman with green eyes appears.

"So, Mr. Zheng, your application for a German student visa has been rejected," she says. "I don't see any reason why you should continue your education further in Germany. You have been allowed to stay here for ten years and now you have the German high school diploma, which allows you to study elsewhere. Within the next thirty days you must leave the country; otherwise the police will take care of your transportation back to China—at your own expense, of course."

I am enraged, but I say in a calm voice, "My parents have German citizenship. Why can't I at least receive a student visa?"

"I can explain this to you," she answers. "Your parents came before the German reunification, and have paid taxes for fifteen years. This fact allowed them to receive the German passport. Your case is quite different. You came after the reunification, when laws concerning working permissions for foreigners were changed. As a foreign high school student you were not allowed to work here. Thus you couldn't pay taxes, which means you don't have the right to apply for a passport. We let you stay here to complete your high school studies. Now you are done, so I don't see any reason why you should be here in Germany any longer."

The explanation is so inhumanly logical. I've lived in Berlin for ten years; I won a nationwide architectural competition and graduated from high school with the fourth-best GPA in my class—and there's no reason why I should be allowed to continue my education in Germany? It's even more inhuman to compel me to leave my German friends, and my parents.

My German friends accept me as one of them, as a German. We go together to the Oktoberfest each year; we talk about German politicians and celebrities; we all dream in German. Before each exam, I realize how much they perceive me as a German. My phone does not stop ringing until they have all called to ask questions about German literature, grammar, and spelling. I make fewer grammar and spelling mistakes than they do. I understand German literature and can analyze it more deeply than they can. My teachers call me "a Chinese tutor for German students." I appreciate this opinion because it means my German friends trust me. I help them with academic problems; in return they affirm that I belong with them, in their lives, in their country. Considering myself a foreigner is actually quite unfamiliar to me, because my whole environment confirms there is a German inside of me.

Of course, my parents do not think so. They see in me their Chinese son, as ever. We talk in Chinese, in our northern dialect. We eat only Chinese food because it is the best we know. However, back in China, I am not perceived as pure Chinese. Every time I visit my relatives, my cousins laugh when they realize that I do not know the famous people in China. People laugh at me as I wait for the green light to cross the street, because no one does that; in karaoke bars the computer stalls when I type in songs I remember from my childhood. Once when I asked my cousin to let me hear his CDs of a well-known Chinese rock star, he refused me. In a belittling voice he said, "You won't understand the social problems he sings about. You didn't live here for the past ten years. You know nothing!" I felt as if I had been hit by lightning. It's true that I haven't lived in China for a long time, and that I know little about it beyond the human rights and environmental problems on the news. I am ashamed of being Chinese on my passport yet not knowing what is happening there.

Here I am, between two countries, with no identification from either Germany or China; a cultural bastard, legally rejected by the one and socially rejected by the other.

As I enter the American Embassy in Berlin, the pleasant atmosphere raises my hopes that I will get into the United States. The room is bright, with American flags mounted in every available spot. A man behind a counter separated from the room by safety glass calls the appointment numbers in German with an English accent. Everyone in the room seems to be nervous but focused. I hear conversations in a variety of languages, mostly Turkish and Yugoslavian. In a small room, an American woman behind safety glass asks me in Chinese why I want to study in America. I am surprised that she speaks perfect Chinese, but I tell her calmly the reasons I have prepared for this interview. After five minutes she says that I should receive the American visa within the next seven days, and wishes me all the best for my study in Boston.

No, I am not in a dream. America is really willing to accept me. I feel honored by this opportunity but it means that I will definitely leave my friends and my family. Strangely, I am not sad at all, but overwhelmed by the fact that I will be allowed to work toward my goals in the one country where it is most possible to succeed. I have already forgotten China, forgotten Germany. I have found the place to be.

"Ladies and gentlemen, we are facing some turbulence. Please fasten your seatbelts."

I feel my grandma's ring in my hand. She must have put it into my pocket this morning. Why? This ring accompanied her for her entire life. When the Chinese Communists came to power, it was the only item she kept to remind us of our Manchurian origin—even though it would have exposed our aristocratic past and given the Communists enough reason to kill everyone in the family. This ring secured the family's survival when she traded it for food during a harsh winter in the 1950s. When life and death were no longer at stake, she immediately traded back for it.

Now it's in my hand and I am not sure how I earned it. Maybe she wants it to bring me luck for my new start in America; maybe she just wants me to have something that will always remind me of her. Whatever others, Chinese or German, friends or relatives, say or think about me, she loves me as a person, as her only grandson. She understands how I feel being caught between cultures. Grandma, don't be worried anymore. America is as diverse as I am, as confused as I am. Maybe I am not going to another country. Maybe I am going home.

Duncan Zheng is from Jilin, China, and graduated from Boston College with a degree in finance. He currently works as an investment banker.